Philosophy and its Public Role

ST ANDREWS STUDIES IN
PHILOSOPHY AND PUBLIC AFFAIRS

Founding and General Editor:
John Haldane
University of St Andrews

Volume 1:
Values, Education and the Human World
edited by John Haldane

Volume 2:
Philosophy and its Public Role
edited by William Aiken and John Haldane

Volume 3:
Relativism and the Foundations of Liberalism
by Graham Long

Volume 4:
*Human Life, Action and Ethics:
Essays by G.E.M. Anscombe*
edited by Mary Geach and Luke Gormally

Volume 5:
*The Institution of Intellectual Values:
Realism and Idealism in Higher Education*
by Gordon Graham

Philosophy and its Public Role

Essays in Ethics, Politics, Society and Culture

Edited and Introduced
by William Aiken and John Haldane

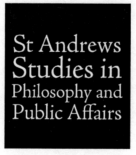

St Andrews
Studies in
Philosophy and
Public Affairs

ia

IMPRINT ACADEMIC

Published in the UK by Imprint Academic
PO Box 200, Exeter EX5 5YX, UK

Published in the USA by Imprint Academic
Philosophy Documentation Center
PO Box 7147, Charlottesville, VA 22906-7147, USA

ISBN 1-84540-003-8

A CIP catalogue record for this book is available from the
British Library and US Library of Congress

Cover Photograph:
St Salvator's Quadrangle, St Andrews by Peter Adamson
from the University of St Andrews collection

Contents

Notes on the
Contributors

William Aiken is Professor of Philosophy at Chatham College, Pennsylvania. He has published in several areas of applied philosophy, principally on quality of life issues and environmental ethics, in journals such as *Applied Philosophy and Environmental Values* and in various edited collections. He is co-editor (with Hugh LaFollette) of two well-known collections of essays: *Whose Child?* (1980) and *World Hunger and Morality* (1995).

John Arthur is Professor of Philosophy and Director of the Program in Philosophy, Politics, and Law at Binghamton University, SUNY. His areas of research include philosophy of law and political philosophy. He is the author of *The Unfinished Constitution: Philosophy and Constitutional Practice* (1989) and *Words That Bind: Judicial Review and the Grounds of Modern Constitutional Theory* (1995); and editor of many volumes including *Color, Class, Identity: The New Politics of Race* (1996), and *Morality and Moral Controversies* (2002).

Bob Brecher is Reader in Moral Philosophy in the School of Historical and Critical Studies, University of Brighton. He is former President of the UK Association for Legal and Social Philosophy and founding editor of *Res Publica*. He is the author of *Getting What you Want? A Critique of Liberal Morality* (1998) and editor and co-editor of several collections including *Liberalism and the New Europe* (1993) and *The University in a Liberal State* (1996).

Richard Brook is Professor of Philosophy Emeritus at Bloomsburg University in Pennsylvania. His areas of interest include the history of modern philosophy, and moral theory. He is the author of *Berkeley's Philosophy of Science* (1973), and of a number of essays in moral theory and applied ethics published in *Ethics*, *Journal of Philosophy*, *Philosophy and Public Affairs* and *Southern Journal of Philosophy*.

David Carr is Professor of Philosophy of Education in the University of Edinburgh. He is the author of *Educating the Virtues* (1991), *Profession-*

alism and Ethical Issues in Teaching (2000) and *Making Sense of Education* (2003). He is also editor of *Education, Knowledge and Truth* (1998) and co-editor (with Jan Steutel) of *Virtue, Ethics and Moral Education* (1999) and (with John Haldane) of *Spirituality, Philosophy and Education* (2003).

James Child is Professor of Philosophy and Senior Fellow of the Social Philosophy and Policy Center at Bowling Green State University. His interests include moral and political philosophy, philosophy of law, business ethics, and philosophical issues in international relations. He is author of articles in *Business Ethics Quarterly, Criminal Justice Ethics, Ethics, Monist* and *Public Affairs Quarterly*. His books include *Nuclear War: The Moral Dimension* and with Donald Scherer, *Two Paths Towards Peace*.

Geoffrey Cupit is Chair of the Department of Political Science and Public Policy at the University of Waikato, New Zealand. He works in the fields of moral, social and political philosophy and has authored a number of articles on issues to do with justice in *Australasian Journal of Philosophy, Canadian Journal of Philosophy, Ethics, Philosophical Quarterly* and *Philosophy*. His book on the subject is *Justice as Fittingness* (1996).

Wendy Donner is Professor of Philosophy at Carleton University, Canada. Her main areas of interest are in moral, social and political philosophy, and the history of liberalism. She is the author of articles in these fields in various journals and collections, and of the study *The Liberal Self: John Stuart Mill's Moral and Political Philosophy* (1991). Her next book will also be on Mill.

Anthony Ellis was Chair of the Moral Philosophy Department in the University of St. Andrews where he was also co-founder and first Academic Director of the Centre for Philosophy and Public Affairs. Thereafter he became Professor of Philosophy and Department Chair in Virginia Commonwealth University. He has published in a number of areas of philosophy, but now works mainly in the philosophy of law. He is currently editor of the journal *Philosophical Books*.

Daniel Farrell is Professor of Philosophy and sometime Chair of the Department of Philosophy at Ohio State University. He works in the areas of political, social and legal philosophy and has published extensively on the issues of threats, deterrence and punishment in journals such as *Ethics, Nous, Philosophical Review* and *Social Philosophy and Policy*.

Bart Gruzalski was Professor of Philosophy at Northeastern University in Boston, before co-founding in California the Pacific Center for Sustainable Living. He has published on moral theory and applied ethics in *Australasian Journal of Philosophy, Canadian Journal of Philosophy, Environmental Ethics, Ethics, Mind* and *Philosophical Studies*. His most recent books are *On the Buddha* (2000) and *On Ghandi* (2001).

John Haldane is Professor of Philosophy in the University of St Andrews where he is also Director of the Centre for Ethics, Philosophy and Public Affairs. He has also been Royden Davis Professor of Humanities at Georgetown University. He is the author (with J.J.C. Smart) of *Atheism and Theism* (second edition 2003), *An Intelligent Person's Guide to Religion* (2003), *Faithful Reason* (2004), and editor of *Philosophy and Public Affairs* (2000) and other volumes.

Jonathan Jacobs is Professor of Philosophy and Director of the Division of Humanities at Colgate University, New York State. He has wide-ranging interests but works mainly in the areas of moral philosophy and the history of philosophy. His books include *A Philosopher's Compass* (2000), *Choosing Character: Responsibility for Virtue and Vice* (2001) and *Dimensions of Moral Theory* (2002).

Rex Martin is Professor of Philosophy at the University of Kansas and was also Professor of Political Theory and Government in the University of Wales Swansea. His fields of interest are political and legal philosophy, and philosophy of history. He is the author of *Historical Explanation: Re-enactment and Practical Inference* (1977), *Rawls and Rights* (1985) and *A System of Rights* (1993). He has also edited the revised edition of R.G. Collingwood's *Essay on Metaphysics* (1998).

Terence McLaughlin is Professor of Philosophy of Education in the Institute of Education, University of London and Fellow of St Edmund's College, Cambridge. He is also currently Chair of the Philosophy of Education Society of Great Britain. He has published widely in Philosophy of Education, and has co-edited a number of collections including *Education and the Market Place* (with David Bridges 1994) and *Education in Morality* (with Mark Halstead 1999).

Andrew Moore is a Senior Lecturer and in the Department of Philosophy, University of Otago, New Zealand. He also chairs New Zealand's National Ethics Advisory Committee. His research and publications are on ethics, political philosophy, and practical ethics, and include recent essays in the *Australasian Journal of Philosophy*, *Bioethics* and *Health Care Analysis*; and in edited collections on *Well-being and Morality*, and *Time and Ethics*.

Lisa Portmess is Professor of Philosophy and Chair of the Department of Philosophy at Gettysburg College, Pennsylvania. Her areas of research include the philosophy of law, and applied ethics. She is the co-editor of two volumes of essays on vegetarianism: *Ethical Vegetarianism: From Pythagoras to Peter Singer* (1999) and *Religious Vegetarianism: From Hesiod to the Dalai Lama* (2001).

William Aiken &
John Haldane

Introduction

Background

Like the first volume in this series (*Values, Education and the Human World*), the present collection of essays grew out of activities of the *Centre for Ethics, Philosophy and Public Affairs*. Since its establishment in 1984 the Centre has run a visiting fellowship programme which in its first twenty years brought some seventy fellows to St Andrews to work on various issues in ethics, moral psychology and social and political philosophy. More than half of this number have come from North America and it seemed apt, therefore, to arrange a conference of former fellows in the United States.

This the Centre did in 2002 with a grant from the *Philosophical Quarterly* and with the hospitality of Chatham College in Pittsburgh, Pennsylvania. The meeting was held in the former residence of Andrew Mellon, the famous Pittsburgh banker and industrialist and sometime Secretary of the US Treasury. As well as providing a beautiful location, having once been home to a major public figure and now being part of an academic institution the setting was apt to the theme of the conference. We are grateful to the President of Chatham Dr Esther Barazzone for permission to use the Mellon House and for her encouraging welcome to the meeting. We are grateful also to the *Philosophical Quarterly* for its financial support of the event.

Given the geographical location of the conference it was to be expected that most participants would be from within the US, but other countries and continents were represented and the contributors to this volume are from Canada, New Zealand and the United Kingdom, as well as from the United States. What unites them intellectually, and what brought them originally to the St Andrews Centre, is a common commitment to the value of deploying the resources of philosophy in the effort to understand and advance discussion of issues of broad theoretical and practical importance.

From the earliest period of the subject philosophers have addressed issues of personal and public values. Pythagoreans, Epicureans and Stoics, as well as Plato and Aristotle, all had things to say about the nature of the public good and what is conducive to it, as well as considering how an individual should live in order to be fulfilled as a human being. The tradition of practical philosophy continued in the West through the middle ages when it was deepened and given systematic treatment in the works of Aquinas and others, and then later in the casuistical tradition which the scholastics inspired. In parallel with these developments may be found Eastern explorations of the individual and common good in Confucianism and Taoism; and then later in the middle east in the traditions of Islamic philosophy.

The European enlightenment and its nineteenth-century democratic legacy saw the merging of Western philosophy and politics in forms that are still with us today. While these originated in the old world they were most extensively realised in the public culture of post-colonial North America. The United States has journeyed a long way in two and a quarter centuries, further perhaps than the European societies from which it originally derived. A decade after the war of independence from Britain a gathering was convened in Philadelphia originally to revise the 1781 articles of confederation. It quickly became clear, however, that something more radical was called for and so emerged the Constitutional convention. The dialectical and rhetorical styles of the contributions to this are immediately recognisable to those familiar with European, particularly British philosophy. The ideas of John Locke and Thomas Reid had arrived in the new world and were shaping its emergent public philosophy.

At the point of the convention's bicentenary in 1987 there was still a sense in the higher reaches of American public culture that questions of policy could and should be resolved by reference to rational deliberation about substantive ends. That is to say it was presumed that policy could be shaped not just by the fair procedures or balanced compromises of liberal contractarianism, but by independently right outcomes, i.e. ones oriented towards objective human goods. Things may now be somewhat different in this respect and they are continuing to change. The demands associated with acquiring the role of world leadership have proved testing of a society that is still developing. The civil rights debate, Vietnam, Watergate, foreign wars, and, certainly not least, the effects of unparalleled affluence have all had an impact upon the ethical confidence of the US. Witness in this connection the domestic demoralisation effected by reports of barbarism perpetrated by the US military in Iraq.

At the same time Europe has faced its own challenges: the adjustment to the decline of industry, the changed expectations of the role of the state, the collapse of the Soviet bloc, new immigration, the changes in individual and family life, the proliferation of new media, and the impact of science and technology. Since some of these factors operate also in North America and elsewhere, and since the US so dominates the English-speaking world, it is unsurprising that Anglophone philosophers in America, in Britain and in Australasia share common concerns and methods. Some of these are in evidence in the essays that comprise this volume.

Philosophy, Society and Culture

The first chapter by John Haldane is a version an address, first given a few months prior to the Pittsburgh conference, to the *American Philosophical Association* on the occasion of its centennial. The essay examines the character and standing of American philosophy now and at the outset of the twentieth century as seen (then and now) from a British point of view. A century ago Britain was itself the unquestioned leader of Anglo-Saxon thought. Now, however, as in so many areas, the US is the pre-eminent world power. This status brings prestige and various benefits but it also carries responsibilities. In considering the latter Haldane recalls some virtues of an earlier generation of American philosophers, especially as they were possessed by William James.

Bob Brecher reasons that, both liberal 'disinterest' and postmodern disavowal of rationality notwithstanding, intellectuals must in some sense be committed to a notion of truth, however circumscribed. Beyond that he argues that practical rationality underpins theoretical reasoning. He suggests that the question of what is to be done is therefore integral to any 'purely intellectual' issue, and further that the objection that intelligence is fit for any purpose true or false, good or bad, can be answered. According to Brecher intellectuals have a particular public responsibility to speak out — one additional to the general moral responsibility of citizens.

In 'speaking out' one may be required to observe a distinctive idea of public reason. According to John Arthur the commitment to this idea reflects an understanding of political legitimacy, by insisting that public justifications be limited in certain respects. He observes that this is doubly controversial, because the idea itself is sometimes thought unrealistic and misguided. Some argue that it is unrealistic because people cannot ignore other reasons, and wrong-headed in insisting that law, for example, should be blind to race and gender. Against these claims, Arthur argues that at its core public reason is a style of impartiality. Properly understood the controversy is not about public reason as such, but about its application.

What norms of public reason we feel are apt reflect cultural as much as any other influences. In his verse and in other writings clearly addressed to issues and problems concerning the post-industrial moral and spiri-

tual condition the poet W.H. Auden jointly identifies the English romantic William Blake, the American progressive educator Homer Lane and
the modern English novelist D.H. Lawrence as 'healers in our land'. He
does so in a way that suggests that they might be held to have been
engaged in some common therapeutic project. In the course of a survey
of their literary and practical works, however, David Carr seeks to show
that despite their undeniably profound psychological insights, their
ideas draw on different sources and point in different socio-political,
therapeutic and educational directions.

The educational theme is continued in Terry McLaughlin's essay on
the subject of values and schooling. McLaughlin is concerned with the
justification of the evaluative influence that schools in pluralist liberal
democratic societies exert on their students. While schooling is not, of
course, synonymous with education, schools remain important institutional contexts in which education is made available to children and
young people, and schooling, like education itself, is inherently value
laden. McLaughlin seeks to show that an exploration of the principles
and predicaments of teacher example in different schooling contexts
throws important light on our understanding of the principles and predicaments relating to 'common' and 'faith-based' schools, respectively.

This distinction represents one kind of deep cultural difference. In her
essay Wendy Donner explores issues surrounding group identity as this
is held to bear upon the legitimacy of certain kinds of liberal policies.
Liberalism is often criticized as being excessively individualistic and
consequently overly concerned with individual identity. Donner, however, argues that liberalism is correct in asserting the primacy of individual identity, and that principled moral agency requires autonomous
individuals who reflect upon and choose their group attachments.
While we are often deeply immersed in social contexts, and our identities are shaped and constrained by gender, culture, class and sexuality,
nevertheless we engage in a process of individuation to construct and
change our personal identities, and in so doing become the sort of secure
and tolerant individuals who can accept difference in others.

Ethics, Economics and Justice

Andrew Moore begins his essay by inviting us to consider the following
case. A patient lies unconscious in hospital and is shortly going to die. At
the death, his partner asks the attending doctor to collect and store
semen from him, to enable her to try for children after his death with the
assistance of IVF. What ought to be done? Moore is here concerned with
the ethical significance of the deceased's consent in potential settings of
postmortem reproduction, and to policy regarding such settings. So far
as the latter is concerned a plausible account of the purposes of public
policy will include the idea that it should oppose unethical conduct, and

not oppose ethically permissible conduct. As Moore notes, however, there is an issue of how to approach these two objectives in contexts where it seems that what would serve one better would serve the other less well.

The challenges facing most of the world's population are more immediate and concern the limitations imposed by poverty. As Geoff Cupit observes, there are considerable inequalities of wealth, political power, education, health care and life-span. While some of these are 'shared around' for the most part this is not so, and some people are much better off overall than others. Cupit examines whether this overall inequality matters. In answer to the question of why we should focus on overall inequality, rather than on specific inequalities he suggests that, providing it makes sense to talk of overall equality and inequality then, if equality is indeed an ideal, it seems reasonable to suppose that it is *overall* equality that is that ideal. This, however, returns us to the issue of whether equality really is a value and leads towards the question of how it may be related to desert, freedom, justice and fairness.

Bart Gruzalski argues that aside from questions of global justice the affluent have reason to modify their material consumption. People often justify the level of First World consumption by arguing that it raises the standard of living. By reference to Amartya Sen's work on capability analysis, Gruzalski reasons that by pursuing their own interest through the purchase of certain classes of highly fashionable goods individuals may actually worsen their lives. He argues that we should therefore encourage development (which does not increase the material bases of our capabilities) instead of growth (which does).

In the essay that follows, Jim Child observes that while the dramatic technological changes of the last fifty years have already had profound consequences for the organisation of economic and social life, those introduced by the internet portend even greater change and threaten traditional political structures. The vast new capacity to process and store information, and the ability and speed of the internet together challenge the concepts of private property and of the nation state. Child surveys recent developments, reviews something of the history of political thought, and explores the problems and prospects now facing us.

Technological innovation always carries social risks, as indeed does any significant material development. Often, however, it is argued that while it is known that there will be some consequent harm if a power plant is built or a new product introduced the risk to anyone in the risk pool is extremely slight compared to the benefits conferred. This is often taken to be a deciding factor in introducing the plant or product into the community. Richard Brook argues that since the probabilities considered are epistemic rather than objective this argument fails. His conclusion is that there is no moral difference between a 'statistical death' and an 'identifiable death'; and that the only consideration should be the total number of likely deaths and injuries.

Rights, Law and Punishment

Issues of public policy arise in fields now structured by the idea of rights. Rex Martin argues that civil rights, as political rights universal within a given society are important, and that they can be justified in relation to what is of benefit to each and all of its citizens. He also seeks to develop the notion of full-bodied human rights under three headings: as requiring effective normative justification; as having authoritative political endorsement; and as requiring to be maintained by conforming conduct and, where necessary, by governmental enforcement. He then applies this notion to particular cases considering to what extent the idea of human rights can be particularised to different cultural preferences and histories.

A compelling complement to this examination is provided by Lisa Portmess who considers the case of miltary tribunals as courts providing neither military nor civilian justice but a distinctive, and contested, parallel legal system with different standards of evidence. Prior to the attacks on the US of September 11, 2001, these issues might have seemed of somewhat specialised interest but the detention of terrorist suspects and their delayed trial has brought the justice of military tribunals to the forefront of public discussion. Lisa Portmess argues that as pressure for greater due process intensifies, with higher standards of evidence, the likelihood increases of indefinite detention of suspects without trial, or of trials in which incrimination by group affiliation substitutes for absent evidence.

Trials lead either to acquittal or to conviction and hence to punishment. It is an ancient and still pressing question of what justifies the latter. Anthony Ellis sets out a theory of punishment according to which it is justified as a form of deterrence. Traditionally deterrence theory has been interpreted as holding that offenders are punished to deter others (or themselves). This invites the objection that it involves an unacceptable use of people. Ellis refines the broad deterrence approach to argue that it would be legitimate, in self-defence, to issue to potential aggressors a threat which in normal circumstances once issued could not fail to be implemented; and he holds that, ideally, this is what our criminal justice systems are like.

Ellis concurs with the view that retribution is an unacceptable warrant for judicial punishment. Jonathan Jacobs argues in contrast that punishment is not merely a strategy of social regulation but is also a mode of public address to rational agents, and part of its moral justification is that it is so. Yet some individuals are rational, responsible agents, even though on account of their characters they are unable to recognise why some of their actions are wrong. Jacobs argues that even so it can be morally legitimate to punish them though they do not, and perhaps cannot, recognise the justice of their being sanctioned.

By tradition the ultimate punishment imposed by society upon those who have violated its laws is the death penalty. Once this was a sanction dispensed for a variety of crimes, but by stages it tended to be reserved for murder and then in some jurisdictions to be dispensed with altogether. Dan Farrell observes that the two most common justifications for capital punishment are the retributive argument and what he terms the 'societal-self-protection argument'. Although the first is the more popular of the two among the public in general, Farrell concentrates upon the second according to which capital punishment is both necessary and justified as a way of preventing (or at least reducing the incidence of) harm to the innocent. He does so because while he judges that there is little chance of changing opinions on the retribution argument he thinks that with regard to the other there is some reason to believe that philosophical progress on the issue of capital punishment is possible.

Conclusion

Readers will judge for themselves what progress is achieved in each of the essays; but we would encourage them also to consider the collection as a totality; as a contribution to the general project of bringing philosophy to the public sphere where matters of common interest are discussed with a view to making or to changing policy. The individual contributors and the editors have their own, sometimes conflicting, views on particular issues; but they are as one in believing that philosophy has a public role and that it is important that professional philosophers seek to discharge it. The present volume and that referred to at the outset (*Values, Education and the Human World*) are the first two sets of St Andrews Studies in Philosophy and Public Affairs. It is planned that future volumes will carry the task of examining issues of importance and broad interest into other areas, as well as revisiting some of those already explored.

I
PHILOSOPHY , SOCIETY
AND CULTURE

John Haldane

American Philosophy and its Public Role

Introduction[1]

The *American Philosophical Association* was founded in New York in 1901, with its first meeting being held at Columbia University the following year. Its foundation was more or less coincident with the emergence of American philosophy on to the international scene and the same period saw the first American Gifford lecturers. A century later the United States dominates the English-speaking philosophical community and is set to remain pre-eminent. This advancement parallels more general social trends, but it is no less remarkable for being unsurprising.

In exploring something of the character and standing of American philosophy then and now I approach the subject from a British point of view. At the outset of the twentieth century Britain was itself the unquestioned leader of Anglo-Saxon thought. Now, however, as in so many areas, the US is the unrivalled world power. This status brings prestige and various benefits but, as global political events testify, it also carries responsibilities. In considering the latter I shall highlight some virtues of an earlier generation of American thinkers, especially as they were possessed by one who a century ago was seen in Britain, and in the States, as representing the best of American philosophy.

Let me begin, however, by recalling older thoughts about the place of philosophy within American culture as these were expressed by two

[1]   Earlier versions of the following were given as an invited address to the *American Philosophical Association* in Atlanta, Georgia, December 29, 2001, on the occasion of the centennial celebration of the founding of the *APA*, and to the conference on Philosophy and its Public Role held at Chatham College, Pittsburgh in June 2002. A longer version of the present essay appears under the title 'American Philosophy: "Scotch" or "Teutonic"', in *Philosophy*, Vol. 77, 2002. The common material reappears in the current essay with the permission of Cambridge University Press. The paper was written during a period of tenure as Royden Davis Professor of Humanities at Georgetown University and I am grateful to the University for the benefits bestowed by this appointment.

other non-Americans; both continental Europeans. The first passage comes from Hegel's *Lectures on the Philosophy of History:*

> Only after the immeasurable spaces of America are filled, and the population of this civil society is pressed together, only then will it be possible to compare North America to Europe . . . only then will the population develop the need for an organized state.
>
> America is therefore the land of the future. In the time to come, the center of world-historical importance will be revealed there. ... It is a land of longing for all those who are weary of the historic arsenal that is old Europe (Hegel, 1837/1988, pp. 89–90).

In the same year that Hegel died (1831), the French Catholic aristocrat Count Alexis de Tocqueville travelled to see the land which the German sometime-Pietist philosopher could only imagine. From the second part of Tocqueville's *Democracy in America* comes the following observation:

> The Americans have no philosophical school, and they care but little for all the schools into which Europe is divided, the very names of which are scarcely known to them. Nevertheless it is easy to perceive . . . that without ever having taken the trouble to define the rules of a philosophical method, they are in possession of one common to the whole people . . .
>
> . . . I discover that in most of the operations of the mind, each American appeals to the individual exercise of his own understanding alone. America is therefore one of the countries in the world where philosophy is least studied, and where the precepts of Descartes are best applied (de Tocqueville, 1839/ 2000, Vol. II, Bk. l, ch. 1, pp. 511 – 2).

I shall return briefly to aspects of these observations, but for now I let them stand as providing their own themes for reflection.

American Philosophy Then and Now

I spoke of approaching American philosophy from a 'British' point of view. Being a Scot and a member of a Scottish University (St Andrews) it would be more apt, however, to speak of a 'Scottish' one, as this may serve to explain the particular and strong sympathy I feel for aspects of the American philosophical tradition, aspects of which, as we will see, owe a good deal to earlier Scottish thinkers.

2001 saw the centenary of both the *American Philosophical Association* and the *Scots Philosophical Club.* The latter is a very much smaller society (by about a hundredfold: circa one hundred as against ten thousand members). The *SPC*'s current membership is less than that achieved by the *APA* within its first or second years; but at the point of establishment of the two societies their membership was comparable, both in numbers and in common heritage. Both societies were formed at a time when the populations of philosophers in Britain and in the United States were much smaller, and the great majority were then more concerned with teaching the subject than with original scholarly activity. They were also more socially and intellectually homogenous, both within and between them. Moreover, it was then possible for the active philosophers to read each other's works fairly comprehensively; in part because there were many fewer of them, but also because they were more closely related in subject matter and style, and in their understanding of the status and scope of philosophy itself.

One of the great changes effected in the course of the twentieth century, and particularly following the Second World War, was the increase in the number of professional philosophers, especially in the United States. The explanation lies in the enormous expansion of higher education: with more colleges and universities and more graduate programmes. As is the way of these things, enlargement has also brought diversification of the field, as the greater numbers of professionals pursue different interests and try to establish distinctive sector niches. At the same time, however, the style of graduate education, the prestige of certain programmes, and the professionalisation of the practice of philosophy have led to a high degree of intellectual conformity. This is essentially that of group identification occasionally, but unconvincingly, masked by non-conformist rhetoric. These various institutional and professional forces have also resulted in a general disengagement from the traditional manner of humane reflection directed towards an educated public.

Related to this is the idea, now voiced by moral philosophers as well as by metaphysicians, that like science, and unlike the arts, philosophy now offers the prospect of unmistakable progress in the solution of certain well-defined problems;[2] and with the promise of such progress comes the prospect of professional advancement. It was once common to speak of a philosophical 'calling' and of a life given to its practice, as one might of a life given to literature, theology or to the study of classical antiquity; now it is typical to speak of philosophical 'career advancement' and of 'research projects'.

A flavour of the contrast is given in John Dewey's autobiographical essay 'From Absolutism to Experimentalism', in which he recalls his education at the University of Vermont where the teaching of philosophy was influenced by what Dewey describes as 'the still dominant Scotch school'. He notes that 'Teachers of philosophy were at that time, almost to a man, clergymen' (remarking again the predominance among them of 'Scotch philosophy'); and later he writes of how, after a year of private scholarship: 'I decided to make philosophy my life-study, and accordingly went to Johns Hopkins the next year (1884) to enter upon that "new thing" graduate work' (Dewey, 1930/1973, pp. 380ff).

---

[2] For a critical discussion of these matters see Haldane (2001).

In comparing the situation of American philosophy today with that obtaining a century ago the most striking differences are the changed conceptions of the nature of philosophy in relation to other fields of enquiry and scholarship, and the changed expectations of its public role in education, culture and society. In regard to the latter I have in mind both the expectations held *by* philosophers, and the expectations others may have *of* them. These aspects are, of course, related. The world takes practitioners as it finds them, and too often it has found philosophers uninterested in the world. The influence of American (and British) thinkers as opinion-shapers in the field of public policy, in the broad cultural sphere, and even in the area of the theory and practice of higher education, has declined throughout the twentieth century. Consider that in post-war Britain, Justin Gosling, Stuart Hampshire, Anthony Kenny, Malcolm Knox, Onora O'Neill, Anthony Quinton, Alan Ryan, Stewart Sutherland, Geoffrey Warnock, Mary Warnock, and Bernard Williams have all been heads of colleges or universities, but that with Lord Sutherland's retirement from the Principalship of Edinburgh University in 2002, Onora O'Neill and Alan Ryan are the only remaining philosopher-cum-educational leaders.

So far as the US is concerned it has been said that John Dewey was America's last public philosopher — and he died half a century ago (in 1952). Certainly outside the academy even America's leading figures exert little, if any, influence. Martha Nussbaum and Richard Rorty may be the best candidates for exceptions to this last claim; though while, like Rawls, they are read by non-philosophers their readership remains largely within the academy, and mostly among those who take a philosophical view of their own subjects (principally political science and cultural and women's studies).

In general the profession has itself to blame for the want of wider interest in it. Even in the fields of applied philosophy, which is not what the world comes to philosophy for, the use of pseudo-technical formulations hinders rather than helps. In speculative philosophy it both adds to the sense, and furthers the fact of the subject's isolation. Increasingly, though late in the day, these effects are being complained about by philosophers themselves. In a recent article C.B. Martin and John Heil lament this situation and offer a similar diagnosis of its causes. They begin as follows:

> Contemporary philosophy of mind, like much contemporary philosophy, has become mired in sterile disputes over technical issues apparently of interest only to professional philosophers. One symptom of the current malaise is the difficulty philosophers have in motivating central themes to outsiders. Attention lavished on possible worlds, the causal relevance of mental content, and supervenience is difficult to justify to anyone who has not been con-

ditioned by an appropriately *comme il faut* Ph.D. program (Martin and Heil, 1999).

It is hard not to recognise some truth in this even if one thinks that the use of technical concepts has brought clarity, precision and progress at least to the extent of identifying possibilities. Whether there has indeed been significant progress in the philosophy of mind is a matter about which I have some doubts, though this is not the occasion to pursue them (see Haldane, 2000).

The Jamesian Philosophy

Over the last century there has been a good deal of traffic of persons, publications and ideas to and fro across the Atlantic; but the general direction of influence and the relative standing of the countries has unquestionably changed. Recent British philosophy has been more focused upon the writings of such as Davidson, Dennett, Kripke, Lewis, Nagel, Nozick, Putnam, Quine, Rawls, Rorty, Scanlon and Searle, than upon the thought of Anscombe, Foot, Geach, Hampshire, Hare, Mellor, Strawson and Winch. Dummett, MacIntyre, Wiggins, Williams and Wollheim are exceptions to this catalogue of American pre-eminence, as in younger generations are McDowell, McGinn, Parfit, Peacocke and Wright; but of these all but Dummett and Wiggins have held, or do hold, full or part-time positions in US universities.

A hundred years ago matters of influence and standing were very different. Americans looked across the Atlantic to Scotland, England, Germany and France. They were also keen to associate themselves with the intellectual traditions that had given birth to Hume and Reid, Locke and Berkeley, Kant and Hegel, and Descartes and Malebranche. This can easily be seen in the writings of the period. The commonly felt sense of respect, and even of deference, is expressed in the following preface to one of the great American works of a century ago. The writer is William James introducing his Gifford lectures of 1901–2:

> It is with no small amount of trepidation that I take my place behind this desk, and face this learned audience. To us Americans the experience of receiving instruction from the living voice as well as from the books of European scholars is very familiar . . .
>
> It seems the natural thing for us to listen while Europeans talk. The contrary habit, of talking whilst Europeans listen, we have not yet acquired; and in him who first makes the adventure it begets a certain sense of apology being due for so presumptuous an act. Particularly must this be the case on a soil as sacred to the American imagination as that of Edinburgh . . .
>
> Let me say only that now that the current, here and at Aberdeen, has begun to run from west to east, I hope it may continue to do so. As the years go by I hope that many of my countrymen may be asked to lecture in the Scottish universities, changing places with Scotsmen lecturing in the States; I hope that our people may become as one people; and that the peculiar philosophic tem-

perament, as well as the peculiar political temperament, that goes with our English speech may more and more pervade and influence the world (James, 1902, pp. 4–5).

This passage invites commentary.[3] First, while James bows graciously before his audience I doubt that he was as awed by the occasion as his words may suggest. He was already admired in Britain as were other American philosophical writers. Another figure already known was his Harvard colleague Josiah Royce. In fact, in spite of James speaking of 'being the first to make the adventure' (of talking while the Europeans listen) he had in fact been preceded as a Gifford lecturer two years before by Royce who spoke in Aberdeen on the theme of 'The World and the Individual'.

The earlier invitation had been issued to James himself, but he sought a postponement, and suggested that he knew someone else who would do the immediate job very well. Royce had been educated at Berkeley, Gottingen, Leipzig, and Johns Hopkins, and notwithstanding significant philosophical disagreements James had already advanced Royce's career by securing his employment at Harvard. So the invitation was issued, which Royce accepted with enthusiasm. Born in Grass Valley during the California Gold Rush and subsequently described as that state's 'gift to philosophy', Josiah Royce was formed a neo-Hegelean and developed his own brand of logic-involving Absolute Idealism. A flavour of his gift to Scotland is given by the following characterisation of *being* as that is implied in the meanings of ideas:

> . . . first, the complete fulfillment of your internal meaning, the final satisfaction of the will embodied in the idea; but secondly also, that absolute determination of the embodiment of your idea as this embodiment would then be present — that absolute determination of your purpose, which would constitute an individual realization of the idea. For an individual act is one for which no other can be sustained without some loss of determination, or some vagueness (Royce, 1899, pp. 338–9).

This sort of thing infuriated Russell and he became no less passionate in his opposition to it even as he grew old. In a National Book League lecture delivered in 1946 and entitled 'Philosophy and Politics' he quotes the primary source and is withering in his sarcasm:

> Of [the Absolute Idea, Hegel] gives the following definition: '*The Absolute Idea.* The idea, as unity of the subjective and objective Idea, is the notion of the Idea — a notion whose object is the Idea as such. and for which the objective is Idea — an Object which embraces all characteristics in its unity'. [Russell then continues] I hate to spoil the luminous clarity of this sentence by any commentary, but in fact, the same thing would be expressed by saying 'The Absolute Idea is pure thought thinking about pure thought' (Russell, 1949, p. 91).

---

[3]   I was first alerted to some of the issues I now discuss by Peter Jones's article on William James (1985) to which I am indebted.

James likewise spoke disparagingly of Hegelean and other 'teutonic philosophy'. He and Russell had their differences, for example, over the theses of the *Varieties of Religious Experience* (of which Russell wrote 'everything is good about the book except the conclusions' (Russell, 1951, p. 252), and over the importance of formal methods: in a letter of 1908 to Russell, James wrote 'my dying words to you are "Say good-bye to mathematical logic if you wish to preserve your relations with concrete realities"' (See Russell, 1951, p. 303). It is ironic, therefore, that following James's death, a year or so later, the status of being America's best known philosopher settled upon the logic-loving Californian devotee of the Universal Absolute.

This leads to my second comment which is prompted by James's remark about the 'Peculiar philosophical temperament . . . that goes with the English speech'. Whatever their differences, James and Russell were appreciative of the classical British empirical tradition and were equally opposed to idealism. That Royce's teutonic metaphysics did not meet with staunch opposition from his Scottish audience is due to the fact that the astringent philosophical styles of Hume and Reid had given way, through a series of transformations, to a Caledonian brand of Hegeleanism. This was associated primarily with the Edinburgh and St Andrews philosopher James Ferrier — author the term 'epistemology' and of its less successful counterpart 'agnoiology' (the theory of ignorance). Ferrier fell under the influence of absolute idealism in Germany which he visited in 1834, bringing back to Edinburgh works by and a medallion of the not-so-late Hegel.

The most ironic of these transformations came at the hands of Sir William Hamilton, Reid's self-appointed chief editor and sometime mentor of Ferrier. As others have done since, Hamilton thought to improve Reid's realism by accommodating it to Kantian epistemology. It will be no surprise, however, that Reidean realists are keen to reject Hamilton's 'improvement'. In his effort to reconcile direct epistemological engagement with the diversity of epistemic perspectives Hamilton spoke of 'the conditioned relativity of knowledge', and such was his prestige that conceptual relativism took secure root in Scotland before it had even been planted on English soil; and in the capable hands of Ferrier it had put forth blooms of Hegelean form and proportion. So it was that Royce could feel that in Kings College, Aberdeen he had an audience that understood him. When I add that the Giffords have always been public lectures attended by town as well as by gown, that may give a sense of how educated a public there was for such lectures, and also how familiar in its broadest features, was Hegeleanism to that audience.

A third comment arising from James's introduction is that any doubt one may have about the sincerity of his opening words of humble appreciation as he began his own lectures is entirely eliminated when it comes to those passages in which he mentions the Scots philosophers. When he spoke of the Europeans 'talking as Americans listened' he went on to identify 'Scottish, English, French or German representatives of the science or literature of their respective countries'. He was himself of Scots/Irish extraction and this may have coloured his estimate slightly; but it is no doubt true that, as he says, his first philosophical reading was of Scots authors: Sir William Hamilton, Dugald Stewart and Thomas Brown. As Dewey later noted, this was generally the case of people of education in nineteenth-century America. Indeed, the influence of the thinkers James mentions, as of the other Scots, who Dewey had in mind (such as John Witherspoon, Hugh Blair and James McCosh) upon the development of American philosophy, even into the twentieth century, is still insufficiently appreciated. (For accounts of this influence see Duncan, 1975; Fowler, 1980; and Fleischacker, 2003.)

It was members of this broad group who introduced to America the idea that philosophy should be fundamental in College education; and it was this that influenced James to write in *Some Problems of Philosophy* that:

> philosophy in one sense of the term is only a compendium name for the spirit in education which the word 'college' stands for in America; something to be associated with liberal education (James, 1911, p. 6).

Elsewhere — in 'The Sentiment of Rationality' — he follows the Scots philosophers in stressing the importance of feeling in moral psychology, and (anticipating Merleau-Ponty) in emphasizing the significance of phenomenal bodily consciousness as falsifying the Cartesian form of the division between mind and body. The first of these, and arguably so far as Hume and Adam Smith are concerned the second also, is a central element in eighteenth and nineteenth century Scots moral science. A third element of that tradition, alighted upon by the pragmatists, (and later rediscovered by 'basic belief' philosophers of religion such as Plantinga and Wolterstorff (Calvinists both)) is the place given to *natural belief* as a category in epistemology. Perhaps the best discussion of this is in Peirce's 1905 essay 'Issues of Pragmatism' where he commends the 'Scotch philosophers' for recognising that 'the original beliefs [are] of the general nature of instincts' (Peirce, 1905, p. 441).

Other metaphilosophical aspects of this tradition also find expression in James's writings. For reasons of space I simply enumerate four of these:

1) *Belief in the need to master effective modes of expression.*
    A.J. Ayer who faults James for his want of analytical rigour nonetheless writes of his prose as follows: 'There are philosophers, such as Hume and Russell, who have written with greater elegance, but no modern philosopher matches William James in the vividness and range of his imagery or the freshness of his humour' (Ayer, 1968, p. 175).

2) *Belief in the value of the public lecture.*
James berates Peirce for neglecting the requirement that, as he put it, 'a lecture must succeed *as such'*.

3) *Belief that the quality of a soul is measured by its practical fruits.*
This suggests a Christian influence. It is not, however, the doctrine of salvation aided by works, but the specifically Calvinist one (whose influence is also evident among the Scots philosophers) of salvation by predestined election; good fruits being evidence of that predestination.

4) *Belief in the social role of the philosopher.*
In the previous passage Ayer writes: 'But aiming, as he mostly did, at a wider audience than that of his professional colleagues, he was more concerned to present his opinions in a way that would appeal to the imagination than to fortify them against minute criticism.'

My fourth comment concerns the set of attitudes that James acquired from his reading of the Scots, which made the Gifford invitation so pleasing to him, and which disinclined him to the German academic tradition in philosophy. I have already quoted him to this effect but the full intensity of his opposition deserves to be registered. In a letter to Schiller in Oxford he writes: '*Vive* the Anglo-Saxon amateur, disciple of Locke and Hume, and *pereat* the German professional.' What he was objecting to here was principally a conception of philosophy as a technical science.[4] In the same letter he writes as follows:

> It is an uplifting thought that truth is to be told at last in a radical and attention compelling manner. I think I know, though, how the attention of many will find a way not to be compelled — their will is set on having a technically and artificially and professionally expressed system, that all talk carried on as yours is on principles of common-sense activity, is as remote and little worthy of being listened to as the slanging each other of boys in the street as we pass. Men disdain to notice that. It is only after our (i.e. your and my) general way of thinking gets organised enough to become a regular part of the bureaucracy of philosophy that we shall get a serious hearing. Then, I feel inwardly convinced, our day will have come (James, 1902/1920).

James's mention of the 'bureaucracy of philosophy' sounds ironic, but I presume that what he means by it is only broad acceptance as measured by reading and teaching among professors and students of the discipline. Like Russell and the British realists, James's hostility to German philosophy was not just to its manner and theoretic pretensions. He also objected strongly to the doctrines of Absolute Idealism. In particular, he

---

[4] According to Schelling's lecture of 1827 'Ueber den nationellen Gegensatz in der Philosophie' (On the National Opposition in Philosophy) the true 'scientific' speculative and systematic philosophy is German; see F. W. J. Schelling, 1996, Vol. 10, pp. 193–200.

wanted to eliminate any scope for Hegelean concepts in the 'new' psychology he and others had been developing. In the work *A Pluralistic Universe* (which had been given as lectures in Oxford in 1909) he quotes and glosses a certain amount of Absolute Idealist metaphysical psychology-cum-psychological metaphysics, and he rejects it fairly passionately.[5] Recognising, however, that this is inadequate in a philosophical context he acknowledges the need for something more dialectical:

> abstract emotional appeals of any kind sound amateurish in the business that concerns us. Impressionistic philosophising, like impressionistic watch making or land surveying is intolerable to experts. Serious discussion of the alternatives before us forces me, therefore, to become more technical (James, 1909).

There is in this something of an element of regret, but the more important point is that James had arrived at a view of the general character of a position on the basis of habituated good judgement and any 'technical' demonstration is secondary to that. This is 'prejudice' only in the sense of pre-judgement. It would be as wrong to suggest that James is not in a position to judge the character of the whole until he has worked through the detail, as it would be to maintain that one was not in a position to make a moral judgement until one had done the relevant abstract philosophy, or assembled a case sufficient to secure conviction in a court of moral law. This is just the sort of thing that James recoiled from and which he feared threatened the development of philosophy in America.

Taking Stock

A century on where do we stand? One comparative approach would be to explore in detail the contents of the leading academic publications then and now. There is not the space to do so here, but nor, I think is there the need, for even a brief inspection suffices to reveal a number of obviously significant points. If one looks at *Mind* for 1900 and 1901 and at the corresponding volumes of the *Philosophical Review* one notices several

---

[5]   At one point in *A Pluralistic Universe* James quotes at length from an essay by Henry Jones which was published in the *Contemporary Review* in 1907: 'For many years adherents of [the idealist] way of thought have deeply interested the British public by their writings. Almost more important than their writings is the fact that they have occupied philosophical chairs in almost every university in the country. . . . Carlyle introduced it, bringing it as far as Chelsea. Then Jowett and Thomas Hill Green, and William Wallace and Lewis Nettleship, and Arnold Toynbee and David Ritchie . . . guided the waters into those upper reaches known locally as the Isis [to Oxford]. John and Edward Caird brought them up the Clyde [to Glasgow], Hutchinson Stirling up the Forth [to Edinburgh]. They have passed up the Mersey [to Liverpool] and up the Severn [to Bristol] and Dee and Don [to Aberdeen]. The pollute the bay of St Andrews and swell the waters of the Cam [Cambridge], and have somehow crept overland into Birmingham. The stream of German idealism has been diffused over the academical world of Great Britain. The disaster is universal.' (James, 1909, pp. 53–4.)

facts. First, that they contain a great deal of history of philosophy, more so than in their sum for the corresponding years a century later. Second, the four volumes also contain a good deal more of what would now be regarded as empirical psychology, that being especially so with *Mind* which had been founded to cover psychology along with philosophy (as was the later established *Journal of Philosophy, Psychology and Scientific Methods*). Likewise the two were later to narrow their scope as psychology separated off as a distinct discipline. Third, there is an evident sense of the emergence of 'pragmatism' as a philosophy authored in the United States and which deserves serious evaluation. The volume of *Mind* for 1900 contains a paper by W. Caldwell bearing the title 'Pragmatism' a precis of which by N. E. Truman also appears in the *Philosophical Review* in the following year. It will be enough, I think, if I quote the beginning and end of Caldwell's (somewhat patronising) account:

> There has recently appeared as one of the publications of the University of California (a society whose activity has already resulted in publications of value to philosophy) a pamphlet by Prof. James, entitled *Philosophical Conceptions and Philosophical Results,* that has 'the uncommon merit of being its authors chief or only express treatment of the question of philosophical method' [quoted from the *Philosophical Review* announcement]

> Pragmatism, then, looked at broadly, is simply the expression, in a phrase, of many important tendencies of the science and the criticism and the practice of our day. It requires however the Criticism of the Categories and the Theory of the Ideas (as interpreted by Aristotle and the Metaphysics of Evolution) [here the author gives obscure references to Plato and to his own work on Schopenhauer] to give it form and reality (Caldwell, 1900).

For those in need of it, Truman's gloss on Caldwell is that:

> Pragmatism must make some important assumptions: a unity of the self with the universe; a criticism of human needs; and a criterion of consequences. It [being] unfortunate that Professor James does not connect the principle with its theoretical basis (*op. cit.*, p. 205).

These are reasonable points to raise, perhaps; but what I would emphasize is the note of pressing seriousness. The atmosphere in these early volumes suggests a pair of campaign headquarters in which the oppositions are being given very serious assessment in preparation for a strategic response. British and American philosophy now no longer stand in that antagonistic, or at least defensive posture towards one another. The situation is rather the inverted Hegelean one in which Britain stands close to being a subsidiary city to Imperial America (as a comparative review of current leading British and American journals would easily show). Setting aside political and psychological questions, whether that is good or bad, or neither, depends in large part on the character of contemporary American philosophy.

Conclusion

Writing in brief and impressionistically, though not, I hope, superficially, my own sense is that things are not as they could or should be in Hegel's land of the future. His observations were penned at a time when America was largely uninhabited and he looked forward to a condition that has long since been realised. For good or ill America is not just a collection of civic communities, it is a state. The deeper question is whether it has ever achieved, or if it once did whether it has now lost, the status of being a comprehensive civil *society*. My own estimate is that if it ever was one it is no longer so — a fact obscured by the dominance and extension of American markets and media.

If America is not just an idea but a political entity, and perhaps a network of regional societies, then the issue to be considered is what role American philosophers may have outwith their narrow professional niches. It is at odds with the spirit of James, Dewey and Peirce — as it is, indeed, out of keeping with the spirit of Mill, Bradley or Russell — to pursue philosophy as if it were an empirical science whose results might be, but certainly need not be of speculative interest to non-practising fellow citizens. The tradition out of which American philosophy grew — the 'Scottish [Scotch] tradition' — was one in which it was assumed that every person had good reason to know the truth about reality and the place of human kind within it.

Certainly at its root that tradition was Christian, but Hume as an agnostic (a deist, or an atheist), as was Smith, as was Ferrier, and so on into the period when Royce and James came to deliver their lectures. The question, therefore, is not: do you have to believe in God to think that philosophy should be presented in a form in which the educated public should be able to understand it? but rather: do you really think it is of an order of general interest and importance to warrant addressing it to the world? There is no doubt whatsoever that James supposed this to be so (as did Royce, Dewey and Peirce), and this belief informs the metaphilosophical commitments I enumerated earlier, and which those others would at least have aspired to, and in some cases conspicuously achieved.

Hegel looked to America to develop a philosophy, and De Tocqueville thought he already saw one in operation throughout the land. For all that professional philosophy has berated foundationalism, and for all that the natural formulation of pragmatism may seem to be coherentist, there is indeed, I think, a general tendency in American thought to seek out and build upon secure foundations. Whether that is a philosophical mistake is something that only philosophy can show. And if it is not a mistake, then philosophers in America should look for opportunities to celebrate this good sense. The truth, however, is that professional philosophers in North America have, for all the pages and conferences of applied philosophy, become largely detached from the wider educated public. This is a serious matter that has no easy or sure solution. There is, however, a clue in the history of American education as James and others in his time understood it. That is to give special attention to the place of philosophy in undergraduate education in the hope that this will re-establish the character and importance of the discipline in the minds of the general educated public. Currently fewer than one per cent of undergraduates in American colleges and universities major in philosophy, a fact not unconnected with contemporary academic styles.

Ironically the growth and aggrandisment of what Dewey termed 'graduate work' has produced a professional culture in which the places that really matter the most for the intellectual health of civil society — the liberal arts and other undergraduate colleges — are seen by aspiring professionals to matter less than the places which, in their introversion and self-absorption, fill their waking dreams, viz., the research-led universities.[6] It is a further irony that of the cultural institutions upon which the educated public draws for ideas and values these latter are of least importance. And since it is through that public's interests and efforts that American society is sustained, academic philosophers would do well to reconsider their position, if only as a matter of prudence.

American philosophy faces a choice of preferred identity. Is it to be abstract, esoteric, remote, speculative and technical, working from idealised forms of the real towards the human, and never quite reaching it, or if having done so finding not much of philosophical interest? Or is it to be a mode of reflection that stays close to the language of common experience, and when drawn to the metaphysical prefers the descriptive over the revisionary? Or can it perhaps fulfil Hegel's hope and fashion a new synthesis — be it a non-Hegelean one? I leave these questions for American philosophers to answer; but in light of our subsidiary relationship to American thought I also ask British practitioners to consider the same issues. What is at stake, after all, is nothing less than the place of philosophy within Western civilisation.

Finally, it is in the spirit of the foregoing that I should emphasize that these appeals are addressed to philosophers conjointly, and to rising as well as to established generations. The necessity of common and intergenerational labour was well-expressed a century and a half ago by a Scot who was once widely read and admired on both sides of the Atlantic. The writer is again Ferrier of St Andrews, writing now not from the

---

[6] In the essay from which I previously quoted, Dewey writes that, 'It is a commonplace of educational history that the opening of Johns Hopkins University marked a new epoch in higher education in the United States. We are probably not in a condition as yet to estimate the extent to which its foundation and the development of graduate schools in other universities, following its example, mark a turn in our American culture.'

special position of Hegeleanism but from that of humanistic philosophy generally:

> [T]he history of philosophy repairs any injustice which may be done to philosophy itself. . . . The great problems of humanity have no room to work themselves out within the limits of an individual mind. Time alone weaves a canvas wide enough to do justice to their true proportions; and a few broad strokes is all that the genius of any one man, however gifted, is permitted to add to the mighty and illimitable work (Ferrier, 1842, pp. 292-3).

Bob Brecher

Do Intellectuals Have a Special Public Responsiblity?

Introduction

As Gramsci put it, 'Everyone is an intellectual . . . but not everyone has in society the function of an intellectual' (Gramsci, 1978, p. 9; translation adapted). In other places and at other times, the suggestion that intellectuals have particular public responsibilities qua their function as intellectuals would hardly be a startling one: from Socrates and Plato, via More, Voltaire, Wollstonecraft and Mill, to Sartre and Russell, there is a familiar tradition of what might be called the morally and politically committed intellectual. Today, however, in a culture which is increasingly treating knowledge as a commodity and the very idea of truth as empty, the thought that those who pursue them have a special public responsibility might seem at best quaint, at worst arrogantly authoritarian. I shall argue that we do nonetheless have such a responsibility; and that this is so because rationality is essentially practical, so that the pursuit of truth, far from being antithetical to practical engagement, demands it. Inherent in such a view of rationality is of course a moral cognitivism; and, while I cannot in the space of an article adequately defend the latter in much detail, I hope to show how an understanding of reason as essentially practical makes it at least plausible. The basic argument, put baldly, is this: the function of intellectuals is to think; thinking, and thus at least on occasion knowing, demands doing; intellectuals therefore have a particular responsibility to engage with the world.

Since this seems to me fairly close to a statement of the obvious, I intend to approach the issue by considering at the outset what might stand in the way of such a conclusion. I shall begin, therefore, with a number of immediate objections to it, and then go on to adumbrate in section II a conception of practical reason, with its corollary of moral cognitivism, on the basis of which I think the two most serious of them may be answered; and go on to argue that the rest can also be met with the help of such a conception. Having outlined its theoretical basis, I shall consider in section III some of the implications of the position.

First, then, the objections. Consider another list of thinkers: from the same Plato, via Francis Bacon, Machiavelli and Hume to Schmitt and Heidegger. What might be a conception of the responsibility of intellectuals which can issue in such very different commitments: from democratic to totalitarian government; from truth to expediency as the guiding principle of political activity; from a humanistic to a racist outlook; from conservatism to socialism and from liberalism to Nazism? Does this not simply show that the ability to reason effectively is one thing and any normative conclusions reached quite another? In Paul Nizan's words — though this is not his position —

> We should not judge philosophers by the light of the intelligence. The intelligence is fit for any purpose, it is good for any purpose, it is adaptable to any purpose. . . . The intelligence is useful in the service of truth or falsehood, peace or war, hate or love. . . . This great virtue has a purely technical character. Prison guards are as intelligent as their prisoners, conquerors as intelligent as the conquered. . . . Intelligence turned against man, intelligence in the service of man: it is only a tool . . . (Nizan, 1971, p. 11).

Such an understanding of intellectual activity as 'only a tool' is inimical to any pretension intellectuals might have to a special public responsibility based on the authority of reason. A 'rationality', after all, which can justify anything from socialism to fascism is hardly the justificatory basis of commitment that its defenders claim [objection 1].

The second objection is a traditional empiricist one: facts are one thing and values another. Since moral and political commitment is fundamentally not a rational matter but rather an affective one, it cannot be a consequence — let alone a basis — of truth-claims. Karl Barth's rejection of liberal theology, whatever its intellectual merits or otherwise, was mistakenly predicated on his horrified response to the spectacle of the entire German theological professoriat — and an entirely liberal one in respect of its theology — supporting the Kaiser's call to war in 1914. Likewise, Ayer's social egalitarianism had no more to do with his philosophical commitments than Heidegger's Nazism with his. One must not confuse either the moral shortcomings or the virtues of those holding a particular intellectual position with the mistaken view that their position itself actually has normative implications [objection 2].

The other five objections may be stated quite briefly. First there is the widespread view that the pursuit of truth is distorted if directed other than disinterestedly, something with which any practical commitment cannot but interfere [objection 3]. Moral and political truths, further-

more, being less than certain, militate against any normative commitment, since that requires the mistaken belief that there exist certainties in
the moral and political arenas — that is to say, the view I defend raises
the spectre of authoritarianism [objection 4]. It also raises the possibility
that the moral or political consequences of a position may become the
test of its truth — in short, it invites a Machiavellian, and perhaps a
Rortyan, pragmatism [objection 5]. And even if these worries can be met,
the life of the mind is anyway too demanding to permit its being diluted
by practical engagement [objection 6]. Finally, even the least acquaintance with the everyday conduct of the paradigmatically intellectual
institutions, namely the universities, offers impressive evidence that
intellectuals are as easily swayed as anyone else by extra-rational considerations [objection 7].

In the next section, then, I shall suggest that there is a cogent alternative to the allegedly value-free conception of rationality on which the
anti-cognitivism of empiricism is partly based (objections [1] and [2])
and that it suggests plausible responses to the rest. In outline, intellectual work, while requiring disinterestedness as a methodological tool,
demands also rationally justifiable commitments: the ideal of disinterestedness *as a goal* rather than as a methodological procedure is a false
ideal (objection [3]). These commitments in turn demand practical
instantiation. Furthermore, such a conception of practical rationality
does not require substantive certainty in the moral and political arenas
any more than in any other, since that is too strong a condition of knowledge (objection [4]); that a rational belief has practical implications does
not imply that its truth is a function of those implications (objection [5]); the
issue of demandingness is misdirected (objection [6]); and intellectuals'
moral and/or political failings are also intellectual ones (objection [7]).

Practical Reason

Let me start by acknowledging that, as I have already suggested, it
would be well beyond the scope of a paper such as this properly to
ground and defend the notion of practical reason I have in mind and the
moral cognitivism it allows: within such parameters, the theoretical
basis of a piece of applied philosophy cannot realistically be adequately
presented and defended at the same time as exploring one of its applica-
tions. At most, it may be made reasonably plausible. In this context,
furthermore, knock-down arguments are not an option: all we can do is
to offer, as Charles Taylor has it, a picture which is the 'best account'
(Taylor, 1989, p. 74) one can offer of the matter.

The theoretical basis on which I think that intellectuals do indeed have
a special responsibility, then, is a notion of practical reason, stemming
from Plato and from Kant, which has it that, far from being antithetical,
thinking and doing are deeply interconnected. So conceived, practical

reason is neither subordinate to theoretical reason (as merely instrumental) nor value-free: that is to say, it is practical reasoning, and not theoretical reasoning, which is in a certain sense fundamental. Thus, for example, Plato's identification of cognitive reliability with value in his Theory of Forms in *The Republic* 508e–509 (see Vlastos, 1965) — and in particular his notion of the Good as the source of cognitive reliability and of value alike — need not be understood as some sort of quasi-mysticism but may rather be taken as a claim not only that right and wrong are matters of cognition, but also that reason is at least in part normative. The exercise of reason which enables us to gain knowledge is an inescapably normative activity, being an engagement with The Good: 'The Good not only infuses the power of being known into all things known, but also bestows upon them their being and existence . . .' (*Republic*, 509b: cf. 505b). Or again, and perhaps more palatably, reasoning is itself a normative activity: as Christine Korsgaard puts it in a Kantian context, '[T]he rational necessity of believing the implications of our beliefs [i.e., reasoning] can only be explained if we regard believing itself as a normative act' (Korsgaard, 1997, p. 248). That is what Kant himself is getting at, I think, when he makes what otherwise seems the odd claim that

> [T]he will is . . . the faculty of desire considered not so much in relation to action (as choice is) but rather in relation to the ground determining choice to action. The will itself, strictly speaking, has no determining ground; insofar as it can determine choice, it is instead practical reason itself (Kant, 1996, p. 13).

The will, it seems — at least in this passage — is a rational capacity, not an affective faculty.

To put the matter more concretely: the question 'Why be rational?' both demands and allows a response which goes deeper than any instrumental value that being rational may have in particular instances — say, not kicking the car when it will not start because that will not help. Rather, being rational is a necessary condition just of acting at all; and acting is what we human beings do. To eschew rationality is thus to deny what we are — a practical contradiction. That is why Aristotle insisted that, if in the course of an argument someone really wanted an answer to the question 'Why be rational?' as if it were an ordinary question — rather than asking for a response by way of elucidating what being rational consists in in the particular context concerned — it would be 'like trying to argue with a vegetable' (Aristotle, *Metaphysics*, IV, 4. 1006a.15). We are indeed thinking things, as Descartes insisted: that is just what we do and what enables us to get things done. But his conception of a 'thinking thing' was passive, of a piece with that of the nascent empiricists to which he is sometimes too simplistically considered to have posited an alternative: and it is that conception which we tend to take as given. But agency is not an 'add-on' to thinking: agents is what we are. The common assumption that, so to speak, we are like machines — normally static, and active only exceptionally, when 'started up' — is mistaken. Rather, we are agents first and foremost, agents who sometimes, and exceptionally, are at rest. We are, in short, no less active beings than thinking ones (I elaborate this in Brecher, 1998, ch. 6, esp. 131ff).

And it is because rationality makes agency possible that it is what characterises us as human beings, distinguishing us from other animals: the traditional conception of human beings as rational animals is misleading if understood as referring only to our *reflective* capacity rather than also to our capacity to *act* appropriately. That is why Aristotle's comment has the force it does: to deny the need to be rational is to deny the normativity underlying our nature as agents and thus to deny our agency, something which is already asserted just in posing the question 'Why be rational?' — not least since thinking (in this case questioning) is itself already an activity. And to do that is performatively to contradict oneself.

Note that in claiming that rationality serves agency I do not mean to imply that it subserves agency, that what makes something rational is after all an instrumental consideration. One of Jean Benda's famous charges against the intellectuals of his day in the western Europe of the 1920s, that they had betrayed reason on account of 'the desire and the possibility for men of letters to play a political part', may be justified more generally if that desire turns into a criterion of right and wrong. But it is one thing to say that rationality subserves action, and quite another to claim that it serves right action. To argue that being rational is a requirement of our nature as agents is not to suggest that 'intellectual activity is worthy of esteem to the extent that it is practical and to that extent alone' (Benda, 1955, p. 121: cf. p. 119); but to reconceptualise 'intellectual' and 'practical' not as opposites but as both of them elements of human agency. Benda himself in fact recognises this when he says that '... Nietzsche, Barrès, Sorel ... would blush to be able to say like Voltaire: "I have done a little good, 'tis my best work"' (Benda, 1955, p. 161). Objection [5] thus fails; there is no question of the practical consequences of a rational belief's coming to serve as criterion of its truth just insofar as they are indeed consequences of that belief.

Two things follow for my argument from a conception of rationality as fundamentally active, not passive, and of thinking as itself an activity the point of which is that it enables us to do things in the world.

First, inasmuch as the main plank of moral anti-cognitivism is removed — the argument that, since moral belief requires moral action, it cannot be rational, since reason (alone) cannot motivate (see Norman, 2001; Dancy, 1995; and Garrard and McNaughton, 1998) — it allows of moral knowledge, understood in terms of consistency. And this in turn

implies that the claim that 'intelligence is fit for any purpose', echoed by
empiricists and postmoderns alike, is mistaken, and that it is not the case
that rationality is simply instrumental, a means of achieving ends which
are themselves not given rationally. For if a course of action which was
apparently rationally indicated turned out to be morally inadequate,
then, it turns out, it was not, after all, rationally indicated in the first
place, just because it was morally inadequate. Something would have
gone *rationally* awry in one's appraisal of it; an inconsistency would
have been overlooked. The spectre of authoritarianism (objection [4])
thus fades away; the only authority that is brought to bear is that of reason. Moreover, the certainty which that affords is very much more often
negative than positive: the certainty that slavery is wrong, for example,
that that is not how human relationships should be structured and governed, does not of itself commit one to certainty regarding a particular
positive view of how human relationships should in fact be structured
and governed — in accordance with the Kantian moral imperative, with
socialist principles regarding ownership of the means of production, or
whatever.[1] It should also be noted here that the charge of authoritarianism, although so often and so loosely levied against a view of intellectuals as having any special authority is anyway an odd one: for if it were
justified, then it would hold for just any attempts to change the world,
intellectuals', moralists', politicians' or anyone else's.

Of course, it is a charge properly levelled by those convinced, like
Richard Rorty, that reason does not have the authority I claim for it. But
even if one does not think, as I do, that Rorty's position, like any relativism, is simply self-refuting, and takes literally his assertion that 'there is
no way to "refute" a sophisticated, consistent, passionate psychopath —
for example, a Nazi who would favour his own elimination if he himself
turned out to be Jewish' (Rorty, 1990, p. 636) (and he is not making a psychological point about such a Nazi, but rather one about the impossibility of any universal rationality) then it is difficult to see what consistent
content the notion of an intellectual might retain at all (and notwithstanding Rorty's own contributions in this regard). More serious is the
view that moral and political questions are radically underdetermined
by rational analysis, so that any claim to rational authority in these matters must be misplaced. If, however, a view such as Hayek's is taken as a
quite general thesis, it too turns out to be a normative one and thus open
to its own charge of illegitimate authoritarianism (see Bousfield, 1999,
pp. 91–6); and if it is taken as the more restricted view that the possibility

---

[1]   There is of course far more to be said about this, especially regarding the extent to
      which the reasons why, for example, slavery is wrong set the parameters of
      possible positive views, and about how moral cognitivism might substantively
      rule out more than it can enjoin. I hope to do so elsewhere.

of rational underdetermination needs always to be considered, then there is a question of authoritarianism only if one mistakenly insists otherwise. But why should one do that? If any particular issue is indeed rationally underdetermined, then the intellectual's first responsibility is to say so and to argue the point: anything else is simply dishonest, in the spheres of morality and politics no less than in any other.

Second, the question of what is to be done cannot be radically separated from the question of what is to be thought: the caricature ivory tower intellectual is an inadequate intellectual on that account — whether regarding the application of theories of thermo-nuclear energy or the consideration of policies and structures internal to academia. The determinedly disinterested intellectual goes wrong in failing to limit disinterest to the investigation of the truth or falsity of a matter and in supposing that retaining disinterest at that stage implies a disinterest in — let alone a lack of interest in — the practical results of their deliberations. Far from retaining a proper neutrality, such an intellectual already takes a particular moral or political position, namely to ignore, or pretend to ignore, the implications of their reasoning. This time to quote Nizan's own view, and extending the point to intellectuals in general,

> [T]hey [philosophers] must no longer be allowed to fool the people, to play a double game. When Demetrius laid siege to Athens, Epicurus stood alongside his fellow Athenians. Epicurus took sides. If our philosophers publicly refuse to do so . . . then even the most innocent adolescent will recognize that, in effect, they *have* made a choice . . . (Nizan, 1971, p. 38).

Commitment in respect of action, far from being a threat to necessary disinterest (objection [3]), is an integral element of the commitment to that pursuit of truth which marks intellectual work. The point was well made, of course, by Marx in his eleventh thesis on Feuerbach, even if he himself offered little by way of explicit argument that, while '[T]he philosophers have only *interpreted* the world; the point [however] is to *change* it' (Marx, 1975, pp. 62–4).

If thinking is a species of doing, then the question of the point of what one is doing cannot but arise. *Why* go to the effort to think? The notion of doing something for its own sake distinguishes actions undertaken instrumentally, in order to achieve some other clearly specifiable end, from actions which do not serve such an end: looking out of the window to see if it is raining before I go out, from looking out of the window to admire the view. But this distinction is not one between actions which have an instrumental end and actions which have *no* end beyond themselves; rather it is between actions which are undertaken directly for the sake of some specifiable end to which they themselves are subordinate, and actions the point of which is altogether different. Even admiring the view, while it does not directly serve some other clearly specifiable end, has some point: pleasure, aesthetic satisfaction, or whatever. The notion of the pursuit of knowledge for its own sake, while usefully marking a contrast with knowledge pursued explicitly for some particular end, is also misleading: for it is not the case that the pursuit of knowledge for its own sake has no point, or even no point other than itself. It serves a very general, and only vaguely articulable, end, such as making the world a better place. It is indeed important that some knowledge be pursued non-instrumentally — not for any other clearly specifiable end, such as allowing supermarkets to pack fruit into smaller spaces — but that does not mean that even the least 'applied' knowledge — say, Babylonian numismatics or Fermat's Last Theorem — has no point beyond itself. The world may well be a better place for the disinterested pursuit of such matters, and I would argue that it is, but to describe them as disinterested is to contrast them with more 'practical' matters the pursuit of which serves other and particular purposes, not to deny that they have any point beyond themselves The insistence on disinterestedness thus fails as an objection to engagement.

As for the objection that the life of the mind is so demanding that practical engagement dilutes the capacity properly to lead it (objection [6]), where that is not disingenuous it is misconceived. First, if my general approach to practical reason is even roughly right, then the distinction between the life of the mind and practical engagement cannot in general be so clearly drawn: as we have already seen, entirely disengaged intellectuals 'in effect. . .*have* made a choice' (Nizan, 1971, p. 38). Second, I am not arguing that each individual intellectual should give exactly the same priority to public engagement or to a particular degree of it — there are entirely legitimate differences in temperament, capacity and circumstances, after all — but rather that some such engagement is required: a basic, if varying, minimum. Exactly the same also holds of course for intellectual engagement: being an intellectual is hardly a matter of all or nothing; even the most other-wordly of intellectuals is at the same time a material being, relating to others. Nor is it the case that every form of intellectual inquiry is equally practical — of course some are more speculative than others. The point, however, is not that particular disciplines have particular implications with respect to public engagement (although some do) but rather that to the extent that anyone is engaged in intellectual work, that is to say, in thinking, they are to that extent also committed to acting in light of their capacity to think, whatever the nature of the particular inquiries they are engaged in and whether or not particular individuals recognise the fact. Not everyone can be a John Stuart Mill or a Noam Chomsky, but, equally, no one can ignore the everyday moral and political engagement which their intellectual capacity both indicates and requires. That is why, to move to the final objection, [7], that intellectuals' 'own backyards' attest how unfit they are to intervene in the public domain, I shall in the next section emphasize the need to 'start at home'. That objection, however, while well-taken, does not show that intellectuals have no special public responsibilities: their failings in this regard, while certainly failings and certainly all too common, attest at once moral-political and intellectual shortcomings. As Plato insisted, one cannot knowingly do wrong.[2]

Intellectuals' Public Responsibilities

There are frequently rehearsed and widely accepted grounds for supposing that, at least in general, those moral and political responsibilities have first claim upon us which relate to people who are in a variety of ways closer to us than others. In any event,[3] if intellectuals do indeed have a special public responsibility to engage in public life on the basis of our social function as thinkers, then unless that responsibility is seen by the wider public to 'start at home' — and that means in the great majority of contemporary, broadly western, cases in the universities which employ us — then our attempt to exercise it is likely to be useless. We will not be taken seriously, whether within the university or outside it. One point, then, in arguing that we have in the first place a responsibility not to go along with the exigencies of the political or financial moment as they affect our own professional lives — that is, to speak out and to act in our places of employment — is that that is a necessary condition of our exercising our wider public responsibilities. The other is that it is in any case, I think, the everyday betrayals in respect of the internal features of contemporary academic life that are in many ways especially insidious in undermining our role. If we deny our responsibilities in those things over which we have most power, whether collectively — either as a profession or as specific sub-groups of academics — or individually, then we are acting in bad faith. And it is a fact which we are all too often inclined to forget or overlook that, compared with very many others, we have a considerable degree of power, even in these days of the increasing commercialisation and managerialism of universities: not least the power to refuse rather than to accede. If we deny that power or simply fail to use it, then we abdicate at once our moral and our intellectual responsibility. It has to be emphasized that I am not suggesting that these examples are more important than wider public issues of our time: poverty, power, war and the like. But it is such issues which are a test of the integrity in the absence of which academics' attempts to address

---

[2]   *Protagoras*, 352b; *Republic*, 510c and ff.; *Theaetetus*, 172c–177c. An excellent, though in my view finally unsuccessful, argument against Plato on this is Berel Lang's (1990, pp. 32ff.). I discuss it in Brecher (1998) pp. 124–7.

[3]   And even if the problems with this view preclude any direct application to the present issue, although its denial seems to me no less problematic (see Geras, 1998, pp. 62–77).

those wider issues are likely to be met with considerable scepticism — and rightly so. In light of that, then, let me offer my view of just a few recent, and all too typical, examples.

In February 2001, Ted Steele, a biologist at the University of Wollongong, in Australia, was sacked by the university's Vice-Chancellor 'after claiming publicly that he had been ordered to boost the marks of his honours students. His comments followed widespread debate in the media over earlier claims by other academics that fee-paying international students were receiving unfair treatment in their assessments.'[4] After some eighteen months, and following widespread protest, he was vindicated.[5] In May 2001, readers of the *British Medical Journal* 'who took part in an online poll'[6] voted by 54% to 45% that its editor, Richard Smith, should resign from his (unpaid) professorship of Medical Journalism at Nottingham University on account of its having accepted funding of £3.8 million from British American Tobacco 'towards an international centre for corporate responsibility (*sic*)'[7] at Nottingham University. To his credit, and having initiated the poll, he did indeed resign. One result was that the Campaign for Academic Freedom and Academic Standards was joined by Sir David Weatherall, Professor of Medicine at Oxford University, in calling 'for external scrutiny of commercial deals',[8] as in his own Institute of Molecular Medicine, '[Y]oung researchers became too heavily tied to their commercial sponsors and were unable to discuss their findings with one another.'[9] These cases are perhaps, at least in the first instance, matters for particular collectivities of academics and for particular individuals. The Quality Assurance Agency and the cyclical Research Assessment Exercise, however, directly affect every academic in the United Kingdom. Unhappily, their activities have been accepted, whether reluctantly or enthusiastically, by almost the entire profession, despite the fact that they are — at best — counterproductive with respect to good teaching and genuine research. Indeed, it is only very recently, after something like a decade of the attrition of academic integrity attendant upon compliance — our own equiv-

[4]   *THES (Times Higher Education Supplement)* May 11 2001, p. 11.

[5]   'Legal and disciplinary procedures against microbiologist Ted Steele have been halted. He is believed to have left the university with all his entitlements paid', *THES*, July 17, 2002, p. 2.

[6]   *THES*, May 18, 2001, p. 2.

[7]   *Guardian*, May 18, 2001, p. 6.

[8]   *THES*, May 11, 2001, p. 2

[9]   *ibid.* The corporate takeover of British universities, following the Canadian example, among others, is well documented by George Monbiot (2000, ch.9). Nor of course is commercial and/or political direction of what purports to be genuine research, often extending to ownership of research findings, restricted to the natural sciences.

alents of the proverbial Soviet tractor production figures — that the university Trades Unions have at last started saying publicly what everyone concerned has known very well all along, namely that '[T]he result is a false picture of university research output and quality . . . [which] . . . damages individuals' careers and fostered discrimination' and that '[P]ut simply, universities are falsifying their returns to hefce as a matter of policy.'[10] Aside from any question of deliberate dishonesty, Gordon Graham's trenchant critique of the research 'assessment' exercise (which, it should be noted, he had initially to publish himself) is precisely to the point — but would that it had been voiced other than earlier:

> The resulting system, in fact, is one in which academic worth is identified with *opinions about* worth. To see the error in this, consider again the case of academic journals. When an article is submitted, the editor, with the assistance of referees, must form a judgement about the worth of the piece, and on the strength of this judgement accept it or reject it. But though there can be good judges and bad, the opinion of even the best does not determine that an essay accepted for publication is intellectually substantial or important. Whether it is or not, is determined by its reception and influence in the wider world and the longer term (Graham, 1999a, p. 63).

'Academic Worth' cannot be judged as the RAE judges it.

The issues I have adumbrated seem to me quite clear, involving as they all do in their various ways basic matters of simple dishonesty: awarding marks for payment; the institutionalisation not of irony but of Newspeak and the power that goes with it; the pursuit of self-interest disguised as disinterested research; deliberate lying; and a pretence that something is what it is not — although in respect of the last case, it seems to be an open question whether the misrepresentation of 'academic worth' is wilful or the result of culpably lazy thinking. Nonetheless, it may of course be thought that my view of these matters is an extreme one, and that some — but surely not all — of these examples are more complex than I am suggesting, involving difficult and contentious judgements about financial realities, the need to make compromises for the sake of an overall good and so on. But then, as in the case of any matters of principle and/or policy which are rationally underdetermined, those who think that should make their case, act on it and be prepared publicly to defend their actions (as for example the Vice Chancellor of Nottingham University has indeed done in the matter of British American Tobacco's generosity). One or other party will eventually turn out to have been mistaken and thus to have acted wrongly; but both will have fulfilled their responsibilities as intellectuals, to think critically and act accordingly. I shall return to this point presently, in the course of discussing Heidegger's Nazism.

---

[10]   *THES*, June 1, 2001, p. 5.

Having said something about intellectuals' immediate responsibility as academics, let me turn to their two wider, but as I have argued intimately interrelated, responsibilities: to truth and to engaging in public life accordingly. The first, I take it, is self-evident, and would not be denied even by those entirely committed to an empiricist view of fact and value. That is to say, it is difficult to see how one can fail to suppose that to be an intellectual is to be committed to the pursuit of truth, and thus to to accept the intellectual responsibilities attendant upon such pursuit, whatever one's particular conception of truth, and thus of a commitment to it. Even certain postmoderns' denials of truth arise in the course of their pursuit of it, their denial itself taken as true — notwithstanding the contradiction involved.

With that responsibility, furthermore, comes a responsibility to engage in public life in accordance with intellectual conviction. To be an intellectual — to have the social function of an intellectual, to contribute to society through intellectual production — is to engage in finding, testing and re-testing reasons; in developing and changing one's views accordingly; and in communicating these processes and their results to others. That is to say, one's job is to think, to be critical. But if thinking is itself an activity, and if the activity which is thinking and the activity which is the implementation of thinking are interlinked — if theoretical reason does not have priority over practical reason — then not to take on the responsibilities which that brings is no less intellectually than morally culpable. To know more and/or to be able to think more critically brings with it a greater degree of responsibility: for not only does 'ought' imply 'can', but — on a cognitivist account — 'can' implies 'ought'. Only if I am able to do so is it the case that I ought to try to save the drowning child; but it is also the case that if I can (try to) save the drowning child then I ought to do so. And the more one can, the more one ought.

Our responsibilities as citizens are equal; but the extent to which we are culpable when we fail to meet them depends on who we are.[11] The train driver and the university teacher are equally responsible as citizens to play their part in the moral and political life of the society in which they live: but the train driver is more culpable than the university teacher if they are drunk at work, simply because in the train driver's but not the university teacher's case that could well result in people's being killed. And in turn, the nursery teacher is likely to be less culpable than the train driver, but more so than the univeristy teacher. But in parallel fashion, the university teacher is more culpable than the train driver if intellectually dishonest or self-deceiving; for that is to betray the particular commitment attendant on each of their jobs. Heidegger was no more, and no less, responsible for the Nazis' coming to power and for

---

[11]   With thanks to Tom Hickey for insisting on this point.

their exercise of it than the train driver transporting people to Auschwitz: but he was more culpable by virtue of his professed commitment to truth and his ability to think (and, in his particular context, the resultant trust placed in him by others on that account). His being a Nazi, important though of course that fact is, constitutes a *different* deformation from the one that I am here concerned with: at least at first, if not at all after the war ended, he was *not* guilty of pretending that his academic role bore no direct relevance to his political activities — quite the contrary. It was only after the war, when he remained silent about his Nazi activities and their significance, that he became dishonest (as well as remaining a Nazi).

Whatever one might think of intellectuals' views and how they put them into practice, and without in the least denying their concomitant responsibilities, they cannot be blamed for denying the moral and political relevance of their role as intellectuals if they do put them into practice, whatever else they may rightly be blamed for. They may indeed share, in some form, the active conception of rationality that I am advocating, however much I might disagree about how they apply it; and that disagreement remains a matter for rational resolution.

Of course, to return to the moral cognitivism which underpins my position, the objection will be made that I am operating with a notion of the moral expert. In a sense I am: if morality is a rational matter, and if there is such an expertise as rational expertise, then it follows that there is moral expertise. But why is that a problem, especially if we remember the earlier point that moral knowledge consists more readily in showing that a particular moral position is untenable rather than insisting that such and such is the correct one. Moral expertise does not imply moralism. Like medical or engineering expertise, moral expertise is neither necessarily authoritarian nor arrogant, authoritative though it may be.

Intellectuals, then, have a special responsibility to engage in public affairs. It is doubtless a matter of temperament, opportunity, etc., whether and to what extent this takes the form of activities such as contributing to the deliberations, and to the decisions, of a whole range of public bodies, committees, enquiries and the like, official or otherwise; teaching, and not forgetting questions of who comes to be a student and how, and who does not; or the more directly political interventions of a Michael Dummett.[12] But we cannot set it aside in the name of 'purely'

---

[12] See his book *On Immigration and Refugees* (Dummett, 2001), which is just the culmination of his efforts over the past two decades on behalf of refugees and asylum seekers. As he argues in the *Guardian*, 23 May 2001, p. 13, we are 'a nation of hypocrites, with a government of hypocrites (who) . . . indignantly denounce the "traffickers in human misery" who smuggle people in (but) [A]t the same

intellectual work, for being intellectuals we also occupy a particular role in the matter of trying to make the world a better place, as Plato long ago recognised in his association of truth with goodness.[13]

time, with our incessant talk of "bogus asylum seekers" [we] in effect deny that there is any human misery'.

[13]   Earlier versions of some of these ideas were presented at meetings of the British Society for Philosophy of Education and the Society for Applied Philosophy; and at the Pittsburgh Conference on Philosophy and its Public Role. I am grateful to participants for their contributions. Special thanks go to John Haldane and Will Aiken for detailed comments, and for their conversation and encouragement to students and colleagues at the University of Brighton.

John Arthur

Impartial Public Reason and its Critics

Three Objections

Public reason and impartiality have had a bad press in some quarters recently. I believe that some of the criticisms are misplaced: they misunderstand the nature of impartiality and public reason, and they mistakenly criticize a particular conception of them, thinking they are criticizing the ideals themselves. In what follows[1] I first describe three oft-heard criticisms of impartiality and (what is presumed to be its twin, public reason). Then I explain the nature of impartiality and its connection with public reason, and conclude with an assessment of the three objections.

Following Thomas Nagel (1986, 1987), who supposes impartiality names the perspective from which political coercion must be justified, Iris Marion Young (1990, esp. ch. 4) gives two reasons for rejecting impartiality — she clearly has especially in mind Rawls's veil of ignorance as an example. First, she says it is 'impractical' and 'expresses in fact an impossibility, a fiction' (pp. 112, 103). She also claims, secondly, that because impartiality is 'blind to sex, race, age and so on' it ignores 'the public and political significance of group difference' and so undermines claims for affirmative action and group based rights (pp. 120, 168). Martha Minow writes in a similar vein that 'The ideal of impartiality implies human access to a view beyond human experience, a "God's eye" point of view . . . [but] humans lack this inhuman perspective' (Minow, 1993, p. 233).

[1] An earlier version of this paper was read at the American Philosophical Association Pacific Division Meetings (2002) and at the Pittsburgh Conference on Philosophy and its Public Role (2002). I would like to thank especially Will Aiken, John Christman, John Haldane, Christopher Knapp and Steve Scalet for their helpful comments.

The artificiality of demands for impartial reason in politics, especially the fact that it assumes people are abstracted, disembodied rational agents, has also led defenders of deliberative democracy like Seyla Benhabib (1996) and Thomas McCarthy (1994) to voice another objection, that those who argue for restrictions on political argument in the name of impartial public reason 'freeze ongoing processes of public political communication whose outcomes cannot be settled in advance by political theory' (McCarthy, 1994, p. 61). It is unrealistic, in other words, to suppose that the basic principles of justice and laws can be determined a priori, in perpetuity; they must themselves be the outcome of an on-going conversation among actual persons able to introduce new information and fresh perspectives into the political arena. To answer these three objections — that impartiality is impractical; that it biases political argument against giving due consideration to ethnic, racial and gender differences; and that it prematurely cuts off or freezes political debate about fundamental matters of justice and rights — it is critical that we come to a clearer understanding of both impartiality and public reason. Though both friends and critics often link the two, the exact nature of that connection has remained mysterious — a fact that has then encouraged critics to misinterpret the limits each imposes.

The Myth of Impartiality?

Critics think impartiality is unworkable: it is a myth that demands what cannot be had. But what then *is* impartiality, that its demands are so stringent? Brian Barry (1995) claims our ordinary concept of impartiality is not a 'strong organizing concept' in ordinary moral thinking because its meaning varies depending on context. There is always, he says, 'some other — and deeper — way of characterizing what is at issue . . . [impartiality's] significance is derivative' (p. 19). This seems to me to be wrong, at least in one important sense. While the concept of impartiality is indeed quite abstract, it is not without meaning. Indeed, to understand public reason — both what it does, and does not, require — we must first understand impartiality.

Perhaps the most familiar context in which impartiality functions is in the courtroom. Judges and jurors who convict based on race, for example, or who acquit based on friendship or financial interest, are paradigm cases of failed impartiality. They relied on improper reasons. Barry is right, though, in one sense: we cannot know whether or in what ways we violate norms of impartiality without a great deal of information about context, and even then there is room for considerable disagreement. Reasons that are acceptable or appropriate in one context may be inappropriate in another, and perhaps controversial in a third.

Impartiality is required in the private sphere as well as in governmental bureaucracies and the courtroom. We expect it of teachers who grade students, for instance, and of parents who distribute benefits to children. Indeed, we often exclude facts from *ourselves* out of concern for own impartiality, because we are not sure we will be able to make the right decision if we have full information. Blind grading procedures on students' essays are one example; orchestra auditions behind a screen are another (as is insisting women who are auditioning not wear high heels behind the screen).

But how, then, does impartiality differ from the idea of simply acting reasonably?[2] One difference is that impartiality focuses on distributional questions, that is, on the allocations of benefits and of burdens by some people onto others. So to fail to act impartially is to act unreasonably, with regard to distribution of rewards, punishment, opportunities and so forth. But is impartiality then just the requirement that people should be reasonable in the context of distributive justice or fairness? Again that is too broad. Imagine a legislator who mistakenly votes for a bill based on how the discussion is framed; perhaps his vote depended on the fact that the benefits rather than costs were emphasized by the committee's report. That legislator acted unreasonably, though his vote is not a failure of impartiality. Framing problems are not impartiality problems, and therefore are not all instances of unreasonableness in the distribution of benefits and burdens are failures of impartiality. Rather, impartiality focuses attention on certain *types* of reasons people tend to use when distributional questions about burdens are answered, reasons involving their own interest, prejudice against groups, or sympathy for those we care about. Because prejudice, personal interest and sympathy are common emotions, and often lead to unreasonable decisions, the concept of impartiality focuses attention on them. It does so in various contexts, from the family and classroom to the courtroom. The point is not that having the prejudice or taking the bribe fails the impartiality test, but rather it is the *unreasonable distributional decision* itself violated the duty to be impartial. So the core of impartiality is indeed fairness, as Barry suggests, but fairness in the sense that we are required to ignore certain reasons having to do with personal interest and prejudice that, in the context, would be wrong to use.

Thomas Nagel understands 'impartiality' much more broadly, to mean 'liberal toleration' in which a political system tries to be 'fair among its citizens' with respect to their divergent and often conflicting religious and other ideas about the good life (Nagel, 1991, p. 153). But while this idea, that the state must remain religiously and morally neutral, is familiar to debates about public reason (as I will discuss shortly) it is different from the requirement of impartiality. Ignoring the reasons

---

[2] I am indebted to Christopher Knapp for pressing this question as well as for other helpful discussions of these issues.

that Nagel proposes — conceptions of the good or valuable life — does not show impartiality as the term is normally used. Indeed one can be impartially motivated to violate moral neutrality when, out of altruistic concern for the welfare of a stranger, one insists the person change his ways. In that case, rather than showing partiality or preference for one's self, family or group, violating political neutrality is perfectly impartial.

Impartiality thus focuses attention on particular respects in which people are unreasonable, namely those where we make decisions involving the distribution of advantages and disadvantages, costs and benefits, and where we know that there is a tendency for people to rely on unacceptable reasons. The concept of impartiality picks out those decisions for special scrutiny. Impartiality therefore rides piggy-back on the specific tendencies people have to be unreasonable. If we were different, then the concept would function differently. If it mattered to people what day of the week they are born on (maybe they have religious views on the subject that creates strong feelings of solidarity with others born on the same day) then the concept of an impartial judgment could come to be regarded as important, even in that context.

Coming now to the first objection, is it true, as Young and Minow claim, that impartiality is a 'myth'? It is worth noting that when we criticize or praise based on impartiality, we do make at least two assumptions about humans' capacity to reason. We assume it is possible for people to ignore or set aside reasons they may be inclined, improperly, to accept, i.e. that people can reach if not perfect at least more-or-less objective conclusions. Second, we assume that people are generally aware of their actual reasons, and are not self-deceived. If humans lack such capacities, then it would make no sense to criticize people for failing to exercise them, as occurs when people are charged with failing to be impartial. It is also important to keep in mind, however, that impartiality does not require people to forget what they know. A partial or biased judge is not criticized for *knowing* the race of the defendant, but for *acting on that knowledge*. The point is not to enforce ignorance (which may be impossible), but to criticize motives.

Defenders of impartiality as an important and workable ideal in politics do not deny that people often fail to be impartial, or that is it sometimes controversial what is and is not a violation of the duty to be impartial. But to say nobody is perfectly impartial all the time, or that controversy sometimes arises around what it requires, is no indictment of the ideal itself, or proof that we should treat it is a 'myth', if indeed that were even possible.

In sum, impartiality picks out specific types of reasons that people should ignore when acting, despite the fact that the reasons might, under other circumstances, be tempting and even acceptable grounds for a decision in another context. Those normally reflect personal or group interest and prejudice. Impartiality is therefore one type of 'epistemic abstinence', i.e. abstaining from relying on a reason.[3] We expect epistemic abstinence in many contexts: requiring that insurance companies ignore an applicant's pre-existing medical conditions, for example, and by insisting that employers ignore a job applicant's ethnic background, political views, previous bankruptcies, and sexual orientation. We also demand epistemic abstinence when police reject ethnic profiling, sometimes despite the fact that profiling could save valuable resources. Indeed even the right to privacy, which provides for concealment of personal information from other people, is a form epistemic abstinence. While others may want to have information in order to make their decisions, norms of law and of morality insist that they are not allowed to gather private information. Epistemic abstinence also extends beyond the demands of impartiality in legal trials when, after a witness has answered an improper question, jurors are expected to ignore what they have heard.

We also enforce epistemic abstinence on ourselves. Sometimes (as in the grading and auditioning cases) it done is out of a desire insure impartiality, though other reasons may also warrant abstinence. Legal systems, for instance, sometimes use exclusionary rules that ban illegally acquired evidence, and testimonial privileges that exclude evidence given by a spouse, doctor, religious adviser, or lawyer. In all these cases, judges and lawmakers have decided that the benefits of ignoring what might be relevant or even vital evidence is worth the costs, despite the fact jurors may reach a wrong (i.e. false) conclusion. Self-imposed epistemic abstinence can also be prudential, as well as legal and moral, as when a person asks not to be told about a bad medical prognosis or chooses to avoid a vivid depiction of the dangers of flying while sitting on a runway.

The reasons for requiring that people ignore or not learn what might in other circumstances be relevant grounds for making a decision vary widely, as my many examples show. Besides the need to make impartial legal and personal decisions, we limit our use of information in order to create zones of privacy where we can be honest and open with loved ones or with professionals, to protect innocents against self-incrimination, to give convicted criminals or financial failures a second chance in life, to pool the risk so that the sick can afford insurance, to lift the bur-

---

[3]   This usage of 'epistemic abstinence' may seem to differ from that of Joseph Raz who writes that 'Rawls's epistemic abstinence lies in the fact that he refrains from claiming his doctrine of justice is true' (Raz, 1990, p. 9). A different way to put Rawls's point, however, is that citizens can, *but need not*, accept a theory because they believe it to be true. Whether Rawls is right that there are good grounds for accepting principles of justice, besides their truth, is the issue Raz addresses. He argues there are not such grounds.

dens of suspicion from racial minorities, or just not to have to worry during a plane's take-off.

Public Reason

I have argued that impartiality is but one, albeit common form of epistemic abstinence. But how then are those two ideas, impartiality and epistemic abstinence, related to public reason? The term 'public reason' has been brought back into wide philosophical usage by Rawls, though in a way that has made it seem more controversial that it is. He has tied it to political liberalism generally, perhaps even to his own brand of contractualism. In fact, however, the core idea of public reason is more general, and less in dispute, than the specific use Rawls makes of it. Properly understood, I will argue, public reason is epistemic abstinence brought to politics. And although impartiality is also a form of epistemic abstinence, it is distinct from public reason in the following sense. Impartiality is a norm that applies to private as well as public actors, involving the distribution of desired and unwanted goods. It is therefore both broader, and narrower, than public reason: broader because impartiality applies to private as well as political actions, and narrower because impartiality is concerned only with distributive issues, leaving aside many other areas where political power is exercised and public reason demanded.

In Rawls's view, public reason is 'characteristic of a democratic people: it is the reason of its citizens, of those sharing the status of equal citizenship. The subject of their reason is the good of the public'(Rawls, 1993, p. 213). Rather than basing political authority simply on the ability to hold power, on God's will, on a natural aristocracy entitled to rule, or even on the outcome of a bargain, public reason's most fundamental commitment — at least Rawls's social contract variant — is to identify institutions and laws that can win the approval of all citizens, viewed as free and independent equals. Justice requires that power be exercised in ways that can win the support or endorsement of all, under conditions in which there is wide diversity of philosophical and religious opinion and a democratic commitment to self-government and to respect individual rights to speech, expression, religion, and association. Public reason thus expresses three related ideals. One is that political discussion and debate is addressed to citizens who are political *equals*. And second, because the aim of politics is agreement among persons, it must proceed in accordance with beliefs all persons share, or may potentially be brought to accept on reflection. So although it cannot assure agreement on any particular political issue, it at least provides a common basis on which to proceed. Finally public reason reflects a distinction between the public sphere and the private. Reasons that are suitable and even compelling in the context of our non-political lives — religious reasons, for example, or affections we may feel toward our religion, ethnic group and family — are distinguished from public reasons. Rawls concludes that public reason insists that public officials, including judges and legislators, as well as citizens in the voting booth, ignore not only their religious beliefs but also their 'comprehensive' philosophical doctrines in general, at least when setting out 'constitutional essentials' (See Rawls, 1993, Lecture VI). The point, then, is that the scope of political argument is different from, and narrower than, reasoning in general. Public reason is a form of epistemic abstinence. The ideal of laws that can be defended to all citizens, viewed as equal citizens, restricts the justifications available to government officials and voters in their exercise of political power.

But Rawls's account, while of great importance, is only one form that public reason takes. There are other, less controversial examples of public reason, and it is important that the discussions of public reason not ignore them. Public reason names the norms of epistemic abstinence in the exercise of political power, and as such, can serve many purposes and reflect a range of political perspectives. Sometimes public reason overlaps with impartiality. It is widely accepted, for instance, that lawmakers should ignore whatever economic benefits they or their friends might personally enjoy as a result of their vote for a statute, just as judges are expected to recuse themselves in cases where they have a personal financial or other stake in the outcome of a case before them. But public reason is also broader than impartiality; it is at work in the electoral process, for example. When accused by the Democrats of proposing his across the board tax cut out of concern for the wealthy, candidate George W. Bush replied that the cut would increase productivity over-all and anyhow, he said, the money is not the government's but the people's. Similarly, when Al Gore was accused of being a lapdog of the teachers' unions for opposing school choice, he went to great pains to explain that it was in the interests of public education and indeed the entire country that parents not be allowed to choose a school for their children.

Public reason is also imposed on legislators under the US Constitution. Among the more colorful examples is *Gorsjean v. American Press Company*, which tested the constitutionality of a Louisiana law requiring newspapers with a circulation above 20,000 to pay a 2 percent sales tax (*Grosjean v. American Press Co.*, 297 US 250 (1936). The statute's constitutional flaw, said the US Supreme Court, was that it was motivated by the desire to silence criticism of the Louisiana political establishment. It was, said the Court, 'a deliberate and calculated device in the guise of a tax to limit the circulation of information . . .' (*Grosjean*, p. 251). The Court knew this in part because when introducing the bill, its legislative sponsors described it as a 'tax on lying' and expressed regret that they could not find a way to exempt the one large paper what had supported Huey

Long's political machine. 'We tried to find a way to exempt the *Lake Charles American Press* from the advertising tax, but did not think we could do it' reported Governor Allen (*Grosjean*, p. 43). Though a tax on newspapers is not unconstitutional per se, said the Court, one motivated by the desire to silence political enemies clearly is. Epistemic abstinence restricting legislative motives is a pervasive feature of free speech jurisprudence, as well as equal protection cases where discriminatory legislative motives are also distinguished from benign ones. So although the *effect* of a writing test given to applicants for positions on the Washington DC police was to exclude many blacks, its use was not unconstitutional because it was did not show '*purposeful discrimination*' against blacks (*Washington v. Davis*, 426 US 229, 1976).

Other First Amendment requirements, that no official religion be established and that free exercise of religion be respected, are also examples of epistemic abstinence and public reason at work. These two religion clauses demand that, although a law may legitimately have the *effect* of burdening or benefiting a religion, the *motivating reason* — the justification of the law — cannot be either the promotion or suppression of religion. There is nothing wrong with paving roads to a church and giving Bible readers eyeglasses, for example, or with requiring blood transfusions and banning child sacrifice in the face of religious opposition. But that is because such regulations rest on a non-religious purpose — a public reason — and not on the forbidden motive of aiding or suppressing religion.

Though in these cases enforcement of public reason involve specific rights, courts have also lent their weight to enforcing public reason in a more general form. In applying the 'rational basis' test, the US Supreme Court demands that at least some semblance of public reason must exist before a law can pass constitutional muster. For example, legislators cannot pass laws whose sole purpose is the furtherance of a narrow group interest.[4] In a 1976 decision the Court explained the underlying purpose of the rational basis test. The legal issue was the constitutionality of a statute making it illegal for anybody other than a medically trained eye doctor to fit eyeglass lenses. Striking down the law, the Court said that legislation must be an 'exercise of judgment' rather than a 'display of arbitrary power' (*Mathews v. De Castro* 429 US 181, 1976, p. 185, quoting *Helvering v. Davis*, 301 US 619, 1937, p. 640). This eyeglass law, the Court reasoned, was based simply on raw political power of the doctors, served no public purpose, and was therefore unconstitutional.

---

[4]   The public purpose need not be the one the legislators actually had in mind, however. It is generally sufficient that there *exists* such a public purpose, whether it was specifically envisioned by lawmakers or not.

Norms of public reason therefore cover a wide range of political roles and are enforced both through informal moral persuasion, the electoral processes, and the Supreme Court interpreting the Constitution. Far from uncommon, both it and impartiality are widely accepted. And though it is not a neutral, valueless viewpoint, public reason is nonetheless a perspective that is different from the one in which all information is weighed that a decision-maker might want to consider. And like impartiality, public reason too is neither rare nor a myth, as critics suggested. Admittedly it is sometimes difficult (or even impossible) for political actors to ignore information once it is known, just as it is sometimes difficult for jurors (or teachers) to set aside their prejudices. But we nevertheless do expect and enforce norms of impartiality and public reason, demanding that both private agents and public officials make decisions based on the right reasons while ignoring others. The specific requirements of impartiality and public reason are sometimes controversial, and will vary depending on the context. But the fact there is often disagreement about some of the specific forms epistemic abstinence is no argument that it is either unimportant or unworkable.

Public Reason and Group Rights

If what I have argued is correct, then although Young and Minow focused their attack on what they termed 'impartiality', in fact their target was actually public reason of a particular sort. Despite their broadly worded criticisms, neither, presumably, wants to reject public reason in all its forms. They clearly do, however, criticize Rawls's conception of public reason, and especially his insistence that people ignore race, ethnicity, class and gender, on the ground I mentioned: that excluding information about race, gender and ethnicity biases political argument against groups rights, affirmative action, and other race, gender, and group-conscious policies. But is that correct?

The answer depends on when and how the specific constraints on public reason actually work, for there is nothing inherent in the ideals of epistemic abstinence, impartiality or public reason that creates such a bias. As I have suggested, virtually everybody accepts these in some contexts, if not others. Nor, however, is there anything in Rawls's particular account of public reason that prevents appropriate weighing of such information. Recall his important (but oft-overlooked) idea of a 'four stage sequence', and that more information becomes available at each stage (Rawls, 1972, section 31). At the first stage the two general principles of justice are chosen, behind a thick veil of ignorance in which nobody knows either their own situation or the details of their society's racial or ethnic make-up and history. But then at the second, constitutional stage, the veil is raised significantly so that a constitutional convention is able to frame the structure of government that, in the circumstances, is most likely to realize the requirements of justice. While delegates are to remain ignorant of *their own* religious affiliations, economic class, race and gender as they adopt their constitutional structure and protect fundamental rights, they are now guided by not only the two principles of justice but also by all other social and historical information about their society that is relevant to the decision at hand — i.e. choosing the constitution best suited to their particular history and social conditions and most likely to realize the two principles in law. Then at the third, legislative stage, the veil is lifted further so that lawmakers now know the specific constitutional structure and the legal constraints they must work within, along with all other relevant information about their society that they need to frame laws (though again epistemic abstinence demands excluding information about *their own* religion, class, ethnic group, financial interests etc.). Finally, at the fourth stage, with laws in place, judges and citizens apply the laws.

Rawls summarizes the implementation process this way, emphasizing the importance of making relevant information available to lawmakers:

> The notion of the rational and impartial application of principles defines the kind of knowledge that is admissible . . . the flow of information is determined at each stage by what is required in order to apply these principles intelligently to the kinds of questions of justice at hand (Rawls, 1972, p. 200).

Rawls sees clearly that the question of when information is made available is important, and requires careful attention throughout the political process. And contrary to its critics, there is nothing inherent in Rawls's veil of ignorance, or in the ideas of impartiality and public reason generally, preventing lawmakers and judges, in the appropriate context, from taking fully adequate account of race, ethnicity and gender, whether in the design of a constitution or in framing laws. The fact they do not know *their own* race, gender or ethnic background does not mean they lack other relevant information about those subjects.

As an example, consider some possible justifications of affirmative action, which might include reparations for past injustices, improved medical care for minorities, and cultural or intellectual diversity on campuses. All of these arguments are open to elected or other officials committed to public reason to make at the appropriate law-making stages. It is clear, therefore, that public reason does not beg the question against affirmative action, bilingual education or group-conscious voting districts. Each can be defended in the appropriate context and using the right sort of (i.e. public) reasons. That is not to say, however, that legislators using public reason would necessarily adopt such policies, any more than they must necessarily reject them. That decision would depend, in the end, on the weight of all the various arguments. But lawmakers would clearly be aware of their nation's racial history as well whatever racial disparities exist among its different groups.

Public reason *does*, however, rule out some defences that might be offered of racial preferences, group-based rights and other similar policies. Because it limits the acceptable reasons to ones that others can reasonably be expected to accept, public reason is incompatible with certain forms of interest group pluralism in which laws are seen as no more than the outcome of bargaining among different groups — racial, economic, or whatever — all competing for political influence and public benefits. Were democratic politics a market-like competition among groups over the advantages laws can bestow on them, then the only rights that would need to be secured would be ones that make sure people actually get what they are supposed to get under the political bargains that are hammered out, or that guarantee democratic government itself such as freedom of speech and press, one person one vote, and the right to run for office. But the constitutional traditions of the United States and Europe include much more that the rights necessary to maintain interest group bargaining processes. By protecting religious freedom, for instance, or the right to privacy, a broader conception of public reason is preserved.

So while Rawls is the first person of recent vintage to discuss public reason, the concerns it expresses are not limited to his work.[5] The United States Constitution includes an explicit provision banning the 'establishment' of a religion, for example — a provision that exemplifies public reason at work. Other democratic governments in Europe and elsewhere sometimes take a more relaxed view of the separation of religion and state, although those same governments do not reject public reason fully, even with an established church. In securing religious tolerance, preventing government from banning minority religions, and protecting the rights of non-believers, they employ a less restrictive conception of public reason, but a robust one nonetheless.

All of this reinforces what I said earlier: that while it is widely accepted in some senses, there is nonetheless great controversy about the extent of public reason's limits. Those controversies cover four, sometimes overlapping, areas. First, *who* is constrained by public reason? Does it apply to judges only, to all law-makers, to all public employees including teachers and bureaucrats, or to citizens generally? Second, which *forms of reasoning* are ruled out? Is it religious texts taken on faith, or does it include private experiences not generally accessible? Third, what is the *scope* of these limits? Does public reason extend to all occasions in which political coercion is used, or only to 'constitutional

---

[5]   Jean Jacques Rousseau emphasized the importance of understanding the vote of legislators not as a private act but as an expression of the 'general will'. See for example Rousseau, *The Social Contract*, Book IV, Chapter 2.

essentials' as Rawls claims? Finally which *subjects* are ruled off the political agenda? Does public reason prevent government from encouraging or establishing one religion or from promoting one ideal of the good life in general? Or does it insist, more broadly still, that laws not be grounded in controversial philosophical doctrines and rely instead only on shared, political ideas? In fact, I have argued, while Rawls does take important, controversial positions on each of these topics, even his own strongly constraining account of public reason allows adequate weighing of race, ethnicity and gender. Other ways of understanding public reason can obviously do the same.

Public Reason and Democratic Deliberation

I now turn to the third objection to public reason that I mentioned. It is the claim, familiar in the work of Jurgen Habermas (1990),[6] Thomas McCarthy, Seyla Bengabib and other defenders of deliberative democracy, that public reason is incompatible with democratic values because it limits the terms in which deliberation can take place. Habermas, for example, writes that 'Moral justifications [of laws] are dependent on argumentation actually being carried out . . . real argument makes moral insight possible' (Habermas, 1990, p. 57). McCarthy writes in a similar vein that public reason 'freezes' political debate by limiting the deliberative process of citizens based on a prior commitment to substantive principles of justice (McCarthy, 1994, p. 61). Amy Gutmann and Dennis Thomson also echo that position, claiming that political truth (including the nature of public reason itself) cannot be determined before democratic deliberation has taken place (Gutmann and Thompson, 1996, p. 44). Only after the deliberative political process has run its course, according these writers, can we know what justice and public reason require.

Again, however, that misinterprets the role of public reason. Its aim is not to uncover political principles that, once identified, will forever remain unquestioned. The presumed 'finality' (to use Rawls's term) of the choice of basic principles behind the veil of ignorance and then, in light of those principles, of the constitution, is a *consequence* of public reason's demand that the law not be tailored to serve the interests or values of particular individuals or groups, unless doing so can be justified to others (Rawls, 1972, p. 135). Finality simply reflects that commitment to public reason by preventing individuals (or groups) from cooking the books, as it were, and choosing a principle they would later be allowed to reject having learned information (such as how they individually have fared) that should have been ruled out.

[6]   John Christman pressed this point as well in his comments on my paper at the American Philosophical Association meetings.

That assumption, of the finality of the choice of principles before legis-lative deliberation takes place, is both a procedural fact of life and a philosophical commitment to rights that constrain legislation. The pro-cedural fact is that there must be a constitution, in the sense of a system of rules constituting a legislature and its practices, before there can be a legislature. (See for example H.L.A. Hart, 1999, chs. V & VII for a discus-sion of 'secondary rules' as a precondition for the existence of a legisla-tive body.) The commitment to rights that legislators are bound to respect is then modelled by Rawls in the four-stage process, as legisla-tors are presumed to be constrained by the constitution and the princi-ples of justice it aims to realize through law. The key point, though, is that the deliberative process leading to the choice of principles, a consti-tution and so on, while it is self-consciously aimed at making a 'final' decision, leaves open to political deliberation which principles and con-stitutional structures would actually be chosen.[7] So rather than indicat-ing an inconsistency, as McCarthy (1994) claims Rawls's own subse-quent re-thinking and re-defining of the first principle of justice is entirely at one with the larger project of choosing principles of justice that govern ordinary, day-to-day political deliberations. Such principles, though 'final', are nonetheless open to revisions qua final principles.

A related point applies to Benhabib's claim that deliberative democ-racy differs from Rawlsean 'liberal theorists' because liberals cannot allow for 'a discourse model of practical debate as being the appropriate forum for determining rights claims' (Benhabib, 1996, p. 78). Again, however, it is not at all clear there is a real difference in the two positions once the Rawlsean or 'liberal' view is made clear. Deliberation and debate about rights can take place at the both the legislative and judicial stages, consistent with public reason. And while it is true that the debate will be 'constrained' by the demands of justice, in the form of a function-ing constitution and limits on legislative powers, there remain two senses in which legislative and judicial deliberations are also open-ended.

Any 'first principles' of justice and rights is bound to be abstract.[8] The task of first identifying and then defining those rights is left for further deliberation (albeit not necessarily by elected legislators rather than

[7]   Although the sense in which deliberation about the institutional structures and procedures by which democratic government is to proceed is in an important sense a pre-condition of democratic government, unless the entire polity is allowed to participate. But even then, the group must accept rules of order before any deliberations can take place. So there is an important sense in which at least some institutional structures and rules cannot themselves be the outcome of democratic deliberation without an infinite regress.

[8]   Rawls speaks only of an 'adequate system' of rights, without naming or defining them at the first stage, behind the full veil of ignorance. Later on, of course, he

courts, though that too remains an open question). Deliberation also takes place concerning the basic principles of justice governing the choice of a constitution. There is nothing preventing people generally, or elected officials, from considering a constitutional amendment, or legislators and judges from deliberating about fundamental rights and revisiting questions about basic justice in the fashion I just described. And again, Rawls is himself clear about this, saying that people can enter the veil of ignorance at any time.

In the end, then, what really divides Rawls and others committed to public reason from each other, and from the critics I have discussed here, are the details — the actual limits that impartiality and public reason impose. At the lower levels of abstraction, where specific rights are identified and defined, there is of course much disagreement, just as there is deep disagreement over preferences based on race and gender. But the ideals of public reason and impartiality do not, by themselves, rule out (or in) any particular conclusion about rights or affirmative action. So my claim here has been, in a nutshell, that at a theoretical level the only real disagreement between defenders of public reason and their critics is perhaps whether or not they disagree.

---

goes on to suggest how he thinks that Courts and Legislators might implement those principles, including naming and defining the specific rights that would comprise such a system. One could accept his general principles, then, while rejecting his claim about what it should mean in practice.

David Carr

Auden's Great Healers

Blake, Lane and Lawrence on Human Nature, Society and Education

Theory and Human Development

It is commonly assumed by those concerned with issues and problems of public policy that some kind of scientific or other theorising about human growth or development might be of some value or assistance to this enterprise. School teaching, social work and various kinds of psychological therapy and counselling spring to mind as fields to which such theorising has been considered appropriate if not actually indispensable. The exponential twentieth-century growth of social scientific theories of development was very much concerned to lend theoretical support and professional credibility to such endeavours, and developmental theories continue to occupy a prominent place in the professional education and training of teachers, social workers and various kinds of clinicians.

On the one hand, of course, one need not doubt that there are features of human development which call for fairly straightforward empirical explanation and understanding: human beings are born, they sexually mature, they age and they die in accordance with scientifically observable physiological principles. On the other hand, the precise logical or explanatory status of developmental claims about the proper course of human intellectual, moral or spiritual growth has always been rather less clear, and professional scepticism about the practical relevance and utility of such claims has continued to be widespread and enduring. I shall here attend to this issue via an examination of the suggestion or assumption of a major modern poet that there are significant psychological and emancipatory lessons to be learned from reflection upon the work of three interestingly different past writers of some influence on modern thought about personal development and social progress.

Auden's Healers

In a fairly early work, W.H. Auden writes:

> Lawrence, Blake and Homer Lane, once healers in our English land,
> These are dead as iron for ever, these can never hold our hand.
> Lawrence was brought down by smut-hounds, Blake went dotty as he sang,
> Homer Lane was killed in action by the Twickenham Baptist gang.
> 'Get there if you can and see' (Auden, 1977, p. 48).

Although neither philosopher nor theorist, W.H. Auden was nevertheless a prominent intellectual of his generation, his poetic works are much preoccupied with what may be regarded as metaphysical, ethical and social questions, and they exhibit a well-educated appreciation of the ideas of a wide range of ancient and modern philosophers, social theorists and other students of the human condition. Much of Auden's work also seems concerned to find psychological and cultural solutions to what he sees as a prevailing modern climate of anxiety and nihilism. In the above passage and elsewhere, he identifies a holy trinity of prominent martyrs to human salvation, who he also seems to have regarded as engaged in some largely *common* project of perhaps 'progressive' liberation from a range of prevailing modern spiritual, psychological and educational disorders of materialism, nihilism, repression and/or *mauvais foi*. However, although I hope to show shortly that the attempts of Blake, Lane and Lawrence to address some of the key questions of human social, psychological and spiritual weal and woe are of real human and philosophical interest, it should also become apparent that their ideas are driven by somewhat different concerns, and that the prospects of distilling some common human panacea from their diverse insights are therefore much less promising.

Blake's Promethian Theology

Blake is a key figure in Auden's redemptive trinity. Auden's 'self-educated William Blake' who 'threw off relations with a curse, with the Newtonian universe' has also been a perennial comfort and inspiration to those wishing to resist social conformity and/or the anti-spiritual trends of secular materialism. In this light, though it may be doubted whether many of those who profess to admire Blake have ever read his not notably pellucid *Prophetic Books*, the central preoccupation of his more accessible *Songs of Innocence and Experience* with a general theme of corruption of divine innocence by the world of material experience —

which Blake held to be potently symbolised by industrial corruption of a more idyllic pre-industrial order — has had enduring appeal.

First, Blake's *Songs* appear to give fairly concise expression to the romantic idea that human nature is basically good or innocent but liable to corruption in the course of civil socialization: despite his own criticisms of Rousseau, Blake seems to have largely endorsed the former's apparent rejection of original sin, and to have shared Wordsworth's view of the child entering the world 'trailing clouds of glory'. But Blake would also appear prone to an equally attractive celebration, more characteristic perhaps of the darker Byronic side of romanticism, of unbridled sensual and instinctual expression. There is evidence that Blake considered the basic sensual impulses of human nature to be good in themselves and to have held that one particularly damaging form of human bondage is *sexual* repression. On the one hand, this is supported by such familiar Blakean aphorisms as 'the road to excess leads to the palace of wisdom' and 'he who desires but acts not breeds pestilence' (both from *The Marriage of Heaven and Hell*): on the other, it is reinforced by evidence of Blake's proposal to savour the fruits of sexual liberation by introducing a domestic concubine into his household — a project which seems to have been promptly nipped in the bud by Mrs Blake (Raine, 1970, p. 29).

But another reason why one might expect Blake to have been of some interest to Auden, is that his work is driven by explicit religious and spiritual, broadly (albeit unorthodox) Christian, interests and concerns: Blake's paintings and poems abound with religious and Christian artistic and mystical themes, influences and references ranging from Dante and Milton to Boehme and Swedenborg. Given Auden's own eventual conversion to Christianity under the influence of a host of ancient and modern religious writers, and his corresponding conviction that some version of the Christian vision offered the most promising antidote to the secular materialism and nihilism of modernity, Blake would certainly have earned a special place in his estimation.

On the evidence of Blake's highly elusive *Prophetic Books*, the general mythopoeic structure of his religious vision could be described as 'Promethean'. The Greek myth of the revolt of the titan Prometheus against the tyrant Zeus is of course best known from Aeschylus's great drama *Prometheus Bound*. In general outline, the Prometheus myth is but one version of a constantly reworked Greek right of passage theme of the rebellion of sons against fathers, but the story also probably assumed some ancient Hellenic significance as a potent expression of free Greek resistance to oriental tyranny and colonialism. Not surprisingly, Promethean themes also abound in eighteenth- and nineteenth-century romantic art and poetry: Percy Shelley wrote directly on the theme in *Prometheus Unbound*, and the idea is also present in Mary Shelley's

56   *Philosophy and its Public Role*

Gothic shocker *Frankenstein*. Still, perhaps the best known appearance of
the Promethean theme occurs in John Milton's great seventeenth-
century literary and religious classic *Paradise Lost*. In this work, however, the tyrannical Zeus and the heroic Prometheus are subject to rather
radical reinterpretation — since it is the Christian God of truth and justice who assumes the role of the oppressor, and the archfiend Satan who
is his tortured victim. But despite Milton's near glamorization of evil in
his deeply ambivalent portrayal of Satan, his poem finally comes down
on the side of theological orthodoxy: Satan is ultimately the free chooser
of evil over good, his 'freedom' is no more than perverted pride, and his
consequent punishment is both merited and just.

Blake's romantic use of the Promethean myth is distinctly more problematic from the standpoint of Christian orthodoxy. In Blake's
soteriology, the resistance offered by a shifting range of redemptive or
salvific figures (Orc, Los, Oothoon and so on) to the tyranny of Urizen is
by and large symbolic of the struggle of spirit over the material and
social forces which conspire to oppress it: in particular, of the struggle
for freedom of basically sound sensual and other impulses over the
weight of received tradition and convention. In this light, Blake's
redeemer is the Jesus who opposes the Pharisees. But the Jesus of Christianity is also crucially he who says 'Not my will but thine be done', and
who is himself the human personification of divine will. Christ is obedi-
ent, whereas Satan and men are not — and it is because Satan and men
were not, that evil came into the world. But the source of evil for Blake is
not the disobedience of Satan or man, but the blindness of Urizen —
symbolised by the oppression of spirit by matter. Urizen is not God but a
demiurge who brings evil into the world with the creation of matter. In
consequence, and worse yet, redemption is not for Blake a matter of
exculpation from original sin via God's grace and forgiveness, but of the
(self-initiated) liberation of basic human sweetness and light from non-
spiritual oppression. In short, Blake's Promethean theology appears to
be at once gnostic, manichean and pelagian.[1]

Two points seem clear: first, that these theological notions have fairly
close social-theoretical echoes or analogues in just that Rousseauian conception of the relationship of human nature to society which informs
Blake's vision of the commerce between innocence and experience; secondly, that no theology to which such notions are central could ever be a
defensible *Christian* theology. On the first point, many of Blake's shorter
poems such as 'Little boy lost' and 'The schoolboy' are entirely consistent with that radical departure from traditional thinking about the role
of institutional or adult pedagogical intervention in the child's adjustment to well-balanced civil association which has earned Rousseau the

[1]   For elements of gnosticism in Blake and Milton, see Nuttall (1998).

reputation (for good or ill) as the founding father of progressive education. For despite widespread modern misconstrual of the distinction between traditional (or teacher-centred) and progressive (or child-centred) education as a difference of pedagogical method, this distinction really turns on much deeper social-theoretical and normative differences concerning the vexed interplay of nature and nurture in the fortunes of human development. Briefly, Rousseau rejects a traditional conception of society, socialization and education according to which an actually or potentially malign (self-interested or anti-social) human nature requires improvement by civil initiation, in favour of a more radical construal of the vices of an otherwise benign human nature as themselves largely outcomes of such initiation. From a theological viewpoint, however, the key Christian idea of God's atonement for human error remains entirely at odds with any such progressive conception of the relation of first to second nature. Rousseau's social theory is thus, if not also gnostic and manichean, certainly pelagian — and therefore just as surely heretical from a Christian viewpoint.

Hence, if Auden's main interest in his great healers lay in the personally and socially redemptive potential of the Christian vision (as was certainly the case with such others of his time as T.S. Eliot), Blake must be an odd spokesman for any such view. To be sure, although there might be some case for focusing upon an apostle of Christ who emphasizes the more sympathetic and forgiving, less judgmental or punitive, aspects of Christian message, it seems undeniable that the need for some self- or other-imposed discipline upon human inclinations regarded as in and of themselves less than perfect and/or potentially quite wayward, is still central to that vision: when Jesus declines to condemn the woman taken in adultery, his advice is to go thy way and sin no more, not to go forth and let it all hang out. Further, his linking of Blake to Lane and Lawrence, who are not especially religious or theological thinkers, and who seem precisely more concerned with the adverse effects on personal growth of repression — even perhaps with the possible benefits of uninhibited sexual expression — suggests that the powers of great personal and social healing in which Auden was mainly interested may have been more of psychological-therapeutic than religious import.

Lane's Developmental Tightrope

Despite the fact that he was something of a celebrity in his day, and that his work would also influence much early twentieth century experimental educational and rehabilitational practice, the name of Homer Lane is nonetheless unlikely to mean much to contemporary readers — although he deserves lasting credit for developing a distinctive educational and therapeutic perspective which may have undergone some distortion or coarsening in the work of his more famous disciple A.S.

Neill. Briefly, Lane was born in the USA in 1876 where he trained as a teacher of woodwork. In the course of teaching in New England schools he became interested in the reform or rehabilitation of youngsters with behavioural problems, and was in 1906 appointed Director of a juvenile detention centre near Detroit named 'The Ford Republic': it was there that Lane first experimented with ideas of self-government. In attempting to address the problems of problem children, Lane was deeply impressed by the work of Freud, not least by psychoanalytic recognition of the adverse developmental implications of repression, which was to provide him with a theoretical key to understanding what he had already observed to be successful about self-government. Lane came to England in 1912 as Director of 'The Little Commonwealth', a self-governing community of young offenders at Evershot Dorset — which, however, came to an untimely end when two female abscondees made allegations of improper conduct (never proved and later retracted) against Lane. In the view of his many friends and disciples, it was the bad public odour in which Lane was cast by this event that ultimately led to his fatal heart attack ('killed in action by the Twickenham Baptist gang') in 1925.

Lane's ideas are to be found mainly in a short collection of lectures posthumously published under the title of *Talks to Parents and Teachers* (Lane, 1954). Not all his educational ideas were original: for example, the idea of self-government as a remedial strategy had been tried by previous reformers and educators. What is mainly new about Lane's approach is his development of such strategies within a more theoretical psychological framework. Basically, Lane employs the Freudian concept of repression to explain what he regarded as the inevitable failure of traditional or conventional punitive approaches to reform. Lane held that his problem children were the victims of various kinds of negative treatment. As long-term subjects of physical and psychological maltreatrment by abusive or uncaring parents, teachers and law enforcers, they were no longer able to associate authority with anything other than rejection and hostility. Lane believed that the only way in which the idea of authority might be cut loose from its negative effects on and associations in the minds of such children was by shifting authority from external sources to the children themselves: through the self-government of 'The Little Commonwealth' or similar institutions, responsibility for establishing and enforcing the rules of the community would be transferred from the teachers to the pupils.

Talks to Parents and Teachers, is a work of rich psychological insights, and there can be little doubt that Lane had a remarkable understanding of the workings of young minds from infancy onwards. More controversially, the accounts of his rehabilitational work in 'The Commonwealth' are full of colourful and sometimes bizarre examples of the highly unorthodox strategies (such as 'spoiling the fun' of antisocial behaviour by joining in with it) apparently deployed by Lane to break the psychological 'constellations' of anti-authority of his young charges. On the other hand, it also seems that Lane's ideas have little to do with any romantic or anti-rationalist uninhibited emotional or sensual expression for its own sake. On the contrary, Lane is more concerned with the fairly down-to-earth therapeutic aim of assisting emotionally crippled children to 'normal' functioning on a fairly conventional appreciation of responsible human agency: he is more concerned with the adverse consequences for mature adult agency of damaged self-esteem and confidence, and with developing strategies for the repair of such damage, than with any quasi-romantic liberation of feeling and emotion. Indeed, Lane is everywhere emphatic that such damage to responsible agency may follow from unrestrained self-expression, no less than from undue constraints on human freedom: in short, repression may take the form not only of abuse but of *coddling*. In this regard, *Talks to Parents and Teachers* offers a stage theory of child development — very much in the tradition of progressive stage theories from Rousseau to Piaget — which is designed to help adult guardians walk the hazardous tightrope between too much and too little attention to the undisciplined instinctual and other demands of the child.

In that case — in terms of our previous gloss on the traditional-progressive distinction — in what sense is it appropriate to regard Lane as a progressive educator? Indeed, we should first notice that Lane's thought and practice was largely informed by a fairly traditionalist conception of the interplay of nature and nurture. For although his psychoanalytic theory sought to explain adult malfunctioning in terms of the repression of basic instincts, Freud also regarded such repression as the unfortunate personal psychic or emotional price to be paid for the higher good of civilized association, and it is arguable that his views on sexuality enshrine quite traditional and conservative assumptions (I have explored this matter in Carr, 1987). True, Lane's view of human nature and its salvific prospects seems less pessimistic than Freud's, and he may appear to put a more romantic or progressive spin on psychoanalytic theory and method. Allthough he follows Freud in holding repression to be a key factor in personality and character development, repression is not for him an agent of civilized control of the Id's dark powers, but a matter of the sociopathic inhibition — under the pressure of parental and other adult mismanagement and abuse — of a perfectly proper will to life and liberty.

But despite Lane's tendency to a Rousseauian rhetoric of the innate goodness of the child, there is nothing in what he generally says about the mechanics of good child-rearing to suggest that either the child or his instincts do not require discipline. In this respect, it may be that Lane's view of human nature steers a more Aristotelian or Lockean course between traditionalist inherent badness and romantic-progressive innate goodness in holding that natural inclinations are in themselves morally neither good nor bad, and that everything depends for developmental good or ill on wise and loving nurture. So whatever sympathy Lane might have had with Blake's anti-repressive remarks on excess and acting on desire, it would appear that the nature he regards as ultimately good is a formed and informed second nature which requires careful cultivation. It is also not clear that Lane would have endorsed Neill's more general educational application — in what would seem to have been the free-for-all of 'Summerhill' — of his unusual techniques with problem children: Lane may have been more aware than Neill that his special methods constituted therapy for some, rather than education for all.

Lawrence's Dualism of Sensibility

Whatever its general literary merit, Lawrence's provocative *Lady Chatterley's Lover* — the focus of a notorious British obscenity trial — provides a useful introduction to the bearing of Lawrence's creative insights on his broader socio-political and educational views. Regardless of its other attractions for readers, Lawrence's novel is mainly concerned to explore the meeting of two quite different worlds as represented by the aristocrat Lady Chatterley and Mellors the gamekeeper. As a product of the working or labouring class, Mellors is a man of little or no formal education whose relationships to others and to the world is direct and affective rather than second-hand or intellectual: he calls a spade a spade — or by some other down-to-earth term. On the other hand, Lady Chatterley's more cultivated and literate sensibilities are the product of an upper-class formal education which ill fits her for such direct or uninhibited relationships. Whereas Mellors is a product of what has been called the 'folk' culture, Chatterley is heir to a quite different 'high' culture. Indeed, the novel represents a rather more up-front exploration of a theme of the artificiality of 'civilized' suppression of affective and instinctual life with which Lawrence was much preoccupied in such rather more significant efforts as *Sons and Lovers* and *Women in Love*.

On the face of it, the encounter between Mellors and Chatterley seems designed to make a familiar Lawrencian point about the honesty, integrity and authenticity of uninhibited feeling over the falsity and hypocrisy of much so-called civilized interpersonal life and conduct: the formally educated or merely 'book-learned' often appear bloodless in Lawrence's work compared with those whose learning is a product of direct practical, feelingful and/or uninhibited experience and engagement. But Lawrence's apparent celebration of instinctual nature is also riven with deep tensions or ambivalences which become particularly evident in those novels which draw on his own experiences as a school-teacher. Thus, in *The Rainbow*, the new teacher Ursula is faced with the problem of precisely taming, in the name of education and civilized values, the brute and potentially violent passions of instinctive nature — and this is a task which she only finally manages by equally violent and brutal confrontation. It seems clear from his fiction that although Lawrence admired the honesty and authenticity of the instinctual life, he did not for a moment hold that the expressions or deliverences of brute nature are invariably (if at all) admirable or virtuous in themselves: on the contrary, he seems to suppose that the only hope for civil order lies in the proper channeling and control of brute instincts. However, the key Lawrencian point is that the proper route to such control cannot lie through imposing an inappropriate formal education on those of primal feeling and instinct: first, any such education could only be a futile attempt to convert sows' ears into silk purses; secondly, formal education for those who are basically unfitted for it can at best only serve to weaken or enfeeble the vital energy or vigour of their basic nature.

All of these tensions come to a rather virulent head in Lawrence's extraordinary essay 'Education of the People' (in Lawrence, 1973). In this not notably coherent mixture of political theory, wild developmental speculation and educational policy — which also contains, amongst other things, a barely controlled outburst on the emasculatory potential of mother love — Lawrence argues for a hierarchical, selective and segregated system of education not far removed from the class-based educational proposals of Lawrence's distinguished literary contemporary, T.S. Eliot. Indeed, perhaps the most surprising point to emerge from close study of Lawrence's fictional and other writings, is that despite Auden's apparent reverence for him as a (perhaps romantic) champion of authentic sensuous feeling over cold reason, a martyr to the cause of spiritual liberation from the artificial constraints of civilized life and order, Lawrence is deeply opposed to any and all pedagogies of self-expression. Indeed, as the perfect type of a traditionalist social and educational thinker — and a very conservative, authoritarian and inegalitarian one at that — Lawrence stands far closer to Matthew Arnold or T.S. Eliot than to Rousseau, Dewey or Neill. Further, although 'Education of the People' probably weighs more heavily in the scales of sheer derangement than anything Blake or Lane might have written, Lawrence's work was to exercise a profound influence on right-wing educational theorising in post-war Britain and elsewhere. Indeed, the ideas of both Lawrence and Eliot — often reinforced by the work of psychometricians — have had enormous impact on those inclined to argue for an alternative or 'popular' non-academic education for 'less able' children, precisely on the grounds that different types of social background and/or natural or acquired sensibility fit people for different roles and functions in life. [2] But Lawrence's ultimately authoritarian attempt to resolve his ambivalence towards uncultivated instinct also raises problems for any estimate of him as a great healer: if, that is, great healing is rightly taken as reconciling great metaphysical, socio-political or psychological dichotomies or divisions.

Philosophy and Theory in Great Healing

We need not doubt the remarkable psychological insights of all Auden's healers. Few imaginative writers have matched Lawrence's ability to identify and well describe the deep respects in which human experience, feeling and motivation are conditioned by differences and divisions of class and gender, and there could hardly be a schoolteacher who failed to relate to his disquieting depiction of the harsh realities of much class-room life in *The Rainbow*. Likewise, Homer Lane was clearly gifted with an equally remarkable understanding, forged at least partly in the fires of direct practical experience, of the minds and motives of often troubled young people from infancy onwards: despite the unfortunate contemporary neglect into which it has fallen, *Talks to Parents and Teachers* remains a potentially richer and more useful source of psychological insight into child-development than the more educationally influential writings of later cognitive developmentalists. Last, but by no means least, Blake's *Songs of Innocence and Experience* have lost none of their power to captivate the hearts and minds of readers from his day to our own, and such short poems as 'The garden of love', 'London' and 'The chimney sweeper' express more poignantly than any other romantic verse the appalling grief and misery that man has so often made of and for man.

It is another matter, however, whether the psychological insights of Blake, Lane and Lawrence are well accommodated in the theological, social-scientific and/or political terms in which these writers sought to give them theoretical expression or significance, and whether these theoretical perspectives are either jointly consistent or severally coherent. With regard to mutual consistency, it is unlikely that Lane and Lawrence would have been very sympathetic to the more religious or quasi-theological aspects of Blake's vision. There is little evidence of any religious or theological interest on the part of Homer Lane, and even if there is a sense in which Christianity and psychoanalytic theory are both 'traditionalist' social-theoretical perspectives, it is hard to see how a psychoanalytic account of the origins of human deviance might ultimately be squared with an orthodox Christian one. Again, although what might

---

[2]   The British educational theorist G.H. Bantock was a key figure in development of the curricular implications of the educational writings of both Lawrence and Eliot. See, for example: Bantock (1973).

be called Lawrence's paganism is not entirely hostile to religious or spiritual impulses, he explicitly holds in his essay 'On Human Destiny' (in Lawrence, 1973) that Christianity can no longer have any real power to address or counter the ills that afflict the modern condition: in this, Lawrence contrasts markedly with his younger literary contemporaries Eliot and Auden both of whom seem to have turned to Christianity for not just personal but social salvation.

Secondly, we have already doubted whether the significant revisions of received theological and social scientific perspectives encountered in the work of Auden's great healers are separately coherent. The religious or theological vision developed by Blake is unorthodox to the point of heresy from a Christian viewpoint, and its claim to human healing seems anyway prone to wreck on the spiritually disintegrative rocks of metaphysical and/or psychosocial dualism and division. Likewise, Homer Lane's less than orthodox reinterpretation of Freudian theory in support of his own more optimistic view of natural inclination appears to place an intolerable strain upon the basic structural assumptions of that or any other genuinely psychoanalytic theory — given that any such theory seems grounded in some notion of inevitable if not also tragic conflict between nature and nurture. Nor, finally, is it clear that Lawrence's authoritarian political and educational proposals at all resolve his deep ambivalence towards natural or uncultivated human feeling and instinct: it is not obvious how brute authoritarian control might be any less liable to damage or destroy the raw vitality of human spirit than its civil or civilized cultivation, and it is hard to see how Lawrence's implacable opposition to educational equality might be squared with any acceptable contemporary liberal-democratic conception of basic human rights, responsibility or citizenship.

But might it not be that the diverse psychological insights of all the great healers are — perhaps with appropriate contextualization — mutually reconcilable within some larger and perhaps also less theoretically loaded perspective on the human condition ? The trouble here is that the psychological insights are not clearly separable in either Blake, Lane or Lawrence from diagnosis and prescription, and we have seen that they are not entirely at one on such matters. For example, it is not easy to see how Lane's absolute abhorrence of corporal punishment — a practice he regarded as always damaging and utterly indefensible — might be squared with Lawrence's quite alarming enthusiasm in 'Education of the People' for the spanking of little bottoms. All issues of child protection aside, and on a charitable view of Lawrence's frequent rhetorical excesses, it seems that the differences between Lane and Lawrence are at least as much of evaluative as of theoretical import. Lane's work is touched throughout by a sympathy and compassion towards his fellow beings in which support and help take pride of place over judgement and punishment. For Lawrence, this is all so much sentimental therapeutic eyewash, one has to be cruel to be kind and any such lily-livered liberal indulgence is surely the primrose path to morally enfeebling dishonesty and self-obsession.

The Inherent Normativity of Great Healing

Although we have argued that the views of Blake, Lane and Lawrence to which Auden appeals in the name of great healing point towards somewhat different psychological and social goals, they all nevertheless represent developmental narratives upon which psychological and social prescriptions might be based. Indeed, although it is anyone's guess what implications Auden held them to have for educational or other professional policy and practice, it is undeniable that the ideas of Lane and Lawrence have had real influence on educators and therapists, and that latter day social and educational policies have not infrequently appealed to cognitive or other modern developmental models to support their prescriptions. It is also likely that the principled professional reflection of many if not most contemporary primary school teachers is informed by a loose Piagetian developmentalism which is thought to have proved (scientifically) that children progress through a series of intellectual stages from concrete to formal thinking. Likewise Piaget and Kohlberg may be supposed to have shown that moral growth is a matter of progress from heteronomy to moral self-legislation. But the above suspicion that the developmental differences between Lane and Lawrence are no less evaluative than theoretical must also give pause to any such blind faith. Insofar as the accounts of Piaget and Kohlberg, no less than those of Blake, Lane and Lawrence, express ideals or visions of human health or flourishing, they would appear to be no less value-implicated than those of Auden's healers. It is not an established *fact* that morality is a matter of (quasi-Kantian) self-legislation, so much as a point of view — and an ethically contested one at that.

One possible implication of such observations is that it may make more sense to regard any and all accounts of human development — Blake's, Lane's, Lawrence's, Piaget's or Kohlberg's — as *normative* or prescriptive rather than scientific theories of human nature. In this regard, however, it may also be held that developmental theories are no worse off than natural scientific or other theories. Under the inluence of social constructivist views of meaning and knowledge hailing from non-realist and anti-empiricist sources, many (pragmatist and other) social theorists and philosophers of science have come to hold that theories are *inherently* normative, and that it is not ultimately possible to draw any clear distinction between observation and theory, or fact and value. The main snag with this view, which has been subject to widespread and uncritical adoption in the application of philosophy to such fields as education, is that it appears liable to different, more or less plausible, construals. First, on radical poststructuralist and postmodern versions, opposition to the fact-value dichotomy has led to wholesale rejection of received distinctions between natural science on the one hand, and ideology, myth and magic on the other: all human narratives are socially constructed — creative fiction rather than objective fact — and no particular narrative may claim epistemic priority over another.

Any such line of argument is clearly problematic, and will not be pursued further here: for one thing, if everything is narrative, then (as Kant might say) *nothing* is — since it seems no longer possible to mark any significant contrast between what is narratival and what is not. More routine idealist or pragmatist talk of the normativity of theory, on the other hand, seems more modestly concerned to indicate that scientific and other theories have socio-cultural sources and origins, and that there is therefore no epistemic access — no 'view from nowhere' — to some value-neutral objective reality. But such modest anti-realism is clearly quite consistent with holding that there is a real distinction between evidence-based science on the one hand and evidence-free (unfalsifiable) ideological or mythopoeic constructions on the other, and to that extent the problem of the deep normativity of developmental theories re-surfaces more or less intact in non-realist or constructivist epistemology. Indeed, the problem of the explanatory status of developmental narratives might be restated by precisely asking whether it is proper to regard them as evidence-based natural sciences or as more like creative myths.

Largely to his credit, this problem is clearly appreciated by perhaps the most influential cognitive moral developmentalist of the last half century, Lawrence Kohlberg — whose work may also be regarded as standing squarely in the pragmatist tradition of Dewey. As a social scientist of moral development, Kohlberg was nevertheless acutely aware of the inherent normativity of accounts of moral growth, and much exercised by the problem of providing some sort of objective empirical support for such normativity. In a much discussed essay on the fact-value issue, Kohlberg (1971) is clearly persuaded that the scientific status of his theory depends upon the identification of some sort of non-normative factual or other empirical basis for moral norms and prescriptions. But to anyone not already in thrall to a particular picture of social science, it should be apparent that Kohlberg's faith in such empirical evidence is quite misplaced, that there are no norm-free developmental facts or processes, and that the idea of moral formation is completely exhausted by its normative content Although children clearly could be educated in the broadly Kantian conception of moral life and conduct of Piaget and Kohlberg, they could also be formed according to other (virtue-theoretical or care-ethical) moral conceptions. Kohlbergians may argue that these other conceptions are mistaken, but it is surely specious to claim that they go wrong in running against the grain of some fictitious empirical moral processes: the normativity of moral developmental accounts goes all the way down (see Carr, 2002a).

But it may now be feared that we are stuck with a particularly intractable version of the fact-value dichotomy which precludes any possibility of *arguing* the mistakenness of alternative normative conceptions: in holding that developmental theory is inherently normative, we may seem condemned to a moral non-cognitivism or expressivism which precludes any role for experiential knowledge in the construction of moral or other norms. However, the enduring modern debate between ethical cognitivists and non-cognitivists confirms that it is still very much an open question whether moral values and prescriptions have a factual or other objective basis. Indeed, moral naturalists have persistently argued that experiential judgements of human harm and benefit do play a crucial role in moral life, not as the statistical data of some sort of moral science, but as *reasons* for *action*: on this (broadly Aristotelian) view, the gap between the scientific and the normative is a difference, not between objective facts and subjective values, but between theoretical and practical reason. More generally, the question whether some form of (naturalist or other) objectivism or some kind of non-cognitivism provides the correct account of the logic of moral discourse itself clearly calls for objective rational argument of a kind that does not depend upon empirical evidence: scientific evidence is no better placed to settle the question between naturalism and non-cognitivism than it is to confirm Kohlberg's account of moral development.

It would therefore seem: first, that insofar as any developmental accounts are normative, they are unsusceptible to evidential disconfirmation — which might also mean that they do not strictly qualify as forms of *theoretical* explanation at all; secondly, that this need not place such accounts beyond rational evaluation or justification. It is also important to appreciate that these points are no less applicable to the insights of Blake, Lane and Lawrence than to those of Piaget and Kohlberg. In this regard, although it is unlikely that many contemporary theorists of education and therapy would greatly warm to any treatment of the insights of Blake and Lawrence — alongside those of Lane — as genuine developmental views, the present focus on Auden's three markedly different healers is meant to be no less instructive than provocative. In short, whilst the perspectives of Lane, Piaget and Kohlberg are, regardless of contrary appearances, really no less thoroughly normative and no more scientific than those of Blake and Lawrence, the insights of Blake and Lawrence may be no less apt for rational evaluation or justification than those of Lane, Piaget and Kohlberg.

Thus, although perhaps few modern social scientists of moral development would regard Blake's highly mythopoeic treatment of problems of human suffering and freedom as much more than a quite unverifiable (if not actually demented) fairy tale, it may be no more than a 'scientistic' prejudice to assume so. Certainly, insofar as Blake's views can be held to add up to a coherent theological position, they may be in no greater epistemic difficulties than other developmental perspectives. To be sure, one might hold that any and all theological claims are inherently meaningless and/or unverifiable forms of personal expression, but moral evaluation and prescription have also been conceived by modern non-cognitivists and expressivists as matters of little more than individual creative aspiration. On the other hand, the wedge that modern non-cognitivism has sought to drive between moral judgement and the world may also be considered a strong point in favour of a moral naturalism which grounds evaluation and prescription in ordinary human sensibility to facts of harm and benefit. By parity of reasoning, however, the best case for rational theology might be said to lie in a theological naturalism in which claims about divinity and salvation are related to familiar human considerations of harm and flourishing (on this point see Carr, 2002b). In this light, to be sure, Blake's apparent gnosticism must be problematic from an orthodox Christian perspective. First, gnosticism inclines to a manichean or dualistic anthropology which raises problems — of a kind incarnational theologies aim to avoid — for conceiving relations between soul and body and/or the divine and the human. Second, more practically, gnostic dualists have often promoted human excesses — of either ascetic self-denial or sensual indulgence — regarded by orthodox Christians as personally and socially harmful. Be this as it may, to whatever extent such considerations undermine the theological plausibility of Blake's vision, they do not necessarily impugn either its reason or sanity — and one cannot doubt that more dubious doctines of psycho-therapeutic liberation than Blake's have been seriously canvassed in modern times.

Normative Reflection in Professional Policy and Practice

As already seen, the various insights of Blake, Lane and Lawrence would appear to be, as well as addressed to rather different spiritual, moral, social and political concerns, not entirely consistent with each other: on the face of it, they would appear to express or represent rather different visions of human flourishing. Insofar as such visions — along with other developmental accounts — are normative rather than scientific, they are expressive of practical (moral) ideals, aspirations and prescriptions rather than theoretical generalities, and are to that extent inherently controversial. What this also evidently means is that although people — such as the admirers of Blake, Lane and Lawrence — are not prohibited in free countries from holding such views, they nevertheless enshrine the kind of 'comprehensive theories of the good' which are generally considered inappropriate bases for public policies of social control and education in liberal-democratic polities. However, recognition that all developmental accounts are normative through and through, must have similarly problematic implications for the common conviction that some theoretically correct story about human development is required for principled professional educational, remedial or other deliberation and practice: if developmental views are irredeemably controversial, what proper role could they play in practical professional decision-making?

To appreciate that developmental accounts lack the evidence-based status of empirical theory is basically to abandon the idea that the professional education of teachers, child psychologists or social workers is necessarily grounded in some empirical science of human development apt for quasi-technological application. Although such professionals certainly need reflection, it seems mistaken to hold that such reflection needs to be always, if at all, theoretical. Indeed, it seems more accurate to locate the need of such professionals for habits of critical reflection in the fact that few of the questions with which they are daily faced readily admit of unproblematic applied science solution. In this respect, there is clearly a case for professional reflection on the insights of Blake, Lane, Lawrence and other great students of the human condition, not as potential technological solutions, but as part of a wider educated appreciation of the ethical complexities of human motive, association and flourishing. Indeed, it is arguable that what teachers and others need no less than those quasi-scientific theories of human behaviour or social science techniques of action research which are nowadays the contemporary *sine qua non* of so many programmes of professional preparation, is the sort of broad cultural initiation which might comprehend — besides some acquaintance with the insights of Blake, Lane and Lawrence — appreciation of the potential for enhanced professional insight of such other great literary figures as Auden himself. What may have been neglected, in the latter day scramble to regulate and technicise such professions as teaching is the need to educate teachers in that deeper moral sensitivity to the complexities of human experience and association — of which great literaure provides one potent source — and out of the dogma that empirical science and technology are the only legitimate routes to professionally worthwhile knowledge and understanding.

Terence McLaughlin

Philosophy, Values and Schooling

Principles and Predicaments of Teacher Example

Introduction

In recent years there has been a wide-ranging philosophical debate about the nature and justification of the forms of complex evaluative influence that schools in pluralist liberal democratic societies exert on their students. Schooling is not, of course, synonymous with education, but schools remain important institutional contexts in which education is made available to children and young people and the organisation and distribution of schooling gives rise to many issues which have philosophical aspects or dimensions, not least because schooling, like education itself, is inherently value laden. Central to much recent philosophical debate are issues relating to the respective mandates for educational influence claimed in pluralist democratic societies by 'common' schools on the one hand and by 'faith-based' (or religious) schools on the other (see, for example, Callan, 1997, 2000; Dwyer, 1998; Gutmann, 1987; Feinberg, 1998; Halstead and McLaughlin, 2005; Levinson, 1999; McDonough and Feinberg, 2003; McLaughlin, 1992, 2003a; Macedo, 2000; Reich, 2002; Salomone, 2000; Thiessen, 2001; and White, 1996).

As befits a discipline that has been described as pre-eminently concerned with a discussion of abstract matters in the abstract, much of this philosophical debate has been conducted at a distance from educational practice. It has become increasingly clear, however, that a philosophical approach of these matters 'from above' educational practice needs to be complemented by a philosophical approach 'from below' if pertinent questions are to be fully illuminated. In particular, contemporary debate has tended to neglect the point that the distinctive forms of educational influence that both 'common' and religious schools seek to achieve are pre-eminently exerted through teachers. I have argued elsewhere that many of the philosophically significant burdens and dilemmas of common schooling require resolution at classroom level via a form of pedagogic *phronesis* on the part of teachers (McLaughlin, 2003a) as do judgements about equivalent burdens and dilemmas in religious schools (McLaughlin, 1999).

One distinctive form of educational influence that teachers exert is through their example. Our expectations of teachers therefore extend to the example that they set to the children and young people in their charge. No adequate discussion of the nature and justification of the forms of educational influence exerted by different kinds of schools can ignore the different kinds of teacher example which these schools presuppose and require. In this chapter I shall seek to show that an exploration of the principles and predicaments of teacher example in different schooling contexts throws important light on our understanding of the principles and predicaments relating to 'common' and 'faith-based' schools respectively.

The chapter has four sections. In the first, as a background to the discussion, I shall outline in general terms the scope of the example of the teacher. In the second section, I indicate how all forms of teacher example can generate significant controversy. The third section addresses the nature of our expectations with respect to the moral example given by the teacher in a 'common' school. In the fourth section I turn specifically to expectations concerning the moral and religious example of the teacher in 'faith-based' or religious schools. Throughout the discussion I will be using the term 'school' in the British sense to refer institutions of learning for students up to the age of 18.

The Scope of Teacher Example

At the outset, it is useful to look in more detail at the range of expectations we have of teachers with respect to the example they set to students, regardless of the sort of schools in which teaching and learning is taking place. In what follows, I shall refer to three (interrelated) categories of teacher example.

The first of these relate to what is seen by many as the main function of a teacher: the teaching of a subject or area of study. These 'subject related' expectations cover a number of different aspects of teacher example. We expect a teacher to give a good example of subject-related competence, skill and flair. We would think little of an English teacher whose own handwriting was illegible, whose imaginative response to poetry was poor or who displayed little love for literature. Similarly, a Mathematics teacher whose own practice of the subject was bedevilled by inaccuracy or a PE teacher who was incapable of displaying effectively the skills being taught would rightly be thought to be giving a poor example to students. Our expectations of 'subject-related' teacher example extend beyond competence, skill and flair. We also expect, among other things, that teachers will give an example of enthusiastic involvement in their subject and in learning generally.

It is important to avoid an unduly narrow view of the significance of 'subject-related' teacher example and to appreciate why *example* is indispensible. In his essay 'Learning and Teaching' (Oakeshott, 1989), Michael Oakeshott illuminates the complexity of the 'inheritance' which teachers must pass on to their pupils. It is not, he claims, a kind of property which could be conveyed by lawyers, requiring on the part of pupils merely 'legal acknowledgement'. On the contrary, it is a wide ranging inheritance of

> feelings, emotions, images, visions, thoughts, beliefs, ideas, understandings, intellectual and practical enterprises, languages, relationships, organizations, canons and maxims of conduct, procedures, rituals, skills, works of art, books, musical compositions, tools, artefacts and utensils (p. 45).

To enter this inheritance, claims Oakeshott, involves both the acquisition of 'information', which can be communicated through 'instruction', and of 'judgement' which, in Oakeshott's view, cannot properly be communicated in such a direct way. For Oakeshott, 'judgement' involves the development of the intellectual virtues (such as disinterested curiosity, patience, exactness, industry and the like) and an awareness of 'style' (the detection of an 'individual intelligence' operating in every 'utterance'). 'Judgement' cannot be communicated by instruction but must be 'imparted' in everything which is taught. Oakeshott writes

> It is implanted unobtrusively in the manner in which information is conveyed, in a tone of voice, in the gesture which accompanies instruction, in asides and oblique utterances, and by example (p. 61).

With regard to the latter, Oakeshott acknowledges his debt to a particular teacher for giving him a recognition of certain important virtues

> . . . I owed it to him, not on account of anything he ever said, but because he was a man of patience, accuracy, economy, elegance and style (p. 62).

The wide ranging sorts of influence over pupils that the teacher has to exert in the 'conversation between the generations' that constitutes education means that the teacher must be a *certain sort of person* who communicates not only knowledge and skill but also (parts of) him or herself.

The requirement that a teacher be a certain sort of person is apparent too in the second category of teacher example to which I shall refer. This category relates to our expectation that the teacher should act as a responsible adult. The kind of example being sought here embraces, and extends beyond, the duties of acting *in loco parentis*. We expect a teacher not only to set an example of prudence, care and common sense in relation to many matters, but also to exemplify broader personal qualities such as balance, wisdom and maturity.

The third category of teacher example is the specifically moral example that we expect a teacher to set. The slogan 'every teacher is a moral educator' captures the important point that a teacher cannot avoid moral responsibility. Education, teaching and schooling are inherently laden with moral values. Moral considerations are deeply implicated in all properly educational aims, relationships and processes. With regard to educational aims, we expect teachers to assume some responsibility for the moral education of pupils and to help (at least to some extent) to form their moral beliefs and character. Many other educational aims have strong moral overtones, such as the development of the 'critical independence' of pupils and the provision of 'equality of opportunity'. With regard to educational relationships, we expect teachers to control and discipline pupils not merely through the exercise of power, but through an appropriate form of authority, with its concern for reason, justification and fairness. We also look for morally resonant qualities such as integrity and respect in relationships between teachers and pupils. With regard to educational processes, we expect teachers to avoid intimidation, indoctrination, discrimination and the like, and to take account of morally significant considerations such as respect for the autonomy and dignity of the pupil.

The moral influence of the teacher is therefore wide-ranging and pervasive, and is inseparable from all other forms of teacher influence. As with these other forms, moral influence is exercised not only (or necessarily) through formally taught lessons, although moral questions can be directly handled in the classroom and arise in relation to aspects of many issues and subjects. A number of morally significant forms of learning, however, cannot take place simply through instruction or discussion. Morally significant qualities of the teacher such as integrity can only be detected in their exemplification. The forms of moral example that may be given by teachers are varied, and include not only actions but also less tangible ways in which attitudes and sensitivities can be expressed, including reactions and gestures. As with other aspects of teacher example, omissions can be highly significant. Teacher example is not confined to matters which are directly intended. The matters in relation to which moral example can be given are similarly varied, as are the contexts in which it can arise.

It is important to underscore the interrelatedness of the three categories of teacher example which I have identified. Moral considerations, for example, permeate both 'subject-related' and 'adult' teacher example. It is also important to note that within each of these categories, the expectations that arise vary as to their status and character. Some expectations have contractual or legal dimensions, in that a failure to satisfy them can involve the possibility of censure, dismissal or legal proceedings. One can readily imagine cases involving subject-related incompetence, lack of adult responsibility or moral failure which fall into this category. Other expectations in the categories relate to our broader expectations of the teacher as a professional, and several of these are matters which might feature in a professional code of ethics (on ethical codes of practice for teachers see, for example, Carr, 2000, Sockett, 1993, Ch 6, the Code of Professional Values and Practice for Teachers of the General Teaching Council for England <www.gtce.org.uk> and the Code of Ethical Practice for the Teaching Profession prepared by the Universities Council for the Education of Teachers <www.ucet.ac.uk>). A number of our expectations of teacher example, however, go beyond the contractually, legally or professionally significant and involve matters of personal preference, aspiration and style.

Controversiality and Teacher Example

As noted earlier, not all forms of teacher example are equally controversial. It might be thought, for instance, that in contrast to 'moral' forms of teacher example, 'subject-related' and 'adult' examples are, or should be, relatively uncontroversial. The qualifier 'relatively' is important here, however, and we should not overlook the respects in which all forms of teacher example can give rise to significant or well-grounded controversy.

With regard to 'subject-related' teacher example, there is much disagreement about what should be taught in schools (the 'inheritance' which teachers are responsible for passing on) and about methods of teaching, and this can be expressed in terms of disagreement about related aspects of teacher example. Those who feel that open critical discussion in the classroom of (say) sensitive political or religious matters is inappropriate may regret a teacher's exemplification of Socratic questioning in relation to current political events or the existence of God, and devotees of a particular author or playwright might criticise the example given by a teacher in dismissing his or her work. Similarly, critics of 'progressive' teaching methods may object to the failure of teachers to exemplify their favoured pedagogic virtues. There are, after all, different traditions of practice within teaching, with different educational perspectives and commitments (McLaughlin, 2003b).

Disagreement about 'adult' teacher example can arise from differences of view on the nature of appropriate adult behaviour, and can be expressed in terms of unease about (say) teachers' dress, linguistic style or demeanour (cf. Carr, 2000, ch. 6). Another source of possible controversy about 'adult' teacher example is the claim that, since teachers 'model' adult life, women and members of ethnic minorities should be properly represented on the staff of a school, and in positions of author- ity, so that pupils are not given a restricted set of perceptions and aspira- tions. Such policies may give rise to controversy about the criteria that should appropriately govern the appointment and promotion of teach- ing staff.

The moral example of the teacher, however, is particularly susceptible to controversy, in part because of the controversial character of the moral domain as a whole in pluralist liberal democratic societies. Con- troversy can focus upon the nature and extent of the moral example which can be expected of a teacher. The issues involved here differ according to particular schooling contexts. I shall therefore consider this matter first in relation to the 'common' school and then in relation to schools with a specifically religious character.

The Common School and the Moral Example of the Teacher

A common school can be regarded as one in which all students are edu- cated together regardless of differentiating characteristics such as reli- gious and cultural background, and which aspires to offer a common conception of education which is seen as embodying an educational entitlement judged as appropriate for members of society as a whole. In the context of the value diversity of a pluralist democratic society, such a school is faced with a complex task with respect to moral influence. In aspiring to offer a common form of moral education for all pupils, such a school lacks a mandate to offer a specific form of moral influence which goes beyond that acceptable to society in general. The sort of moral influ- ence which the common school can exert is illuminated by the familiar, albeit problematic, distinction between 'public' and 'non-public' moral- ity in a pluralist democratic society, which can be accepted for the sake of the present argument. Roughly expressed, 'public' values can be regarded as those which, in virtue of their fundamentality or inescapability, can be insisted upon for all democratic citizens and for all reasonable and decent persons in general. It is in relation to common or 'public' values of this kind that the common school strives to exert a sub- stantial and non-negotiable moral influence. It is therefore unhesitant in its advocacy of (say) kindness, toleration and honesty and its rejection of (say) cruelty, racism and deceit. In virtue of their strong commitment to the 'public' values, common schools cannot be accused of lacking a moral basis or of aspiring in any general way to value neutrality.

With regard, however, to values which are not 'public' or 'shared', the common school cannot exert a similarly strong and unambiguous moral influence. Such values are significantly controversial, often because of their connection with particular overall frameworks of belief which are themselves matters of disagreement and dispute. The moral significance of a canonically invalid marriage, for example, can only be appreciated within the broader framework of Catholic belief and practice. Such values can be described as 'non-public' not because they are, or can be, completely isolated in all respects from the 'public' domain, but because they cannot (either on principle or in practice) be imposed upon all citizens through the exercise of political power, or through a common form of education. In relation to such 'non-public' values the common school therefore lacks a mandate to shape either the beliefs or personal qualities of pupils in a way which assumes the truth or normative force of values of this kind. The common school must in these matters exert a principled forebearance from influence. It cannot, for example, express disapproval of (say) re-marriage after divorce on the religious ground that since divorce has only legal and not moral force, the couple in question is living in a state of permanent adultery. Nor can it exert a substantial and non-negotiable moral influence against cohabitation outside marriage on grounds which appeal to religious norms. In relation to religious matters, the common school has the role of developing the understanding of pupils and their capacity to make their own critical responses, judgements, and decisions. In important respects, the common school must regard questions of 'non-public' value as 'open', not in a sense which implies a relativistic view of them, but which insists that their public status inhibits the assumption and transmission of them in a definitive way.

The moral influence of the common school in a pluralist democratic society is therefore two-fold in character. On the one hand, it seeks a unifying and universalising influence, 'transmitting' the common and non-negotiable values, principles and procedures of such a society, and securing appropriate forms of respect for, and allegiance to, them on the part of pupils. On the other hand, the school seeks a diversifying and particularising influence with regard to significantly controversial moral questions where the demands of diversity and pluralism are acknowledged. In relation to such matters, the common school encourages on the part of pupils appropriate forms of understanding, open-mindedness, critical judgement and tolerance.

The moral role of the common school which has emerged in this sketch, together with the queries and difficulties to which it gives rise, requires much fuller elaboration and discussion, which I have attempted to provide elsewhere (McLaughlin, 2003a). For our present purposes, however, the sketch can serve as a basis on which the nature and extent of the moral example expected of the teacher in the common school can be brought into focus.

The two-fold character of the moral influence of the teacher in the common school is reflected in the nature and extent of the moral example which the teacher is expected to give. With regard to 'public' values such as kindness, care, fairness, impartiality, benevolence and the like, the teacher can be expected to offer a clear and unqualified example which mirrors the clarity and forthright commitment of the school to values of this kind. Teachers cannot opt out, for example, of providing an example of non-racist attitudes and behaviour. The claim that teachers in common schools should exemplify 'public' values is, however, more complicated than it may seem at first sight in the light of the fact that many of these values, properly understood, are themselves complex and morally textured. For example, the common school needs to achieve a fine-grained understanding of 'respect' on the part of its students. 'Respect' should not be presented as requiring the necessary approval of the choices which people make within the limits of their rights on (say) relativistic grounds, nor should 'civic' respect be presented as the only form of respect. Teachers therefore need to exemplify, particularly in the classroom, a form of respect which is sufficiently rich to satisfy the educational aims of the school. More generally, Callan's account of the nature and demands of the attitudes, habits and abilities required by public virtue (Callan, 1997), some of which are subtle and complicated, have their implications for teacher exemplification. A further complication for this task arises from the fact that the common school should be concerned with the *fit* between the public and the non-public views which students affirm.

With respect to 'non-public' values, the common school cannot *require* a teacher to 'model' an aspect of 'non-public' belief, such as a particular form of religious practice. It may not *forbid* a teacher providing such an example, providing that it is made clear that no processes are involved which suggest that pupils are being directly and unfairly persuaded to subscribe to the values involved. Thus many Christian teachers who work in common schools see themselves as having a vocation to provide a personal example of Christian commitment to pupils. The school may have no objection to the commitment of the teacher becoming clear to pupils in various contexts, as long as the teacher in question does not attempt to directly encourage his or her pupils to become religious believers in unacceptable ways. In general, therefore, where a teacher does offer an example related to 'non-public' moral value, the common school requires that that teacher offer an additional example of principled forebearance from influence and an encouragement of pupils to think for themselves on the matters at stake. The difficulties inherent in making a judgment about when 'undue influence' is being exerted, or when a proper encouragement to pupils to think for themselves is being given, highlights the complexity of the practical judgements needed in relation to matters of this kind. An interesting question concerning the 'non-public' domain and teacher exempification concerns the extent to which a teacher's own views on controversial questions should be revealed in classroom discussions of such matters.

One important issue which arises in relation to the extent of the moral example which can be expected of the teacher in a common school is the relationship between the 'professional' and the 'personal' life of the teacher. In relation to the moral example of the teacher — and indeed the role of the teacher more broadly — the 'professional' and the 'personal' cannot be separated from each other in any very simple way. The professional responsibilities of a teacher cannot be isolated from the qualities which the teacher possesses as a person (on these matters see Carr, 2000, Hare, 1993). In contrast, in the case of some professions, it is possible to envisage a less strong connection between the personal characteristics of the professional and his or her professional competence. However, the strong connection between the 'professional' and the 'personal' in teaching needs to be understood carefully.

The issues involved are usefully illuminated by a recent discussion by David Carr. In his consideration of the close relationship between the moral role of teachers and their moral personhood, Carr insists that '. . . it is the normal expectation that decent or right values will be exhibited only by those who hold them' (Carr, 1993, p. 195). Although 'hold' is somewhat ambiguous (as between, say, 'believe in' and 'live by'), the general point here can be accepted. However, Carr goes on to claim that '. . . values are not the sort of qualities that a person assumes in one context and sheds in another; since they crucially define what or who a person *is* they can only be expected to assert themselves across the different contexts of life in which an individual operates' (Carr, 1993, p. 198). Further, Carr argues, '. . . an effective teacher of values can only be the individual who clearly exhibits them in his personal life' (Carr, 1993, p. 205). Whilst there is a good deal of truth in both of these observations, their interpretation in relation to the moral role of the teacher needs some care. There is a certain ambiguity in the notion of the 'personal life' of the teacher. A distinction needs to be drawn between the 'personal' and the 'private'. For reasons mentioned earlier, the 'personal' has wide ranging significance for the professional work of the teacher, but the significance of the 'private' is less easy to judge. Drawing a distinction between the 'personal' and the 'private' gives rise to the question: Are *all* the 'contexts of life' in which the teacher operates relevant to his or her professional role? Carr does point out that what a teacher is like as a 'private person' is a not a matter of indifference and he gives homosexuality and extra-marital cohabitation as examples of the sorts of aspects of the lives of teachers which parents are inclined to worry about (Carr, 1993, p. 195). He does not, however, give a full account of how these matters should be handled.

How might the domains of the 'professional' and the 'private' be distinguished with regard to the teacher in a common school? This is no easy task. A solution to the problem can, however, be developed along the following lines. First, the 'professional' role of the teacher can be seen as relating directly to his or her work in school in its various aspects. As indicated earlier, this role is inseparable from the personal qualities of the teacher, and for this reason it is impossible for the teacher's 'personal life' in this sense to remain wholly irrelevant to, or concealed from, pupils: the 'professional' includes significant aspects of the 'personal'. Underpinning the professional role of the teacher are the 'public' values described earlier, and the attitude toward 'non-public' values which was also described. Second, it is possible, and necessary, to delineate a 'private' domain of the 'personal' life of the teacher. This is the context in which the teacher lives his or her life in a fuller sense, including the living out of a personal vision of life as a whole governed by 'non-public' values. Teachers in common schools do not expect that their own religious faith (or lack of it), political beliefs or domestic arrangements will be seen as matters which have a bearing on their professional role, provided that these matters do not intrude inappropriately upon that role. A teacher's 'private' life cannot, however, escape some degree of moral assessment. This is particularly the case when an infringement of 'public' values is involved. Thus a teacher's conviction for theft, violence or child abuse could not be regarded as a 'private' matter, even though the offences may not have been committed in school. Many matters involving 'non-public' values relating to the teacher's life outside school might, however, be seen as of no concern to the professional role of the teacher in the common school. Therefore if teachers are living in a homosexual relationship or re-married after divorce, this should not be seen as relevant to their professional work. There has been in recent years an expansion of the 'private' domain of teacher's lives, compared to earlier times when teachers in common schools were expected to embody a much wider range of moral qualities and virtues than is now found acceptable, in part because of the complex part which religion has played in the development of public schooling in England and Wales (on this matter see, for example, Tropp, 1957).

The suggestion that matters involving 'non-public' values relating to the teacher's life outside school is of no relevance to the professional role of the teacher needs, however, to be handled with caution. Within the 'private' domain of the life of the teacher there is a 'public/private' area, where some aspect or aspects of the private life and belief of teachers may come into the public domain. This may be through the direct statements of teachers, or by the visibility of (say) their political activities or domestic arrangements in the vicinity of the school.

Kenneth Strike draws attention to a complex 'middle ground' between, on the one hand, matters which are clearly part of the teacher's private life and in relation to which interference is justifiable only on very strong evidence of their causing educational harm and, on the other, matters which either in virtue of their direct harm to students or their illegality do require interference. This 'middle ground' he argues contains

> ... activities that usually are not illegal and that may have some degree of legal protection as part of a right of privacy but that are found to be immoral or offensive by some part of the community (Strike, 1990, p. 196).

What is particularly difficult about such matters is that

> There is no moral consensus about them, they may be held to be part of the individual's private sphere regardless of whether they are thought to be immoral, and their effects on students are difficult to ascertain (p. 197).

The existence of this 'middle ground' is underscored by the fact that common schools exist in social, cultural and political contexts which are complex and changing. The evaluative basis of such schools cannot be solely derived from considerations of abstract principle. If it is accepted that a principled distinction between 'public' and 'non-public' values is broadly tenable, it is important to note that what is in fact regarded as signficantly controversial, and therefore as a public or a non-public matter, will vary in different contexts and over time. We do not enjoy a stable consensus about matters in the 'middle ground' to which Strike refers. It is therefore not possible to map a very clear distinction between the 'public' values (which might be thought to govern the 'professional' role of teachers including its 'personal' aspects) and the 'non-public' (governing their 'private' life). This will call for discretion about the extent to which matters in the 'private' domain are made public. These difficulties are reinforced by close attention to the mandate of the common school. Strictly speaking it is required to have an 'open' view on matters of non-public value. But it might be thought that a teacher known to have a certain position on a 'non-public' matter is jeopardising his capacity to teach in an even-handed way.

The demands upon the moral example of the teacher in the common school are therefore not straightforward. Complex practical judgement in relation to this matter is called for as it is in relation to the aspiration of the law to specify 'reasonable requirements' for the behaviour of teachers without unjustifiably restricting their liberty.

The Moral and Religious Example of the Teacher in the Faith School

The issues which arise concerning the moral example of the teacher in a faith or religious school are clearly different from those which arise in the common school as a result of the wider mandate for the exercise of educational influence which faith schools enjoy. In contrast to the common school, the educational influence of the faith school can be based on an overall philosophy of life. Thus, in the Catholic school, for example '. . . a specific concept of the world, of man, and of history is developed and conveyed' (Sacred Congregation for Catholic Education [1977] — hereinafter CS — para 8). Faith schools can be described as seeking to achieve non-common educational aims in a non-common educational environment (Halstead and McLaughlin, 2005). The non-common educational aims to which most faith schools aspire are to present a particular religion as true, together with a range of beliefs, values and attitudes (including those of a moral kind) which follow from this, including the aspiration to form the religious commitment of students in some way. Aims such as these are non-common in that, in pluralistic liberal democracies, they are not shared by society as a whole, although care should be taken to avoid giving the impression that there are no significant overlaps between aims of this kind and those of the common school. The educational environment of a faith school is non-common in that it is precisely intended for a particular group within society and not for society as a whole, even if, for various reasons, admissions to the school may extend beyond these boundaries. In virtue of these distinctive aims and environments, faith schools can expect a greater scope of moral example on the part of its teachers than can common schools, and this expectation can extend to religious example as well.

The centrality of the example of the teacher to the educational mission of faith schools is strongly emphasized. Thus the teacher in the Catholic school is seen as one who not only transmits knowledge but forms human persons by communicating Christ (Sacred Congregation for Catholic Education [1982] — hereinafter LWCF — para 16). He or she must provide a 'concrete example' of the Catholic concept of the human person (LWCF paras 18, 22), be a source of spiritual inspiration (LWCF para 23), extend horizons through their personal faith (LWCF para 28) and provide a wide ranging example of faith witness (LWCF paras 32–33; 40–41; 59). For reasons such as these the life of Catholic teachers is seen as involving not merely the exercise of professionalism but of a personal vocation (LCWF para 37) in which '. . . they reveal the Christian message not only by word but also by every gesture of their behaviour' (CS para 43).

It might be thought that these requirements of teacher example in the faith school are appropriate only for certain teachers in the school, such as those concerned with the teaching of religion and holders of key leadership roles. However, at least at the level of principle, this conclusion cannot be drawn so easily in the case of many faith schools. Catholic education, for example, aims to provide a holistic educational experience. This 'holistic dimension' is one of the major reasons why the church considers that separate Catholic *schools* are such an important part of its educational mission. Therefore it seeks to 'integrate . . . all the different aspects of human knowledge through the subjects taught, in the light of the Gospel' (CS para 37, see also paras 26, 33–43). What is involved in this wider Catholic influence on the general curriculum of the school is complex, as is the broader question of the distinctive character of the life and work of the Catholic school as a whole. The aspiration, however, to provide an integrated or holistic educational experience is clear. There is therefore a need for all teachers in the school to share a common purpose and commitment — so that 'unity in teaching' and the development of community can be achieved (CS paras 29, 59–61).

The range of things which teachers are expected to exemplify in the faith school is therefore wide ranging. If these expectations are to be construed non-platitudinously, they require, amongst other things, a formation for teaching which in its nature and scope goes far beyond what is currently envisaged by most faith communities. In the case of Catholic schools, for example, there has been a tendency for Catholic teacher education to be seen as requiring no more than the addition of a few elements to teacher education generally conceived. It seems clear, however, that from the point of view of the expectations of exemplification, a much fuller kind of personal and spiritual formation is needed for teachers in Catholic schools (McLaughlin, 2003b). A focus on the expectations of exemplification also invite closer attention to what some of the expectations actually mean and imply. This is the case, for example, in relation to the integrative aspects of the Catholic school. What must a maths teacher exemplify, for example, in integrating mathematics with the light of the Gospel?

The requirements of faith schools with regard to the moral and religious example given by their teachers would seem to call into question the distinctions between the 'professional', 'personal' and 'private' lives of teachers which were drawn in the case of teachers in common schools. In the context of the common school it was argued that the 'private' life of the teacher (the context in which he or she lives out his fuller vision of life governed by 'non-public' values) can be seen as separable from his or her professional role, subject to compatibility with public values and sensitivity to 'middle ground' issues. It would seem, however, that the 'private' lives of teachers are inseparable from the moral and religious example which they are invited to give in the faith school. It is precisely this expanded expectation of teacher example which has led to criticism of faith schools, especially when such schools are supported to some extent by public funds.

The most obvious aspect of the private lives of teachers which is seen as part of the example they must give in the faith school is their own religious belief and practice. This example would seem to extend also to other aspects of lifestyle and behaviour relating to and required by religious belief and practice. Thus a Catholic school, for example, might be thought to have grounds for censuring or dismissing a teacher who is openly co-habitating in a sexual relationship outside of marriage (including homosexual relationships) or is living in a marriage which is canonically invalid on the grounds that their example in these matters is undermining the influence of the school by contradicting its teaching on important issues.

Two approaches to such cases which are designed to allay the difficulties they present are not wholly convincing. The first approach is to argue that compassion and forgiveness for individuals are more important Christian virtues to emphasize and exemplify than judgements of individual guilt. This approach is illustrated by cases such as the following: A teacher who is the Deputy Head of a Catholic school informs her headteacher that she is pregnant as the result of a casual, regretted affair, and offers her resignation on the ground that her position in the school is incompatible with her being an unmarried mother. The Head, supported by his governors, rejects the resignation because he sees compassion and forgiveness as prior Christian virtues to be exemplified to pupils. Further, the Head argues, in not having an abortion his colleague is specifically exemplifying for pupils the right thing to do in this situation from the point of view of Catholic teaching. Cases such as these are not, however, straightforward. The pedagogical impact of the decision of the Headteacher may indeed be to exemplify the virtue of compassion, but is also capable of exemplifying a justification of the original actions of the Deputy Head. The pedagogic influence arising from decisions such as these is ambiguous. The second approach is to argue that if there is a concern in such cases with scandal, then as a matter of contingent fact most people today are not in fact scandalised by such behaviour. This, however, is to construe 'scandal' as mere subjective offence rather than as a stumbling block to faith. The very fact that people are not subjectively offended may demonstrate that they are indeed scandalised in the sense of the term which concerns the church.

These considerations, however, do not remove a range of difficulties relating to wide ranging expectations of teacher example on the part of faith schools of the kind which has been indicated. A number of points are relevant to the further pursuit of these difficulties. First, as a matter of practical reality, many faith schools have to employ teachers who are themselves not members of the sponsoring faith of the school. Here, the most that the school can expect is that the teacher in question will be invited to support and aims and ethos of the school in some agreed and specified way and not to undermine them. Second, difficult judgements are called for in relation to the selection of the elements of exemplification which are judged worthy of emphasis by the faith school. Why matters of sexual morality, for example, rather than kindness or generosity? Third, the position in the school held by a particular teacher is highly relevant to expectations with respect to teacher example. The requirement to set an example of the appropriate kind is more stringent on holders of important posts. Fourth, the extent to which various forms of perceived counter-witness is in the public domain is a significant matter.

Conclusion

The current philosophical debate about the nature and justification of the evaluative influence exerted by common and faith schools respectively on their students specifies in the case of both types of school kinds of influence which are complex and subtle. In the case of common schools, for example, it is necessary for students to understand the nature, scope and significance of the distinction between 'public' and 'non-public' values and to achieve a proper grasp of notions such as 'respect'. In the case of faith schools, students are being formed in a faith tradition but also being invited to approach it critically and to relate it to the wider values and practices of the broader society. In both kinds of school, relevant forms of educative influence are exerted pre-eminently by teachers. In some quarters, the task is seen in an over-simple way as requiring, for example, the judicious selection by teachers of curriculum content and the adoption of forms of teaching which emphasize discussion.

However, a focus on the forms of teacher exemplification which the two kinds of school presuppose and require opens up a much richer perspective on the nature and coherence of the kinds of educative influence which they are invited to exert and upon what is involved in putting these into practice. The present chapter has sought to identify some of the principles which might be proposed in relation to the forms of teacher example expected in each context. In the process a range of predicaments has emerged which relate not only to the individuals involved, but are also significant in relation to the justification of the principles themselves, and of the forms of complex educative influence from which they arise.

Wendy Donner

Is Cultural Membership a Good?

Kymlicka and Ignatieff on the Virtues and Perils of Belonging

Introduction

> The essential task in teaching 'toleration' is to help people see themselves as individuals, and then to see others as such — that is, to make problematic that unthought, unconsidered fusion of personal and group identity on which racism depends.... If intolerant groups are unable, or unwilling, to perceive those they despise as individuals, it is because intolerant individuals are unable or unwilling to perceive themselves as such. Their own identities are too insecure to permit individuation; they cannot see themselves as the makers of their individualities, and hence they cannot see others as the makers of theirs either (Ignatieff, 1995a).

Current dialogues in political philosophy feature strong claims about the importance of group identities. Liberalism is often criticized in these debates as having difficulty accommodating such group identities, as being excessively individualistic and consequently overly concerned with individual identity. However, claims about the overarching nature and primacy of clashing group identities — national, racial and gender — tend to cancel each other out. I argue in this paper that liberalism is correct in asserting the primacy of individual identity and that principled moral agency requires autonomous individuals who reflect upon and choose their group attachments. Liberal selves are deeply immersed in social contexts, and their identities are shaped and constrained by their gender, culture, class and sexuality. Yet such agents are not determined by their group identities, and they engage in a process of individuation to construct and change their personal identities. In so doing they

become the sort of secure and tolerant individuals who can accept difference in others.

In the first part of this paper, I examine critically Will Kymlicka's arguments in *Multicultural Citizenship* (Kymlicka, 1995a) that cultural membership is a Rawlsian primary good. I argue that Kymlicka's arguments
are too weak to establish this foundational claim. I then turn to Michael
Ignatieff's exploration of nationalistic attachment, and examine how his
use of Freud's notion of the narcissism of minor differences sheds light
on the harmful aspects of nationalism. This examination raises the moral
dilemmas of identity construction and otherness with which defences of
national attachment must comes to terms.

Kymlicka:
The Nature of Culture and Cultural Membership

Kymlicka aims to defend a liberal theory of minority rights and to
explore how 'minority rights coexist with human rights, and how
minority rights are limited by principles of individual liberty, democracy, and social justice' (Kymlicka, 1995a, p. 6). His argument that liberalism is consistent with and requires an accommodation of cultural
membership is now a familiar feature of his writings. In this book he
returns to the theme as backdrop to his arguments for a wide range of
group-differentiated rights for national minorities living in liberal societies.

One focus in this paper is on Kymlicka's underlying claim that cultural membership is a Rawlsian primary good. The claim that cultural
membership is such a good imposes some stringent requirements upon
the case that needs to be made, and I argue that Kymlicka's arguments
do not meet these conditions. The claim that something is a Rawlsian
primary good is not merely the claim that it is an important good, but
goes far beyond this relatively modest view. It is 'a good which people
need, regardless of their particular way of life' (Kymlicka, 1995a, p. 214,
n. 11). While Kymlicka's arguments for special group-differentiated
rights hinge upon establishing that membership and participation in
one's own societal culture is a Rawlsian good which requires protection,
this claim has wide application to a number of compelling questions.

Kymlicka marks out some patterns of cultural diversity that are common in modern liberal societies. His defence of minority rights depends
upon various separations and distinctions, some familiar and uncontroversial, others more likely to raise questions, and some frankly and
admittedly stipulative. Political communities contain and incorporate
different sorts of minority groups. According to Kymlicka, 'multiculturalism' is a term that can lead to confusion and can obscure the important
distinction between what he calls national minorities and ethnic groups.
A national minority, or nation, is 'a historical community, more or less

institutionally complete, occupying a given territory or homeland, sharing a distinct language and culture'(p. 11). Countries that contain more than one nation are multinational states. These nations may be incorporated into states involuntarily, through conquest or colonization, or voluntarily, 'when different cultures agree to form a federation for their mutual benefit' (p. 11). Such national cultures usually 'wish to maintain themselves as distinct societies' and so typically demand self-government (p. 10). Canada contains three nations — English Canadian, Quebecois (this nation was, until recently, called French Canadian), and Aboriginal peoples — and the United States also has a number of national minorities such as Aboriginal peoples and Puerto Ricans. Several nations — Welsh, Scots, English and Irish — cohabit Britain.

In contrast, according to Kymlicka, ethnic groups are incorporated into a society through voluntary immigration of individuals and families. The standard pattern of such groups is to integrate into the larger society, and while 'they often seek greater recognition of their ethnic identity, their aim is not to become a separate and self-governing nation alongside the larger society, but to modify the institutions and laws of the mainstream society to make them more accommodating of cultural differences'(p. 11). National identity, according to Kymlicka, is confined to nations, and nations are also distinct from political communities or states. Political communities can inspire only limited sorts of loyalty or allegiance, and not forms of national identity. Kymlicka summarizes his mapping of the terrain:

> I am using 'a culture' as synonymous with 'a nation' or 'a people' — that is, as an intergenerational community, more or less institutionally complete, occupying a given territory or homeland, sharing a distinct language and history. And a state is multicultural if its members either belong to different nations (a multination state), or have emigrated from different nations (a polyethnic state), and if this fact is an important aspect of personal identity and political life (p. 18).

This is, he says, his stipulative definition of 'culture' and 'multicultural'(p. 19). Debates about culture and nationalism can quite easily get bogged down because different parties are using terms in ways that put them at cross-purposes and/or contribute to their talking past each other. There is no harm done if stipulative definitions help to clarify points at issue. However, Kymlicka's concepts of culture and cultural membership have the effect of diverting attention from some of the most significant points of contention concerning nationalism. Here he sets aside some important senses of 'culture' which are regularly invoked in discussions of belonging and identity, and this has the effect of obscuring important questions and prematurely ruling out certain perspectives. Firstly, he leaves out many non-ethnic social groups who have been excluded from mainstream society. Groups such as women, workers, gays and lesbians, that is, groups based on lifestyle, voluntary asso-ciations, and groups founded on social and political commitments, are often said to have cultures around which members build their identity and sense of belonging. These are sub-cultures or localized cultures. The second excluded sense of culture is broader, rather than narrower, than Kymlicka's stipulated sense. 'At the other extreme, using "culture" in the widest sense, we can say that all of the Western democracies share a common "culture" — that is, they all share a modern, urban, secular industrialized civilization, in contrast to the feudal, agricultural, and theocratic world of our ancestors' (p. 18).

Finally, Kymlicka returns to his chosen sense of culture to clarify one of his major themes. He emphasizes that he is not referring to racial groups but rather cultural groups not based upon race or descent. A lib-eral conception of minority rights must define

> membership in terms of integration into a cultural community, rather than descent. National membership should be open in principle to anyone, regardless of race or color, who is willing to learn the language and history of the society and participate in its social and political institutions (p. 23).

Michael Ignatieff's distinction between 'civic' and 'ethnic' nationalism — a distinction which is widely invoked — is interpreted here by Kymlicka as holding that 'national membership should be based solely on accepting political principles of democracy and rights, rather than integration into a particular culture' (pp. 23–4). It is also set to one side. I return to this issue below. Kymlicka's survey of the terrain sets the stage for his argument that cultural membership is a primary good.

Societal Cultures as Context of Choice

The first step in Kymlicka's argument for the value of cultural member-ship revisits earlier, by now well-known, claims about the dependence of liberal freedom and autonomy upon a cultural context. Individual freedom, according to Kymlicka, is bound up with membership in soci-etal cultures, the cultures of national groups. Modern societal cultures revolve around shared memories and values as well as common institu-tions and practices'. Its members share a 'vocabulary of social life, embedded in practices covering most areas of human activity . . . [and] institutionally embodied — in schools, media, economy, government, etc.' (p. 76). In a modern liberal society, the dominant culture has the power to integrate a wide range of groups and individuals, in particular recent immigrants. Such immigrants arrive with their own languages and history, but these are no longer embodied in institutions, and the process of integration has the effect of enriching and diversifying the dominant culture. In contrast, national groups wish to remain as 'dis-tinct societies' and to retain their practices and institutions and resist integration into the dominant culture. Thus immigrants and members of national minorities relate to the dominant culture in radically dissimilar ways. Immigrants contribute to and participate in and are assimilated into the dominant culture, in the process making it more diverse and pluralistic; national groups remove and insulate themselves from the dominant culture to preserve their distinct societal culture and all of its institutions. As part of this protective function, it is important for members of national minorities to have access to their own culture.

Participation in societal cultures protects people's freedom, the fundamental liberal value. Condensing earlier formulations of this major theme, Kymlicka says that liberalism

> grants people a very wide freedom of choice in terms of how they lead their lives. It allows people to choose a conception of the good life, and then allows them to reconsider that decision, and adopt a new and hopefully better plan of life (p. 80).

There are two preconditions for leading a life that is good. The first is what Dworkin calls the endorsement constraint, which says that we must 'lead our life from the inside, in accordance with our beliefs about what gives value to life' (p. 81). The second is that we must be free to question our beliefs about the good, and 'be able rationally to assess our conceptions of the good in the light of new information and experiences, and to revise them if they are not worthy of our continued allegiance' (p. 81). Our culture provides the information and examples for this questioning, as well as conditions necessary to acquire a perspective on different options for the good life. Liberal societies allow people the freedom to form, pursue and revise their conceptions of the good life, and provide the conditions which make it possible for members to carry out these commitments and plans. These commitments of liberalism, according to Kymlicka, directly lead us to the importance of cultural membership, because societal cultures are the context of choice for decisions about the good life.

> Put simply, freedom involves making choices amongst various options, and our societal culture not only provides these options, but also makes them meaningful to us (p. 83).

The shared vocabulary of a culture underlies its range of social practices and institutions, and to understand the cultural narratives requires understanding of the history and language on which they depend. So the central claim is that participation in and an understanding of the language and history of a societal culture are needed to have available vivid and meaningful options. Another precondition for exercising the freedom of forming and revising our conception of the good is the possession of self-respect that comes from having the worth of our choices about the good confirmed. Cultural membership, by giving meaning to the range of options, is also crucially related to self-respect.

Kymlicka concludes that there is an intimate relationship between individual choice and the cultural context. In particular what is needed is for individuals to have access to their 'own' culture.

Objections to Culture as a Context of Choice

Kymlicka's notion of a cultural structure as a context of choice cannot bear the weight his argument requires of it. Sociological claims are essential in arguments about culture, and it is difficult to specify exactly how much evidence is sufficient to lend credence to claims about the need of such a context. But Kymlicka's claims about culture do not even meet a minimum standard. There are too many counterexamples to his key thesis.

Firstly, his position is marred by the looseness of his notion of culture. His descriptions of it are so vague and lacking in character that it is difficult to understand why people would feel particularly attached to this culture, rather than another, similarly colourless one. However, the more we specify in detail the character of our culture, the more room there is to question whether we feel comfortable in or even owe allegiance to this, more fully specified, culture. One question that Kymlicka does not sufficiently attend to is this issue of the conditions under which it is principled to give up our allegiance to our culture and move beyond it. Kymlicka emphasizes the option of persons' choices to reform their culture; he evaluates differently, and inconsistently, their choices to give up or move beyond their culture, should it strike them that it is no longer worthy of allegiance. These latter choices are treated as regrettable or peculiar rather than as equally worthy options.

There are other general objections to his characterization of societal cultures as the context of liberal choice. The second objection is that there is no good reason resolutely to stick to societal cultures as this context. The actual contexts of choice for agents can be both broader and narrower, and indeed such contexts can fluctuate and change. The point is that in an age of global communication, options are not rendered meaningful or vivid simply by our culture. Kymlicka prematurely rules out discussion of global or North American or Western culture, but for many people these wider cultures do function as their social context of choice. People make choices to move among different cultures precisely because these wider media have presented vivid options. They travel and discover that they feel more at home in a culture other than their birth culture. The opposite pull can also work to narrow options. The power of ethnic communities within liberal cultures is stronger than Kymlicka acknowledges; the children of immigrants often find themselves under severe pressure to restrict their choices to those valued by their communities, and to forego moving out into the dominant culture. It is unrealistic to argue that only a societal culture can fulfil this function.

The next general objection focuses on Kymlicka's characterization of liberalism. In moving closer to a communitarian position, I claim that he gives up too much of the spirit of liberalism. At least one historical liberal, John Stuart Mill, would have strongly rejected jettisoning central liberal values and accepting a view of society as limiting our lifestyles and individuality as Kymlicka recommends. It is plausible to read many of Mill's eloquent comments in *On Liberty* as a resounding rejection of this view of society as setting and making meaningful our range of options.

> Persons of genius are ... more individual than any other people — less capable, consequently, of fitting themselves, without hurtful compression, into any of the small number of moulds which society provides in order to save its members the trouble of forming their own character (Mill, 1977, pp. 267–8).

Mill adds that

> the despotism of custom is everywhere the standing hindrance to human advancement, being in unceasing antagonism to that disposition to aim at something better than customary, which is called, according to circumstances, the spirit of liberty, or that of progress or improvement.... The progressive principle ... is antagonistic to the sway of Custom, involving at least emancipation from that yoke; and the contest between the two constitutes the chief interest of the history of mankind (p. 272).

Tomasi agrees with this worry. He says,

> liberalism, a doctrine that historically defined itself against the conservatism of the ancien regime, has a deep motivational connection with ... a belief in the possibility of social progress, especially as a result of personal experimentation (Tomasi, 1995, p. 591).

Social progress depends upon people who are willing to reject the limitations set by their culture. If Kymlicka's response is that this counts as a transformation of culture, then his position is so diffuse that it cannot fulfill his argumentative requirements.

Tomasi also points out a further problem with the unidimensionality of Kymlicka's analysis. Cultural membership is our anchor, Kymlicka says, and so 'if a culture is not generally respected, then the dignity and self-respect of its members will also be threatened' (Kymlicka, 1995a, p. 89). Tomasi notes that

> self-respect is an extremely complex psychological phenomenon and Kymlicka's argument underestimates the myriad ways members of...groups are able to secure self-respect for themselves (Tomasi, 1995, p. 590).

That is, self-respect can be enhanced by fighting oppression and harmful stereotypes, as well as by making choices that go against the grain of our culture and reject our culture's traditional estimation of options. This opens up some rather large and thorny questions about 'the politics of recognition' and it is important to search for the right balance. However, there is a danger that arguments for the importance of 'recognition' encourage members of minorities to hand over their power to others. If others do not value members of oppressed minorities, this should lead them to resist, not accept the consequence of diminished self-respect to which Kymlicka's argument leads.

The Value of One's Own Culture

Kymlicka's arguments for the claim that people need access to their own culture are also weak. He addresses the question of why members of a national minority need access to their own culture, rather than access to the dominant culture. His initial response is an argument from analogy. This proposal 'treats the loss of one's culture as similar to the loss of one's job'(Kymlicka, 1995a, p. 84). Analogical arguments are rarely conclusive, and this one is especially weak. The critic asks why the relevant cultural context cannot be broader than one's 'own'. Why do we need to be bound by our own culture? The relevant comparison is culture to culture. Kymlicka's initial response raises a point that bolsters his opponent's case rather than supporting his own. For many people, the loss of their job or their vocation would be far more regrettable than the loss of their culture. They would gladly switch cultures in order to pursue their vocation, because their vocation is much more basic to their self-respect and sense of identity than is their cultural membership. Academics, for example, notably are willing to pursue their dreams across borders. This particular example works against Kymlicka's thesis and underscores the limitations of his perspective.

But this is just one example, albeit a telling one. To assess the overall case requires scrutiny of his argument for his foundational claim that cultural membership is a primary good, i.e., 'a good which people need, regardless of their particular way of life'(Kymlicka, 1995a, n. 11, p. 214). Ignatieff states that

> as a cultural ideal, nationalism is the claim that while men and women have many identities, it is the nation that provides them with their primary form of belonging (Ignatieff, 1995b, p. 5).

This claim, he says, correctly, is contestable and not 'intuitively obvious'. 'It is not obvious, furthermore, why national identity should be a more important element of personal identity than any other'(p. 6). Since the claim is, as Ignatieff says, contestable, one would reasonably expect Kymlicka to devote considerable effort to defending it. However, he begs the question on this foundational point. He says that, the choice to leave one's culture can be seen as analogous to the choice to take a vow of perpetual poverty and enter a religious order. . . . Liberals rightly assume that the desire for nonsubsistence resources is so normal — and that the costs of forgoing them so high for most people's way of life — that people cannot reasonably be expected to go without such resources, even if a few people voluntarily choose to do so . . . material resources are something that people can be assumed to want, whatever their particular conception of the good.

Similarly, I believe . . . we should treat access to one's culture as something that people can be expected to want, whatever their more particular conception of the good (Kymlicka, 1995a, p. 86).

This reply is inadequate. Since Kymlicka treats his claim not as the contestable statement it surely is, but as one so obvious that liberals can simply 'rightly assume' it, he straightforwardly begs the question at a crucial juncture of his discussion. Those persons who voluntarily choose to give up this 'normal' good are treated as curious anomalies. The very cases that need to be explained and accounted for are brushed aside as examples of regrettable peculiarity. One example of this is Kymlicka's use of ad hominem in his review of Ignatieff's own book on nationalism. Ignatieff's book, Kymlicka claims, 'tell[s] us something about the psychology of cosmopolitan liberals at the end of the twentieth century'. They feel 'threatened and confused' about the resurgence of nationalism. Ignatieff is a 'citizen of the world whose ambitions took [him] beyond [his] country's border'(Kymlicka, 1995b, p. 133). Ignatieff's commitments and life choices are uncharitably described as ambitions; his sophisticated and reflective approach to confusing and threatening phenomena is dismissed, and a simplistic analysis of a complex problem is substituted.

Ignatieff's own comments convey much more about the many facets of the experience of moving outside the boundaries of one's own culture. In a review of two books by Polish writer Czeslaw Milosz, Ignatieff comments:

exile usually generates a fair number of melancholy thoughts about a poet's banishment from his native language. Milosz's poetry seems to confound these cliches, both defying loss and accepting its inevitability:
'But the shape of lips and an apple
and a flower pinned to a dress
were all that one was permitted
to know and take away.'
Yet just as he knew that he had to leave behind the provincial mediocrity of Wilno, so he seems to have understood that his mature poetry flourished on his duality: living in two places in his mind and belonging ultimately only to himself . . . Milosz seems to have been galvanized by exile (Ignatieff, in *New York Review of Books*, March 23, 1995, p. 39).

Any adequate liberal theory of the good life must be able to accommodate and evaluate the entire range of choices, and include a reasonable assessment of choices made either to remain in one's birth culture or to move beyond it. Yet Kymlicka's view appears to devalue at least some lives which the core principles of liberalism judge to be among the most meaningful and valuable.

But the peculiar anomalies will not go away. Their numbers are legion. Voluntary immigrants, one group Kymlicka discusses in the book, are included in this class. Of them he says,

> while many immigrants flourish in their new country, there is a selection factor at work. That is, those people who choose to uproot themselves are likely to be the people who have the weakest psychological bond to the old culture, and the strongest desire and determination to succeed elsewhere. We cannot assume a priori that they represent the norm in terms of cultural adaptability (Kymlicka, 1995a, n.14, pp. 214–5).

Nothing on a topic with so much empirical content can be assumed a priori. But this group's choices and commitments directly challenge one of Kymlicka's fundamental claims. A more convincing and robust response is required to defend his theory.

The other prong of Kymlicka's argument emphasizes the high costs to those who do voluntarily give up their initial cultural membership. Kymlicka describes their sacrifice:

> But even where successful integration is possible, it is rarely easy. It is a costly process, and there is a legitimate question whether people should be required to pay those costs unless they voluntarily choose to do so (Kymlicka, 1995a, p. 85).

> We cannot be expected or required to make such a sacrifice, even if some people voluntarily do so (p. 87).

Kymlicka's arguments thus far in response to objections have been surprisingly weak. The arguments that follow threaten his entire enterprise. Recall that the point of defending the good of cultural membership is to protect individuals' freedom to lead a good life. The freedom to choose and revise our plan of life is a bedrock value of liberalism. In reality, achieving such a life rarely happens without great costs and sacrifices, as Kymlicka agrees. He says, 'it is not easy or enjoyable to revise one's deepest ends, but it is possible, and sometimes a regrettable necessity' (p. 91).

Kymlicka's argument is fundamentally inconsistent in its treatment of and evaluation of the costs of individual autonomy and freedom on the one hand and of freedom from cultural belonging on the other. Costs and regret are present in both cases. In the first case, this is taken to be an often inevitable part of the process of leading a good life; in the second case, this is taken to be the sort of sacrifice which no one should reasonably be expected to make, and which most persons reasonably would wish to avoid. In other words, it is an absence of a Rawlsian primary good. Consider the picture painted by Kymlicka of the burden of moving from one culture to another, and consider if this picture were to be applied consistently to the burden of liberal freedom.

The costs of choosing our own plan of life and painfully revising our conception of the good are so high that we should not reasonably expect most people to make the sacrifices required to lead such a life. The 'crisis in faith' in which we may 'come to see that we have been wasting our lives, pursuing trivial goals that we had mistakenly considered of great importance' (Kymlicka, 1991, p. 202) is simply too difficult for most people to endure. So we should not expect them to take on the task of reflecting upon and revising their conception of the good, should new experiences give them the opportunity to question their commitments. Instead, we should allow them to rest secure in their unquestioned beliefs and commitments, aware that a passive response to the life that has been set for them by the options and limitations of their culture is good enough. The examined life is just too costly and burdensome for most people.

However, instead of recognizing and backing away from this inconsistency, he pursues and develops this line of thought, deepening the conflicts within his argument. He refers to Margalit and Raz's proposed answer to the question of why cultural bonds are so strong. It is so difficult to switch cultures because cultural membership plays such a strong role in self-identity. One reason is that 'national identity is particularly suited to serving as the "primary foci of identification" because it is based on belonging, not accomplishment'. A quote from Margalit and Raz follows:

> Identification is more secure, less liable to be threatened, if it does not depend on accomplishment. Although accomplishments play their role in people's sense of their own identity, it would seem that at the most fundamental level our sense of our own identity depends on criteria of belonging rather than on those of accomplishment. Secure identification at that level is particularly important to one's well-being.

Kymlicka sums up. 'Hence cultural identity provides an anchor for [people's] self-identification and the safety of effortless secure belonging'(Kymlicka, 1995a, p. 89).

This is a bizarre appeal to philosophical alchemy, for, from the base metal of a cultural context of passive, safe, effortless, secure belonging we hope to conjure the pure gold of liberal freedom and accomplishment. It is difficult to comprehend how a liberal defence of a social context of choice that enables people to construct and revise their plans for good lives has resulted in acclaiming passivity, safety and effortless belonging.

How did the argument come to this pass? How did a commendable effort to narrow the gap between liberals and communitarians and to respond to some cogent communitarian critiques of the liberal view of the self and context of choice end up radically undermining those liberal values most deserving of respect? Kymlicka's arguments countering early communitarian critiques of the liberal self are justly celebrated for exposing the weakness of many of those objections. The liberal self is not atomistic and unencumbered, and liberalism does pay attention to the social conditions that enable rather than thwart freedom. But bringing to the fore the liberal defence of a social context of choice does not require us to turn that context of choice into one that limits and impedes, rather than enables choice and encourages people to expand their options and move beyond set boundaries. It is the characterization of the context, the narrowness with which it is described, the insistence that only one sort of social context, the societal culture, is appropriate and 'normal' for people to be embedded in, that are the roots of the problem. Our identities have many facets, our belongings are also multiple and fluid, and our boundaries are to be challenged and pushed back, not accepted as 'givens'.

Ignatieff on Nationalism

The limitations of Kymlicka's depiction and evaluation of cultural membership reveal the need for a more expansive, balanced and realistic account of it. Cultural membership, or nationalism, is not the colourless and innocuous phenomenon that Kymlicka puts forward; it can be an evil as well as a good, and it has a dark and dangerous potential and underbelly that must be acknowledged and placed in perspective in any adequate account. One of the weaknesses of Kymlicka's account is that it exhibits very little understanding of the phenomenon of nationalism. Ignatieff, having borne witness to the horrific aspects of nationalism and its sometimes-grim genocidal results, as well as having reflected upon it, has a much more thorough, balanced and realistic picture of it as the multi-faceted phenomenon it is. Societal cultures do not function simply as the backdrop or context in which people construct their identities; nationalism, to a greater or lesser extent, constitutes people's identities. This qualifier 'greater or lesser' is important, and brings to the fore the central question of what is a principled construction of identity. Autonomous agents do not merely choose a conception of the good, but they also choose to accept or transform their identities. Construction of good lives and construction of self-identity are intimately connected projects. Another weakness of Kymlicka's account is its ignoring of the role of identity construction in relation to attachment to culture.

Ignatieff says that

> as a political doctrine, nationalism is the belief that the world's people's are divided into nations, and that each of these nations has the right of self-determination, either as self-governing units within existing nation-states or as nation-states of their own. . . . As a cultural ideal, nationalism is the claim that while men and women have many identities, it is the nation that provides them with their primary form of belonging
>
> . . . As a moral ideal, nationalism is an ethic of heroic sacrifice, justifying the use of violence in the defense of one's nation against enemies, internal or external.

These interconnected claims are reinforcing.

> The moral claim that nations are entitled to be defended by force or violence depends on the cultural claim that the needs they satisfy for security and belonging are uniquely important. The political idea that all peoples should struggle for nationhood depends on the cultural claim that only nations can satisfy these needs. The cultural idea in turn underwrites the political claim that these needs cannot be satisfied without self-determination (Ignatieff, 1995b, p. 5).

Further, crucially, nationalism sets out the conditions under which violence is justified when the right to self-determination of a nation is threatened. This is one significant reason why nationalist attachments and identities call for justification, because it is claimed that violence is warranted to defend these needs and values.

One central distinction within Ignatieff's system is that between civic and ethnic nationalism. He argues that a central moral battle is the one between defenders of these two types of nationalism, and that civic nationalism is morally defensible, while ethnic nationalism is not. So he defends nationalism of a certain kind, and he does not downplay the importance to people of having a cultural home and a sense of belonging.

> Civic nationalism maintains that the nation should be composed of all those — regardless of race, color, creed, gender, language, or ethnicity — who subscribe to the nation's political creed. This nationalism is called civic because it envisages the nation as a community of equal, rights-bearing citizens, united in patriotic attachment to a shared set of political practices and values (p. 5).

> Ethnic nationalism claims, by contrast, that an individual's deepest attachments are inherited, not chosen. It is the national community that defines the individual, not the individuals who define the national community . . . what gave unity to the nation . . . was not the cold contrivance of shared rights but the people's preexisting ethnic characteristics: their language, religion, customs, and traditions (pp. 7–8).

The sociology of ethnic nationalism is unrealistic even though the psychology of belonging may appear compelling.

While this description of forms of nationalism is more illuminating than Kymlicka's, and while it is heading in the right direction in terms of clarifying the moral quandaries posed by nationalism, it requires further refinement. It is more helpful to see things not in terms of a strict division or dichotomy of these two types of nationalism, but instead in terms of a continuum of kinds of nationalism which exhibit different mixes of these two salient elements. For the purpose of evaluating types of nationalism, it is more illuminating to conceive of societal or national cultures as containing both civic and ethnic elements, and then to explore which forms are more or less morally defensible. Then Ignatieff's point can be recast to make the claim that morally defensible forms of nationalism are those that accord the strong central place to civic elements such as political practices, values and symbols. Immigrants who arrive in a culture, as well as their children and grandchildren, can readily identify with and take on as their own such civic elements without feeling excluded by their lack of participation in the history of the culture. Values, symbols, and political practices are things which, in principle, anyone can choose to identify with and share. Kymlicka claims that immigrants integrate into a culture by learning its history. But, according to nationalists, what binds people together is their experiences of a shared history, not their learning about it second-hand. The bonds of shared history are exclusionary elements of a culture that must be balanced by civic elements that hold together people of diverse backgrounds and history.

Ignatieff applies a critical scrutiny and a degree of scepticism to overblown statements of the importance of national identities. Further, he argues that in its overblown form nationalism can be a 'fiction of identity, because it contradicts the multiple reality of belonging. It insists on the primacy of one of these belongings over all the others' (p. 16). It can turn into a lethal fiction. Ignatieff is perceptive about the link between belonging and its use in the justification of violence, as well as the link between identification and attachment on the one hand, and the exclusion of strangers and outsiders on the other.

Nationalism promotes goods like belonging and community, but in so doing it can operate so as to turn history into myth, and thus become a dangerous fiction. The identities and histories of nations do not float in isolation; they are relational, and depend upon the identities and histories of the other. Referring back to the example of nationalism in the context of the former Yugoslavia, Ignatieff makes several claims about identity construction.

Firstly, 'identity is relational. A Serb can't define himself except in relation to Croats, and vice versa . . . the one a tragic mirror of the other'. Secondly, 'identity is divided: nationalist ideology does not swallow up personal identity. The fit is never perfect'. Finally, 'nationalism does not simply "express" a preexistent identity: it "constitutes" one. It divides/separates/reclassifies difference. It does so by abstracting from real life. It is a fiction, an invented identity. A form of narcissism'(p. 141).

Ignatieff claims that while nations are partially characterized by their histories, this is not problematic in itself. It becomes problematic when history is turned into distorted myth or lethal fictions about the past. Witnessing the devastation of the conflict between Serbs and Croats in Croatia, he claims that such distorted myths play a large role in the downward spiral. The spiral begins

> in the most ordinary form of cowardice, the one everyone of us knows only too well — telling lies about the past. . . . When Vaclav Havel said that people need to live in truth he also meant that nations cannot hope to hold together if they do not come to some common — and truthful — version of their past (pp. 34–5).

What happens all too often is that a truthful version of the past is judged to be not glorious or stirring enough to maintain the emotional ties that nationalists sometimes claim are necessary to bind together a people. Then fictitious versions of the past are put forward without due regard to their dangerous consequences.

David Miller's analysis of the place of shared history in nationalism falls prey to the dangers pointed out by Ignatieff. Miller maintains that

> veil-drawing is also required in the case of national history. Renan remarked that 'to forget and — I will venture to say — to get one's history wrong, are essential factors in the making of a nation' (Miller, 1995, p. 34).

Miller adds, 'national identities typically contain a considerable element of myth' (p. 35). For example, 'various stories are concocted about the past history of the people' and the history is constructed on 'artificial inventions' which are 'fraudulent' (pp. 34–5). However, he continues, we should not dismiss such national identities, but we need to examine their function in nation building.

> For it may not be rational to discard beliefs, even if they are, strictly speaking, false, when they can be shown to contribute significantly to the support of valuable social relations (p. 36).

Such myths serve purposes.

> They provide reassurance that the national community of which one now forms part is solidly based in history, that it embodies a real continuity between generations (p. 36).

However, this appeal to false history is hollow. It is self-defeating and inconsistent to attempt to reassure people that their history is real when in fact it is concocted, fraudulent, and wrong. An example that is offered by Miller in an attempt to bolster his case instead underscores the problem. The example is of 'a happy and loving family which is supported by the (false) belief that all the children are the biological offspring of the parents'(p. 36). This is a desert island example. Family lies like this can rarely, in real life, be maintained, and when the child discovers the deception the results are typically devastating. Analogously, the lies of a nation's history operate as destructive 'lethal fictions'.

Ignatieff's analysis of nationalism is illuminating; it makes us understand why people are prepared to use violence in its defence, as well as why it is often linked to intolerance. The analysis is organized around Freud's notion of the narcissism of minor difference. Freud argued that

> the smaller the real difference between two peoples, the larger it was bound to loom in their imagination. He called this effect the narcissism of minor difference. Its corollary must be that enemies need each other to remind themselves of who they really are. . . . Without hatred of the other, there would be no clearly defined national self to worship and adore (Ignatieff, 1995b, p. 22).

Ignatieff observes Freud's 'emphasis on ambivalence, or conflict within identity itself: feelings of difference fighting against feelings of recognition'(p. 17). Ignatieff asks, 'how is it that differences that from the outside seem to be reducing are increasing "on the inside"'? (p. 18). This is explained by the phenomenon of narcissism.

> The facts of difference themselves are neutral. It is narcissism that turns difference into a mirror. In this mirror, the narcissist does not see the others in and for themselves; he sees them only as they reflect upon or judge himself (p. 19).

Narcissism is passive and self-absorbed. It leads to intolerance in part because intolerant people are not interested in those who are the supposed objects of their hatred. Nationalism, then, can be understood as the process by which identity is transformed into narcissism, and neighbours are transformed into strangers. The legitimate projects of provision of collective belonging and security and redressing inequalities of power and allowing people to speak for themselves are also transformed. The antidote to all of this is democratization and empowerment. Ignatieff also analyses the problem in terms of autism. Since outsiders cannot understand, they are not worth listening to.

Autism and narcissism are connected, for both are processes of closing off and refusing to listen to or learn from those seen as other. The problem is not identity assertion; having collective identities is a good thing. 'The problem is the systematic over-valuation of the self that goes with narcissism, and the mythic distortions of others that go with it', including the devaluing of strangers and outsiders (p. 20). Freud pursued this line of thought in *Civilization and its Discontents*, noting that groups can be bound together in love 'so long as there are other people left over to receive the manifestations of their aggressiveness' (pp. 20–1). Instead, the differences that ought to count are those among individuals, not those among groups.

What follows throws into even greater relief the problems with Kymlicka's defence of effortless secure belonging.

> It is worth speculating that if intolerant groups are unable, or unwilling, to perceive those they despise as individuals, it is because intolerant individuals are unable or unwilling to perceive themselves as such. Their own identities are too insecure to permit individuation: they cannot see themselves as the makers of their individualities, and hence they cannot see others as the makers of theirs either. . . . On this account, the narcissism of minor differences is a leap into collective fantasy which enables threatened or anxious individuals to avoid the burden of thinking for themselves or even of thinking of themselves as individuals (p. 23).

Tolerance depends upon resistance to an uncritical fusion of individual and group identity.

Cultural and national identities, like other sorts of group identities, are not merely relational, as Ignatieff points out, but they are also inherently exclusionary. The very process of constructing an identity involves creating boundaries of inside/outside. For this reason, among others, defenders of even moderate forms of nationalism need to do more to establish their case than simply establish the value of, need for, or interest in, attachment to a national group. Since the very process of identity construction creates boundaries and marks off groups who can then become the targets of oppression and aggression, defences of nationalism must come to grips with the dilemmas posed by such identities. It should be noted that these inside/outside boundaries do not operate merely to mark off members of other states. They also divide members of multinational states. As well, they mark out members of subcultures who are often seen as being less than full members of the nation.

Iris Young's analysis of what she calls the ideal of community and the politics of difference is a compelling account of these dilemmas. She argues that 'any move to define an identity, a closed totality, always depends on excluding some elements, separating the pure from the impure' (Young, 1990, p. 303). Moreover, these processes often create reactions that are unconscious and they serve to separate out groups within a society. The ideal of community undermines respect for those seen as different, as those with whom one does not identify. Young's own solution is to turn to what she calls the ideal of city life; an unoppressive city is one that promotes 'openness to unassimilated otherness' (Young, 1990, p. 319). It is an ideal that suits people who must live together as strangers. She argues for a version of identity construction in which people view themselves as multi-faceted, plural, and engaged in a continuous process of change; such a subject offers numerous entry points for identification with a variety of others.

Actual individual lives do not fit well within broad social categories. The requirements of following the scripts laid out as 'proper' for individuals who are members of groups are often experienced as coercive and burdensome, especially as most actual individuals are members of many such social groups and would be hard pressed to live out so many, often conflicting, narratives. If we can change the frame of the debates of contemporary identity politics to acknowledge individuals who must negotiate complex identities and construct personal identities by choosing, as liberals argue, which group identities are most worthy of their allegiance and most fitting for their life plans and commitments, we could move yet further along the paths of both resolving the dilemmas of conflicting group identities as well as advancing the cause of liberal tolerance of difference.

Young's analysis of the problem and her proposed solutions are too complex to be examined in detail in this paper. However, her insight concerning the problem of otherness echoes the concerns expressed by Freud and Ignatieff about the hazards of nationalist identification. A defensible account of cultural membership needs to come to grips with these dilemmas, and to search out means to counterbalance the harmful tendencies inherent in the process of national collective identity construction. There are at least two separate routes to this that could be pursued; both of these have been raised in this paper, but call for much greater exploration.

The first route calls upon the resources of what Ignatieff labels civic nationalism. Defences of nationalism sometimes put too much weight on the emotional component of nationalist bonding, i.e. that national communities are held together by the emotional attachments to those with whom you identify. However, this sort of emotional bond operates most strongly in face-to-face and small group interactions, and cannot be relied on to hold together large groups, and to protect oppressed groups within a society. The counterweight of civic nationalism's resources, 'the cold contrivance of shared rights' is a realistic alternative (Ignatieff, 1995b, p. 7). To live together peacefully does not require passionate emotional attachment; on the contrary, these ties can be saboteurs of peaceful community. Strong institutions are needed to support rights when respect fails.

The second route calls upon some traditional resources of liberal moral theory, such as liberal autonomy, empathy, and moral identification. These also act as counterweights to the elements of identity construction which create strangers, outsiders, and the other. This second route offers a variety of opportunities to constrain the harmful elements of nationalist attachment. Both of these routes are promising leads in the puzzles posed by the need to balance liberal freedoms and nationalist bonds.

II
ETHICS, ECONOMICS AND JUSTICE

Andrew Moore

Postmortem Reproduction, Consent, and Policy

Introduction

Consider the following 'focus case':

> A man has suffered an accident or rapidly progressing illness, and he is now unconscious in hospital. It is clear that he is shortly going to die. At the death, his partner asks the attending doctor to collect and store semen from him, to enable her to try for children after his death with the assistance of IVF.

In any such case of postmortem reproduction, the fundamental human facts of reproduction and death would come strikingly together. Not surprisingly, there is disagreement about the ethics of postmortem reproduction, and about policy regarding it. After confirming the feasibility of sperm retrieval after death, and outlining the relevant procedures, a standard urology text observes that: 'the ethical appropriateness of such retrieval is the most important issue surrounding its use' (Goldstein, 1998, p. 1363). The present paper addresses just those issues concerning the significance of the deceased's consent to the ethics of health professional response in potential settings of postmortem reproduction, and to policy concerning such settings.

There have been some reports from clinical practice of doctors regarding the deceased's consent as not necessary for ethically acceptable postmortem reproduction (eg., Strong, 1999; Strong *et al.*, 2000; Douglass and Daniels, 2002). The clear majority position in the relevant bioethics literature, by contrast, is that the deceased's consent is necessary for ethically acceptable postmortem reproduction. Discussion below centres on the comparative merits of these two positions. There are two main sorts of acts on which this issue might concentrate. One is collection for the purpose of postmortem reproduction. The other is postmortem reproductive use. In general, discussion below centres on the first sort of act, but

applies also the second. In the focus case, collection of sperm for purposes of postmortem reproduction would be from a man who is irre-
versibly incapable of consent or dissent, and would be performed at the
time of, or shortly before or after, his death. There are several techniques,
none of them especially invasive in physical terms (see, eg., Strong *et al.*,
2000).

The public profile of postmortem reproduction, and demand for it,
are reportedly both increasing (see Batzer *et al.*, 2003, p. 1265; and
Douglass and Daniels, 2002). Those jurisdictions that have addressed
the matter at a policy level have tended also to put consent requirements
in place (Strong *et al.*, 2000, pp. 740, 742). Several authors have
impressionistically commented that young men rarely anticipate fatal
illness, and fewer still set out what they would want done with their
sperm in that circumstance (eg., Bahadur, 2002, p. 2771; Moore, 2001,
p. 11). There have also been a few reported cases in which individuals
have done both these things (eg., Ramsay, 2000). To date, however, there
appear to be no systematic empirical studies of what people would
want, were they to die unexpectedly.

This paper proceeds as follows. In the next section, various cases of
postmortem reproduction are outlined. Claims about the significance of
consent have implications for all these cases. Keeping this range of cases
in mind also helps with assessment of the argument in the focus case.
Section 2 responds to the question: 'When is there consent to postmortem reproduction?' It makes a series of general points about consent,
and examines their application to postmortem reproduction. Section 3
takes us to the heart of the matter: 'In postmortem reproduction, how
important is consent?' It assesses three rival answers: (i) 'Consent is not
at all important', (ii) 'Consent is an ethical requirement', and (iii) 'Consent is an ethical factor but not an ethical requirement'. Section 4 concludes the paper with brief reflections on policy concerning postmortem
reproduction.

Varieties of Postmortem Reproduction

Some published discussions describe a range of possible cases of postmortem reproduction (see, eg., Strong, 1999; Strong *et al.*, 2000, p. 740;
Soules, 1999; Orr and Siegler, 2002; American Society for Reproductive
Medicine, 2004). In the following more systematic account, postmortem
birth, pregnancy, and conception are distinguished from one another
and outlined, and what one might call the context of consent is commented on. For brevity's sake, things are set out rather starkly, with little
humanising context. The cases are set out against an assumed background of a female/male couple with a joint wish to have a child.

Consider first postmortem births. In these cases, conception and part
of pregnancy take place in an ordinary and familiar way, but then one

parent dies before the child is born. It might be the child's father, mother, or even both. The father-death cases are familiar, for example through stories of 'war children'. But it is rarely noted that the child's being born postmortem might or might not have the deceased father's consent. This point is revisited below. In mother-death cases, the woman dies during her pregnancy, but her body is supported medically to allow for her child to be born after her death. Again, in mother-death cases, the child's being born postmortem birth might or might not have the woman's consent.

In postmortem pregnancy, a couple typically achieves conception extra-corporeally, through use of IVF techniques, and one or more pre-embryos are stored. Then one or the other parent dies, or both do. In father-death cases, his partner has one or more pre-embryos implanted after his death. If she has a fertility difficulty with implantation or gestation, however, she might instead pursue third party implantation and pregnancy, for purposes of either surrogacy or donation to others. Each of these sorts of postmortem pregnancy and later childbirth might or might not have the father's consent. Now suppose it is instead the mother who dies. Postmortem reproduction in this setting would involve her partner's pursuit of embryo implantation in and pregnancy of another woman, for purposes of either surrogacy or donation. Again, in either case, this postmortem pregnancy and later childbirth might or might not have the consent of the now-dead woman.

In postmortem conception, all three aspects of reproduction picked out above — conception, pregnancy, and childbirth — occur after parental death. Again, it might be the man's death, the woman's death, or both. In one variant of the father-death case, his sperm has already been collected and stored. In another, the focus case above, it is collected at the time of his death, or shortly before or after. In vitro fertilization and implantation would then follow, after his death. Conception and implantation might both be with his partner. Alternatively, perhaps because of a fertility difficulty, one or both might instead be with a third party, for purposes of either surrogacy or donation. Postmortem conception of all these sorts might be with his consent, or without it.

Consider now the mother-death sort of case. In one variant of this, ova or ovarian tissues have already been collected from her and stored. There are difficulties with the reproductive viability of such tissues, but these are diminishing with technical developments over time. If she dies, her partner might pursue implantation in and pregnancy of a third party, for purposes of either surrogacy or donation. In a different sort of case, ova or ovarian tissues are collected at or near to the time of her death, with fertilisation and implantation after her death. Fertilisation might typically be with sperm from her male partner, but could be with sperm from a third party. In light of such a process, implantation in a third party woman is then a possibility, for purposes of either surrogacy or donation.

In all the above cases, the request for postmortem reproduction is assumed to come from the partner of the dead person. But it might come from the family of the now-dead person, or it could come from both. In the latter case, the contents of the requests might differ, or coincide. If they differ, then conflict is strictly unavoidable only if there are too few gametes or pre-embryos to satisfy all the requests. Each party's views regarding the authenticity and appropriateness of the other's request would of course also generate some further potential for conflict.[1]

When is there Consent to Postmortem Reproduction?

This section makes some arguments about the nature and varieties of consent, contrasts facts of consent with reasonable belief regarding consent, distinguishes some different forms of expression of consent, and distinguishes what is consented to from the matter of whom it is expressed to. Its arguments also apply, with relevant minor changes, to dissent. Topic by topic, the implications for postmortem reproduction are also examined.

If I may spend my money how I choose, then it is plausible that the ethics of your taking some of it from me depends at least in part on my consent. If I am not entitled to alienate my life, on the other hand, then my consenting to your taking it does not alter the ethics of your taking it. Cases such as these suggest that one's ethically significant consent is directed at what someone else does or proposes to do to something over which one has a claim or entitlement. In the central case, one actually consents, and is 'in the maturity of [one's] faculties' (Mill, 1859/1977, chapter 1, paragraph 10) and is thus fully competent to do so.

Consider the following argument that there cannot be actual consent to postmortem reproduction. Consent is a sort of action; necessarily, postmortem reproduction would occur only after one's death, and one cannot then perform any actions; therefore, one cannot consent to one's

---

[1]   The case of postmortem reproduction can illuminate other debates also. Consider, for example, the conditions for parenthood, in the sense of primary responsibility for a child's care and rearing. Postmortem reproduction seems to be a counter- example to the claim that a relevant *genetic* relation is sufficient for parenthood. The possibility of postmortem conception shows that such a relation can be formed after one's death, when one cannot acquire any further rights or responsibilities. Similar issues arise for intentional, causal and gestational accounts of the sufficient conditions for parenthood. Good general discussion of these conditions, albeit overlooking the significance of postmortem reproduction cases, can be found in Bayne and Kolers (2003). For an excellent survey of the conditions for *legal* parenthood, primarily but not only in the New Zealand setting, see New Zealand Law Commission (2004).

own postmortem reproduction. In reply, however, we can note that during one's lifetime, one can actually consent to or dissent from actions, such as those constituting postmortem reproduction, that others might perform after one's death. This argument for the impossibility of consent to postmortem reproduction consequently fails.

An act of hypothetical consent is one that is not actually performed, but would have been performed in relevant circumstances. In some writings, it can be difficult to tell whether it is actual or hypothetical consent that the author has in mind. Strong et al illustrate the parallel point concerning desire. They say it is at least sometimes reasonable to claim that 'a married man would desire to promote the interests of his surviving wife' (Strong *et al.*, p. 743). Their idea is perhaps just that he would desire this if asked about the matter, but perhaps instead or also that he now actually has the desire that 'my wife's interests be promoted, should I die before she does'.

It might be thought that merely hypothetical consent has no actual ethical significance. Consider this, from Ronald Dworkin: 'A hypothetical contract is not simply a pale form of an actual contract; it is no contract at all' (Dworkin, 1989, p. 18). This remark is charming, but false. Hypothetical contract is of course not a kind of actual contract, but it is a kind of contract nevertheless. Dworkin really means to argue that hypothetical contract has no actual ethical significance, and the same thought can be applied also to consent. But Dworkin does not here offer any argument for such a conclusion regarding either contract or consent. Furthermore, it is plausible that merely hypothetical consent does have ethical significance. Suppose, for example, we know from previous expression of his Jehovah's witness religious beliefs and from broader general expression of his wishes, that the man bleeding heavily at the accident would dissent from having any blood transfusion.[2] Assuming that his actual dissent from this operation would have actual ethical significance here, it is plausible also that his merely hypothetical dissent would have actual, albeit lesser, ethical significance too. More specifically, it would have actual significance for the ethics of health professional response to him, even when they know he has not actually dissented from such an operation.

Turn now to matters of consent's content and scope. The arguments made below on this topic are generally expressed in terms of actual consent. They generalise also, with relevant minor changes, to hypothetical consent, and to actual and hypothetical dissent.

If I consent to eat that oyster, and that oyster is the oyster that has very high toxic algal loading, it does not follow that I consent to eat the oyster

---

[2]   I owe the example to Martin Wilkinson.

that has very high toxic algal loading.[3] More generally, consent to q does not entail consent to what is logically implied by q, identical with q, in the nature of q, or caused by q.[4] The reason is that the person who has consented might fail to understand these things. Insofar as the further implications of what one consents to are opaque to one, one does not consent to those further things. Consent's 'opacity' is often overlooked. It is nevertheless important, for postmortem reproduction and for much else. It severely limits argument from any premise that a person consents to one thing, to a conclusion that another thing has that person's implied, implicit, indirect, inferred, or tacit consent.

Alongside the opacity of consent, and constrained by it, sits the fact that both hypothetical and actual consent can be either general or specific. A general consent can include numerous specifics. For example, your relatively general consent to my deciding everything when you die might include your more specific consent to my deciding what to do with your remains when you die. It will do so as long as you believe that when you die you will leave remains to be dealt with. Or suppose I consent to your using my sperm after my death to create a child. If I believe this process would involve fertilization, implantation, pregnancy, and childbirth, then my general consent to postmortem reproduction includes consent to all these more specific things.[5]

Suppose a man and woman have agreed to try for children together. It does not follow that he has agreed to her using his gametes to try for children after his death, should he die before she does. He might not even have contemplated the possibility. Now suppose a couple instead has an agreement to try not to have children. Again, it does not follow that he has agreed she should not use his gametes to try for children after his death, should he die before she does. This point has not been noticed in the literature, though it has been contradicted.[6]

Suppose a man has actually consented to facilitating his partner's intentions, and promoting her interests, subject only to qualifications and exceptions he says he will work out as these arise. If he has contemplated the application of this general consent also to postmortem situa-

[3]   I here adapt a point made about desire by Wiggins (1991) p. 6.

[4]   I here draw on the work of O'Neill (2003) pp. 5–6.

[5]   If one can consent only to something that is offered, then both parties must believe these things.

[6]   Thus Orr and Siegler (2002), p. 301: 'if a man had steadfastly refused to have a child while alive, it would be ethically wrong to honor a request to retrieve his sperm for [reproductive] use after his death'. They write this despite their acknowledgement (p. 302) that if a man has consented to 'live' reproduction, it does not follow that he has consented to postmortem reproduction.

tions, then he has thereby also consented more specifically to facilitating her intentions in such situations.

Consider now a slightly more specific consent. Suppose a man has agreed to his partner's dealing with his remains however she thinks appropriate, should he die before she does. It seems a plausible conjecture that this wish is widely shared by those in good intimate relationships. If and only if he has contemplated postmortem reproduction as falling within its scope, this relatively general consent also involves actual consent to postmortem reproduction.

In the sorts of circumstance discussed in the previous two paragraphs, the man's consent is actual rather than merely hypothetical. It is also in the first instance relatively general in scope. Postmortem reproduction is a matter of more specific acts that fall within the scope of these general consents. Were there to be such actual consent in a given case, consent considerations would support the women's request, and a physician's agreement to facilitate her request, for assistance with postmortem reproduction. This is not to say that postmortem reproduction in such cases would be ethically acceptable. Recall that this paper restricts its attention to the ethical significance of consent considerations in such settings.

Discussion so far in this section has concerned features of the act of consent, and especially whether it is actual or hypothetical, and whether its scope and content is general or specific. Call such matters 'facts of consent'. These are one sort of thing, and what it is reasonable for others to believe regarding them is another. To see the distinction more concretely, suppose I privately thought through a matter over which I had an entitlement, wrote down a consent to the actions of others with regard to that matter, then put the note away somewhere known only to me. These are some of the facts of consent in the case. Suppose also, however, that all evidence available to others regarding my will on this matter points to its being the opposite of what I have written down. Here the facts of consent come clearly apart from the matter of what it is reasonable for others to believe regarding those facts.

In the literature, facts of consent are often run together with others' reasonable beliefs about those facts, and the two can be difficult to disentangle. For example, many (eg., Strong, 1999; Strong *et al.*, 2000; Batzer *et al.*, 2003, p. 1265) regard 'reasonably inferred consent' as a distinct kind of consent, but it is strictly speaking not a form of consent at all. It is instead a matter of others' having reasonable beliefs as to the fact of a person's actual or hypothetical consent in a case. Strictly speaking, such belief can be reasonable even in certain cases where there is in fact no consent at all, actual or hypothetical, in the case.

Once the main point of the previous paragraph is clearly seen, a further important issue arises. Suppose I am considering what I should do, and that the matter of your consent to my act bears on what I should do. Is it the facts of your consent or otherwise that have that bearing, or is the ethically significant matter instead what it is reasonable for me to believe those facts to be? One might call the first view factualism, and the second view evidentialism.[7]

It will be assumed below that the significance of your consent to the ethics of my action depends on what it is reasonable for me to believe you have consented to, or would consent to, and not on the facts of consent. The parallel assumption will be made also regarding the ethics of policies concerning the role of consent in postmortem reproduction. If reasonable belief in consent is what matters, then there is consequent need for attention to focus on general and operational standards for such belief. One needs at least some tools with which to answer the question: 'When is it reasonable for a health professional to believe an individual has consented or would consent to postmortem reproduction?' Those whose focus is on actual consent tend also to argue that it is reasonable to believe one has this only if that consent is written, and is explicit or specific (eg., Douglass and Daniels). One rationale for this very stringent approach is a conflict of interest consideration. As some have noted (eg., Orr and Siegler, 2002; Strong), the partners and families who would typically be the best sources of non-written evidence are typically also those who wish to pursue postmortem reproduction. In practical effect, however, any such requirement will tend to exclude nearly all the evidence that partners and families might be able to bring to the situation. One could do a lot worse than place some trust in a person's loved ones, even where they do have a potential conflict of interest. A less stringent standard, argued for by Strong, would require that the person concerned has explicitly addressed, and has in that context specifically favoured, allowing certain others to purse postmortem reproduction using his or her gametes, but would not require that this be in written form (Strong, 351). Strong would require such consent to be specific, but this should be liberalized to accommodate the arguments made above that where the matter is 'transparent' to the consenting party, general consent includes

---

[7]   It is well recognized that act consequentialists must choose between these two approaches, which are sometimes (eg., by Crisp, 1997, pp. 99–101) called 'actualism' and 'probabilism'. It is much less widely recognised that the same sort of issue arises quite generally for normative ethical theories. Should virtue ethics assess rightness of action in terms of what a virtuous person would actually do in the circumstances, or in terms of what it would be reasonable for the agent to believe a virtuous person would do in the circumstances? Should contractualism assess right action in terms of what rational persons could in fact not reasonably reject, or in terms of what it is reasonable for the agent to believe rational persons could not reasonably reject? Similar issues arise for Kantians, rule consequentialists, Rossian pluralists, and so forth.

also the relevant specifics. A further refinement is this. Where there is a very limited time window for collection of gametes for purposes of post-mortem reproduction, the significance of consent considerations should be assessed and acted on in that information-poor setting. If that leads to gamete collection, then any subsequent decision about use should be a matter for further appraisal. What it might then be reasonable for the health professional to believe regarding the person's consent or other-wise might by then have changed, with richer information to hand. Where there is no significant time on collection, on the other hand, health professional appraisal of the evidence regarding consent to post-mortem reproduction should proceed simultaneously for acts of both collection and use.

It is well recognised that what one consents to is distinct from how one expresses that consent. When I put my attractive proposal to you, for example, you might consent verbally, perhaps even on audio-tape or video, or instead in writing. Perhaps you might just do so in some con-ventionally well-understood non-linguistic way; for example, by responding to my 'May I sample your Central Otago pinot noir?' by sim-ply pouring some into my glass. It is less frequently noticed that the mat-ter of whose actions one consents to is distinct from the matter of whom one expresses that consent to. I might consent to being an organ donor at the death, for example, but express this only through instructions to the official who loads the details electronically onto my driver license. Ramsay discusses the case of a man who died and left a note consenting to his fiancée's reproductive use of his gametes, but does not mention whether or not he expressed this consent to her. Sometimes in the litera-ture on this topic, it is unclear whether a point is being made about con-sent's content, or instead about its expression. For example, consider the claim (Strong, 347) that explicit prior consent to postmortem reproduc-tion is 'consent that the man gives to health care professionals'. This might just be the obvious point that consent to health professional assis-tance is a required part of explicit consent to postmortem reproduction. But it might (also) be the more questionable claim that to count as such, explicit prior consent to such health professional assistance must be expressed to that health professional. On Strong's behalf, one should perhaps also add that he might have had in mind here primarily the operational requirements for policy, rather than the ethical fundamen-tals about the nature of consent. There is further comment below on the policy issues.

In Postmortem Reproduction, How Important is Consent?

On what basis does consent have ethical significance? One standard answer is that it is a matter of respect for autonomy (eg., Strong, 1999,

p. 348). A rival answer is that consent instead plays only the more modest role of protection against deceit and coercion (eg., O'Neill, 2003). No view on this issue will be taken in this paper, which will appeal only to an intentionally vague notion of 'respect' as a basis of consent's ethical significance. Whatever the basis of consent's importance in general, the question addressed in this section is instead 'How important is consent to the ethics of postmortem reproduction?' Three rival answers are considered, each in turn.

(i) Consent is not at all important

It might be argued that there cannot be postmortem interests or postmortem respect, or that neither of these can have ethical significance, and hence that a man's consent or otherwise to postmortem reproduction cannot have ethical significance. On this view, there can be no consent-based or dissent-based ground either in favour of or against postmortem reproduction. Consent and dissent considerations are simply silent in the setting of postmortem reproduction. Its ethics is determined by other considerations (Robertson, 1998).

It will be assumed below that there can be ethically significant postmortem interests and postmortem respect. I have nothing to add to the significant literature in which others have argued for these claims.[8] In effect, then, this position is here acknowledged just to be set aside unrefuted by any argument made in this paper. In light of this, sceptics about postmortem interests and postmortem respect should perhaps treat much of the discussion below as responding to the question: If there can be ethically significant postmortem interests and postmortem respect, what is the ethical significance for them of consent?

Setting aside very general doubts about the possibility of ethically significant postmortem interests and respect, it is plausible that one can have an interest in reproducing postmortem. As Strong has argued, reproduction even in this setting can constitute a key contribution to person creation, can be an affirmation of love, and can create a special link to future generations (Strong, 349–50). As he further argues, it is also plausible that one can have an interest in not reproducing postmortem. For instance, one might wish to avoid reproducing in circumstances one considers undesirable for rearing (Strong, 350), and one might count postmortem circumstances amongst these. Or one might have an interest in reproducing only when one is an active and voluntary participant, a condition that most forms of postmortem reproduction do not meet. Note also the possibility of rival 'objectivist' and 'subjectivist' accounts of the conditions under which one has such interests. On an objectivist

---

[8]   For an excellent survey of and contribution to that literature, see Wilkinson (2002).

view, certain of the above are favourable or unfavourable interests for individuals, whatever attitude those individuals might actually or hypothetically have toward them. On a subjectivist view, there is an actual or hypothetical 'attitude condition' on any such thing's counting as a favourable or unfavourable interest.

(ii) Consent is an ethical requirement

Many claim that consent is a requirement for ethically acceptable post-mortem reproduction; that the practice is unethical without consent. Thus: 'a person's gametes . . . should not be used for procreative purposes without the person's consent'.[9] Furthermore, if consent is a requirement for right action, and if action is either right (ethically permissible) or wrong (ethically impermissible), then non-consent is sufficient for wrong action. This too is taken below to be part of the 'consent requirement' view. Note that this requirement can take an 'actual consent' form, or instead a 'hypothetical consent' form. Either way, if it also takes an 'evidentialist' rather than 'factualist' form, then there are various possible places at which one might set the standards for reasonable belief that there is consent in this or that particular case.

The consent requirement implies that if the man in the focus case has not consented, then postmortem reproduction is wrong. Furthermore, if Strong is correct that practically every case of postmortem reproduction to date has proceeded without consent, then it implies that 'practically every case of sperm retrieval after death or PVS to date has been ethically unjustifiable, due to the absence of . . . consent' (Strong, 354). Whether he is right about practice to date depends in part on arguments made above about the conditions under which consent that has a broad general content also includes consent to more specific things.

Those who endorse a consent requirement on ethically acceptable postmortem reproduction tend to treat it as obviously plausible. Perhaps because of this, the literature generally presents under-developed arguments for it, and in some cases no argument for it.[10]

Strong argues that if done without the consent of the man in question, postmortem reproduction uses, and is disrespectful toward, the previously living person (Strong, 351–3). Rather than argue directly for this thesis, however, he instead sets out to illustrate that it is wrong to violate the consent rule. He does so by reference to a Californian case in which preembryos 'were transferred to recipient couples without the consent of the couples who were the progenitors of the preembryos, resulting in live births in some cases'. This was a misuse of persons because of 'the

---

[9] Strong (1999) p. 352. Similarly: Douglass and Daniels (2002) pp. 263, 279; Soules (1999); and Batzer *et al.* (2003) p. 1265.

[10] For example, Douglass and Daniels (2002).

relationship between respect for persons and the special meanings pro-creation can have for individuals' (Strong, 1999, pp. 352–3). There is, however, an obvious disanalogy here that Strong overlooks. Disrespect and misuse in the Californian fertility clinic case arises from failure to ask those who created the pre-embryos what their wishes were, even though doing this was readily practicable. If the same sort of approach is practicable in case of postmortem reproduction, but health profession-als nevertheless proceed without making any such approach, then it too would be a case of misusing and failing to respect persons. Given that this is generally not practicable in the setting of postmortem reproduc-tion, however, there is no such ground in that case on which to base a claim of disrespect.

Bahadur argues for a consent requirement, on the grounds that post-mortem reproduction profoundly affects core values the person had whilst alive, and that if it proceeds without consent, then it writes a highly significant life-chapter that is not authored by the person con-cerned (Bahadur, 2002, p. 2773). In broad terms, Bahadur's thought seems to be that if one reproduces in a way that is not self-authored, this makes one's life go seriously worse. The suggestion here seems to be that there is a consent condition on the avoidance of seriously negative inter-ests. But why believe this, given one's possible favourable interests in postmortem reproduction, as outlined above? In addition, some believe they have no postmortem interests (eg., Robertson); and others believe that an actual or hypothetical con-attitude on one's own part is a neces-sary condition of one's having any serious unfavourable interest in a matter. Bahadur seems committed to rejecting all such views. Third, and most importantly, even if Bahadur is right that in this area there is a con-sent requirement on the avoidance of seriously unfavourable interests, it does not follow that there is a consent requirement on morally right acts of postmortem reproduction. As so far developed, the possibility is still open that other interests might outweigh even strong unfavourable interests in postmortem reproduction.

It might be argued that there is a requirement of informed consent because there is a right to determine one's own reproductive fate (eg., Batzer *et al.*, 2003, p. 1265). More modestly, one might argue that there is a right not to reproduce, at least where the person has not performed any activities, nor been negligent in any respect, involving risk of reproduc-tion.[11] Plausibly, this is the situation of the man in the focus case of post-mortem reproduction with which this paper opened.

If there is a right not to reproduce, then it is plausible that it would be violated by a person who proceeded with postmortem reproduction in the face of actual dissent, or perhaps even in the face only of hypothetical

---

[11] I am indebted to Martin Wilkinson for discussion of this sort of option.

dissent. Such a right might also be violated if it were reasonably practicable to elicit the person's consent or dissent, yet there was a failure to do so. But why think it a violation of such a right where it is not practicable to secure any expression of consent or dissent, and where no reasonable belief can be formed as to what that person's expression of will, if any, would have been? Even if there is a right not to reproduce, it is not clear why one should regard this as violated by postmortem reproduction that proceeds without consent or dissent, either actual or hypothetical, having taken all reasonable means to uncover any pre-existing consideration of this sort in the case, and all reasonable means also to generate any such new considerations.

I conclude that the arguments so far made for a consent requirement are poor and unconvincing. Proponents of this position have so far done little to convince the uncommitted that the ethical significance of consent in postmortem reproduction takes the form of a consent requirement. Arguments broadly of the 'right not to reproduce' kind seem the most promising start-points for strengthening this work.

I turn now to objections to any consent requirement. Three of these are considered below.

Consider the following argument: if there is a consent requirement on postmortem reproduction, then there is a consent requirement on all one might do with a person's postmortem remains; but in that case, nearly all that is done in contemporary cultures to nearly all of us when we die would be unethical; but this is very implausible; therefore, there is no consent requirement on postmortem reproduction.

Any general consent requirement on actions that deal with persons' postmortem remains would find nearly all such acts to be unethical. The reason is that few of us express any will as to what should be done on these matters, and even conjectures about what persons would consent to would typically be speculative. Reflection on and discussion of such topics is very rare, at least in many contemporary societies. Would he prefer to be buried or cremated, or some third thing? Would she favour organ or tissue donation? Would he prefer his remains to be disposed of as soon as is feasible, or instead to be used first to facilitate the funereal and grieving processes of those who knew him? What style of embalming would she favour? Would he have any preference about the design of the death rituals or celebrations of those who knew him? Would she wish proceedings to be overseen by someone who knew her well, or instead by a religious official? Few of us have communicated our thoughts on such matters to others, or even thought them through for ourselves.

The best critical response to the foregoing argument is perhaps to seek grounds to distinguish postmortem reproduction from other things that are done with persons' remains, such that justification can be found for the existence of a consent requirement in only the former case. Again, the most promising territory to explore might be that of the alleged right not to reproduce. At present, however, this is a promise of a possible reply to the objection, rather than an actual reply to the objection.

Here is another objection to any consent requirement on postmortem reproduction. The leading instances of proposed postmortem reproduction are instances of action between intimates in an area of their intimacy. In such situations, a dissent requirement for wrong action is more plausible than is a consent requirement for right action. These two sorts of requirement are inconsistent with one another; because if dissent is necessary for wrong (impermissible) action, then non-dissent is sufficient for right (permissible) action, and therefore it is false that consent is necessary for right action. So it is plausible that there is no consent requirement here.

One possible reply to the above argument is that a dissent requirement is too permissive toward those who would do bad things to those who have not thought, or not had the opportunity, to dissent. Bear in mind, however, that this dissent requirement is intended to apply only to intimates in the domain of their intimacy. Most of his family would typically not fall within its scope, on matters of postmortem reproduction. Bear in mind also that a dissent requirement would be supplemented with reasons to give opportunities to dissent, in settings where important matters might be at stake.

Another possible reply to the above criticism of a consent requirement would follow Archard's suggestion that even for intimates in the domain of their intimacy, the standard should be consent rather than non-dissent if the activity is sufficiently novel (Archard, 1998, pp. 27–8). And postmortem reproduction is surely sufficiently novel. In my view, Archard's suggestion is reasonable only if we add to his 'sufficient novelty' trigger the further condition that it is reasonably practicable to secure the person's expression of their consent or otherwise. In those cases of postmortem reproduction where this is not reasonably practicable, I think it unreasonable that even sufficient novelty on its own should trigger a requirement that intimates, wishing to act in the domain of their intimacy, must to something that it is no longer reasonably practicable for them to do.

Here is a further objection. If there is a consent requirement on postmortem conception, then there is a consent requirement on postmortem reproduction in general, including on postmortem birth. Therefore, any such birth without the consent of the man concerned is unethical. Such births typically do not have the consent of the man concerned. Therefore, such births are typically unethical. But this is implausible. Therefore, it is implausible that there is a consent requirement on postmortem conception.[12]

One response to the above argument is to claim that men typically do consent to having children, and then to claim that this typically includes a more specific consent to her giving birth to their child, should he die during her pregnancy. Even if all this is true, however, it is implausible that the ethical acceptability of women's giving birth to children in such settings depends on the happy contingency that men in this way always do attend to all the relevant consents. There are also many cases in which men do not consent to have children, even if they do consent to actions that carry a significant likelihood of generating children. And here as in other contexts, consent to have children together in the ordinary course of life does not necessarily imply consent to the other party's having such a child, should one die before that child is born.

The overall picture is this. To date, only weak and sketchy arguments have been developed in favour of a consent requirement on postmortem reproduction. There are, on the other hand, some serious objections to such a requirement. In light of this, there is at present some reason to reject it. It is also important to examine whether any rival view of consent's ethical significance fares any better in this setting. To this matter the argument now turns.

(iii) Consent and dissent are ethical factors, not ethical requirements
The main idea of the factor approach is that in relevant circumstances, consent counts in favour of action and dissent counts against it.[13] A further sketch of this approach follows.

According to the factor approach, actual consent and dissent count most, but hypothetical consent and dissent count too. If you cannot find any of these in the case, then you have reason to look harder for them. If there is no actual consent to or dissent from a proposed action on the part of any relevant person, then you have reason to seek this, if doing so is reasonably practicable. Even if there is already consent to or dissent from an action, there is reason to seek more robust or more nearly current consent or dissent, again if reasonably practicable. If seeking it is not, or if one cannot secure it even after making all reasonable attempts, then neither actual consent nor actual dissent counts in the case. If and

---

[12] This argument presents particular difficulty for Douglass and Daniels (2002) who claim both that there is a consent requirement on postmortem conception (pp. 263, 279), and that postmortem birth raises no significant ethical issues (p. 261). But the argument is also more generally difficult for friends of a consent requirement.

[13] The notion of an ethical factor is developed in both general and particular terms by Kagan (1998).

only if there is no hypothetical consent or dissent consideration in the case either, then consent-independent considerations settle the ethics of the matter.

A strength of the factor approach, unlike the consent requirement or the dissent requirement, is that it does not force one either to choose between the claim that consent counts and the claim that dissent counts, or to offer an exclusive division of the respective domains in which each of these does count.

It might be objected that the factor approach would allow people to do horrible things to others, whenever those others had not thought to dissent. This might be thought to follow from the claim that in the absence of any consent or dissent, all such considerations are silent in the case. To this, however, two replies can be made. First, consent and dissent are not the only factors, so either the proposed act is wrong independently of consent and dissent, or its wrongness depends on consent or dissent. In the former case, it will be unethical for others to do this thing to you, even if you are permanently beyond consent and dissent. In the latter case, their doing it to you cannot be wrong. Second, as emphasized above, mere absence of actual or hypothetical consent or dissent is not sufficient for all such considerations to be silent. We have reason to elicit relevant persons' consent or dissent, if reasonably practicable, and also to identify any hypothetical consent considerations in the case. If at the end of this we still have no consent or dissent considerations whatever in hand, then it seems sensible to conclude that such considerations are silent in the case, and that the ethics of the matter are to be settled by other factors.

More work is needed on the details of the 'consent factor' view. But enough has been said, I think, to establish it as a serious rival to the dominant 'consent requirement' approach. It is also worth exploring further what the consent factor approach would imply across a broad range of other contexts in which consent requirement approaches have tended to predominate. One such context is sexual ethics (see, eg., Archard, 1998). Another is research ethics (see, eg., Declaration of Helsinki). And no doubt there are many others beyond these two. In some such settings, the implications of the two approaches for practice and policy might not come far apart. The most significant differences between them emerge in settings such as the one canvassed in this paper, involving issues of how to treat those who do not now have the capacity to consent or dissent, and who are likely not to have left any significant record of any views they might have had on the matters in question.

Policy Regarding Consent in Postmortem Reproduction:
Preliminaries

This short concluding section of the paper will make only a few programmatic remarks about policy concerning postmortem reproduction.

One central issue concerns the purpose of policy in this area. Two promising candidate purposes are to oppose unethical conduct, and not to oppose ethically permissible conduct. One important issue will be how to approach these two objectives in contexts where it seems that an initiative that would serve one better would also serve the other less well. Another, more philosophical issue concerns whether such goals are to be understood in the broadly consequentialist terms of minimizing the 'amount' of unethical conduct, or instead or as well, in terms of the achievement of more expressive purposes to oppose such conduct.

A further significant issue is whether, as Strong has argued, it is especially objectionable for a policy to oppose ethically acceptable actions (Strong, 1999, pp. 354–5). Strong argues that this generates a particular burden of justification on those whose policies do have or would have this effect, to show that the virtues of their policies cannot be had through any less intrusive policy.

Finally, even a well-developed policy argument grounded in the argument of this paper will be subject to some important limitations of scope. One of these arises from the fact that the argument of this paper has addressed only the consent and dissent considerations in postmortem reproduction. The scope of any policy conclusions built upon it would be similarly restricted. Another restriction arises from the many transaction and transition issues that arise when one sees any policy proposal in the setting of a particular polity to which it is intended to apply. Such issues vary considerably from polity to polity. It hardly needs to be emphasized, then, that this paper has not presented a completed argument that 'consent factor' policies should replace 'consent requirement' policies. In the setting of postmortem reproduction and in many other settings, the paper's argument does nevertheless give us reason to revisit the broad and unsatisfactory consensus in favour of the latter sort of approach.[14]

---

[14] My thanks to Martin Wilkinson, and to participants in the conference on which this volume draws, for discussion and comment on an earlier version of this paper. I am especially gratefully to John Haldane for his comments and encouragement.

Geoffrey Cupit

Three Ways to Value Equality

Introduction

There is much inequality in the world — inequalities of wealth, political power, health care and life-span, educational and cultural opportunities, and so on. Some of these inequalities are shared around so that they tend to cancel out, but to a large degree this is not so, and some people are much better off overall than others. This is manifest on any plausible way of measuring how well off people are overall.

The issue I want to consider is whether this overall inequality matters? Is it objectionable? It may be asked why we should focus on overall inequality, rather than on specific inequalities. The answer is that, providing it makes sense to talk of overall equality and inequality — and I will assume it does[1] — then, if equality is indeed an ideal, it seems reasonable to suppose that it is *overall* equality that is that ideal. If inequalities really did cancel out, then, as far as equality is concerned, it would seem that specific inequalities would not matter.

To be concerned about inequality[2] is to be concerned about how well off one person is compared to another: it is to be concerned about *comparative* or *relative* well being. A desire for equality, then, is to be distinguished from a desire that those who are badly off (absolutely) be better off (absolutely). This distinction is manifest when the two come apart, as when (the figures representing overall well being) we have a choice between:

Option A	Option B
Alan 1	Alan 1
Beth 1	Beth 2

---

[1] Thus I will assume that commensurability is not a problem, and that there is some 'currency' in which the required comparisons can be made. What that currency might be I shall not consider.

[2] Unless the context indicates otherwise, I will use 'equality' and 'inequality' to refer to *overall* equality and inequality.

My concern will be with equality, which I will take to be distinct from how well or badly (absolutely) those who do less well do, and thus from such issues as the appropriate priority (if any) to be given to improving the position of the worst off.

How might equality be defended? It is useful to distinguish between two types of argument for equality: those that assert that equality is a good — that it has value — and those that do not. I want to focus here exclusively on the former — that is, on what we may call the teleological arguments for equality.[3] It is plausible to suppose that not all arguments for equality are teleological arguments. An argument which seems best understood as a non-teleological argument is: all people are equal (in some fundamental sense); in order for people to have been treated as equals, (significant) overall inequalities must be avoided; hence overall (approximate) equality is required if no one is to have been treated inappropriately (wronged). This argument focuses on the importance of *treating* appropriately. It seems that it does not — or need not — make the claim that equality is a good, and to the extent that this is so it is an example of the type of argument for equality that I shall not consider here.[4]

The central issue faced by any teleological argument for equality is: Why think equality has value?[5] It might be tempting simply to assert that equality just is valuable — and perhaps to claim that, since at some point all justifications come to an end, egalitarians are as free to assert the value of equality as others are to assert their values. But the claim that equality is itself valuable has an intuitive implausibility, and this implausibility places a burden of proof on anyone who wishes to assert it.

The implausibility of simply asserting that equality is a value is clear if we consider the question: Who is equality good for? In the case we considered earlier, although Option A is better as far as equality is concerned, it may be said that there is no respect in which it is better for either Alan or Beth. But if there is no respect in which it is better for either

---

[3] Here I follow the distinction between telic or teleological, and deontic or deontological, arguments for equality drawn by Parfit (1991). See also McKerlie (1996).

[4] For discussion of the deontological argument see McKerlie (1996), especially pp. 280–5. I have discussed some of the difficulties associated with the claim that people are equals, and attempted to argue that people ought to be treated as equals, not because they are equals but because they are individuals, in Cupit (2000).

[5] There are other issues. Even if we accept that something is valuable we may still ask why this gives us reason to bring it about, and, in particular, to maximize it. In this paper I focus on equality, and I leave aside, therefore, challenges to teleological arguments in general.

(or for anyone else), how can it be in any respect better? How can something be valuable if there is no one it is valuable for? Wouldn't it be fanatical — crazy — to sacrifice anyone's interests to pursue an end that is in the interests of no one?

Now there may be a satisfactory reply to this question. Perhaps there are impersonal values — things that are valuable without being valuable for anyone. Or perhaps inequality is always bad for those who have less.[6] Or perhaps equality is in some way good for people without there being any specific individual for whom it is good on any specific occasion. Or perhaps there is some other way to deal with this problem. Exactly how this issue is to be addressed seems best left until we understand why equality is valuable — if indeed it is. At some point, however, this issue must be faced; it cannot simply be ignored and thus we cannot simply assert that equality is a value.

How might it be argued that equality is a value? The kind of argument that may be given depends on the kind of value equality is taken to be. It is a commonplace to distinguish two ways in which something might be of value: valuable as a means (or instrumentally valuable), and valuable as an end. How are these notions to be understood? In its purest form, to be valuable as a means — *merely* as a means — is to be valuable by virtue of being conducive to some (valued) end, the means being distinct and separate from the end. By contrast, to value something (exclusively) as an end is to value it for its own sake — not for its impact or effect on anything else. It is to hold that something is valuable when considered separately, distinctly, and independently.

Understanding valuable as a means and valuable as an end in these ways leaves room for a third way of being valuable: valuable not independently, but by virtue of connections to other values, those connections not being merely instrumental. To think something valuable in this way is to suppose that it has value (when it does) by virtue of its having a place in a network of (sometime) values. I shall refer to these different ways of being valuable as 'instrumental value', 'independent value', and 'connected value' respectively. The term 'connected value' deliberately leaves open the nature of the connection to other values. To use a more specific term — 'interdependent', 'constituent', 'organic' — would be to presuppose a relation that might exist in some cases but not in all. Could overall equality be valuable in any of these three ways? I want to consider these three possibilities in turn.

---

[6]   Cf. '. . . since what is bad about inequality is its unfairness, inequality is clearly a bad suffered by individuals' (Broome, 1991, p. 199).

Equality as an Instrumental Value

Many arguments against specific inequalities are instrumental in form. Inequalities of wealth are said to undermine fellowship[7] — and without fellowship and a sense of community goes stability, peace, and all that peace makes possible. Without fellowship the life of man is likely to be not only 'solitary' but 'poor, nasty, brutish and short'. Can we argue in a similar way against overall inequality?

It might be said that instrumental arguments — relying not on conceptual connections but on effects achieved through complex social and psychological processes — are, by their nature, uncertain and at best contingent. This may be so. How far it matters, however, depends on what our interests are. If our interests are philosophical and concern theories of value, instrumental arguments may be of little interest. If, however, we simply wish to know whether equality is valuable, we might not much care whether the value is contingent or necessary. If, for all practical purposes, inequality really does undermine fellowship, community, peace, and all that requires peace, then we might say that that is good reason for us to value equality — even if there are possible worlds in which the contingent connections in question do not hold. Thus, perhaps, we should not dismiss instrumental arguments for equality merely on the grounds that they can do no more than show equality to be a contingent value. Perhaps being a contingent value is enough.

Nevertheless there are reasons to doubt that instrumental considerations can provide good grounds for thinking overall equality valuable. In setting out these reasons I will focus on the argument for equality from fellowship (or community) since this seems a particularly plausible form of the instrumental argument.

One way to cast doubt on the claim that equality is instrumental to some valuable end is to insist that it really does have to be *inequality* that is detrimental to the end, and not some feature that may often be found with inequality but is distinguishable from it. For example, it is often the case that when there is inequality, someone has taken more than their share and has done well at the expense of others. In the classic example, a cake is divided between n individuals, each of whom has the same claim to the cake, and one takes a share larger than $1/n^{th}$. Now it is hard to imagine how such behaviour could not be damaging to fellowship and

---

[7]   In a very early (1954) party political television broadcast for the British Labour Party, Attlee summed up what his party had to offer in these words: 'Well, you know, there's nothing better than the motto that we have in this Borough [Walthamstow], by our greatest citizen, William Morris — 'Fellowship is Life' — we believe in the kind of society where we've fellowship for all. You can't get that in a totalitarian society, you can't get that while there's grave inequalities in wealth. That is the hope of the world, and we offer fellowship in our own country and fellowship with all other countries.' (Quoted in Harris, 1984.)

community. But this does not show that *inequality* undermines fellowship: fellowship may require that people do not take more than their
share or profit at the expense of others, but inequality may not have
these accompaniments. If you are better off than me, and could be even
better off without affecting me, then your being even better off, though it
increases inequality between us, may not constitute taking more than
your share, nor being better off at my expense.

The question, then, is whether *inequality* is detrimental to fellowship?
Is there any reason to suppose that it is? Rawls identifies 'a natural
meaning of fraternity' as 'the idea of not wanting to have greater advantages unless this is to the benefit of those who are less well off', and suggests that family members 'commonly do not wish to gain unless they
can do so in ways that further the interests of the rest' (Rawls, 1971,
p. 105). Now this allows, of course, that some increases in inequality are
consistent with fraternity — increases where those who are worse off do
better as a consequence. But this, it might be said, is because in this case
the disvalue of the additional inequality is offset by the value of the
improvement in the position of those who have less. But what of cases
where those who do less well do not benefit from an increase in inequality? Rawls' remarks suggest that such inequalities are detrimental to
fellowship. But is even this true?

We may agree that to have a sense of fellowship is to hope that among
the ways in which we can improve our own lot will be ways that
improve the lot of our fellows; and not to choose those ways when they
are available is detrimental to fellowship. Fellowship means being concerned not just about oneself: it means caring about others' interests, loving one's neighbour or fellow. But the less fortunate may love too. And a
part of fellowship, surely, is delighting in the good fortune of others —
including those better off than ourselves. If a more fortunate member of
one's family has the prospect of doing even better (at no one else's
expense), would it not be detrimental to fellowship to want her or him to
forego that prospect? If fellowship really did require that where some
must remain in a state of depravation, all must, then we might doubt that
fellowship is to be cherished — and doubt also that such fellowship
underpins stability. But this is not what fellowship requires. That it is not
inequality that undermines fellowship can be seen if we consider a case
such as Oates' noble act on Scott's expedition. Here a less well off member of a community sacrificed his interests in the interests of the better
off. Even if such an act increased inequality, it would still be, surely, an
act of fellowship.[8]

---

[8]   It might be said that while Oates' producing this increase in inequality was not at
       all detrimental to fellowship, Scott's producing it — say by simply leaving Oates
       behind — would have been. And, of course, this is true. But that does not show an

We may say, then, that where there is inequality there will often be forms of behaviour — taking more than one's share, profiting at the expense of others, failing to show due concern for others, and so on — that are detrimental to fellowship. But it does not follow from this that *inequality* is detrimental to fellowship. Indeed there is good reason to think that considerations of fellowship, other things equal, provide a reason *not* to constrain inequality, and are better seen as supporting priority for those who have less, rather than as an argument for equality.

A second reason to doubt that instrumental considerations can provide good grounds for thinking overall equality valuable focuses on the point that we are here concerned with *overall* equality. To see how this argument comes about consider what we might call the argument against inequality from competitive considerations. As we have noted, to be concerned about equality and inequality is to be concerned about relative levels. Now one reason to be concerned about relative levels is that relative levels can affect absolute levels. If you and I are in competition — for a job, at an auction, or in a battle — what matters is not our absolute level of experience, available funds, or military strength, but who has more. A standard objection to inequalities of wealth and power, then, is based on competitive effects: your having more can make me worse off (absolutely) than I would otherwise be.

Do competitive consideration arguments apply if our concern is with *overall* equality and inequality? It may be argued that they do not for, it may be claimed, whatever our measure of overall well-offness is, competitive effects will already be included, and to take account of them again would be to double count. Hence although competitive considerations may be of the first importance when deciding what effect specific policies and specific inequalities will have on how well off overall different people will be, they are no basis on which to argue against overall inequalities.

So far the argument has been used to support setting aside competitive considerations. But the argument might now be applied to the instrumental effects of inequalities. Thus it may be said that instrumental effects on overall inequality will also have already been taken into account. If fellowship (or whatever it is that equality is instrumentally valuable for) really is valuable, this will result in at least some of us being better off. But our being better off will already be reflected in how well off overall each of us is. That being so, instrumental effects can have no further role in the evaluation of the overall inequalities. Thus instrumental arguments for equality — such as those from fellowship — though

---

increase in inequality is detrimental to fellowship. It shows that some behaviour that increases inequality is detrimental to fellowship — not a conclusion that should occasion surprise.

highly relevant to the assessment of how well-off each of us will be if different policies are pursued, must be irrelevant to an assessment of those
overall inequalities.

It is important to note that the argument here relies on a claim about
the need to avoid double counting. The argument is *not* that overall
assessments are in some sense 'final assessments' and cannot, therefore,
reflect (even in part) inequalities in those assessments since that would
require a further assessment to be made after the (*ex hypothesi*) final
assessment has been made. That argument, were it valid, would apply
not merely to instrumental arguments but to all arguments regarding
the value of overall equality. But such an argument is not valid. The disvalue of an inequality in overall well-offness can itself be included in
overall well-offness.[9] The point about instrumental arguments is that,
the value in question being exclusively *instrumental*, there is no value
that has not already been included. Hence there is nothing needing to be
added — and to do so would be double counting.

There is, however, a response to the application of this double counting argument to the instrumental effects of equality. The argument is
compelling only on the assumption that the whole value of whatever
equality is taken to be instrumental to is reflected in (different) people's
good. Take the argument that overall inequality tends to undermine fellowship. Presumably the value of this fellowship means that at least
some people are better off. But the question is whether *all* of the value of
the fellowship will have been captured. Or could the fellowship be valuable in a way that is not reflected in its being valuable for anyone? After
all, we earlier left open the possibility of equality itself being valuable
without there being anyone it is valuable for. Why might not equality be
instrumentally valuable to something that is valuable in this way?

This response may be sound as far as it goes — but it does not leave
things quite where they were, for the upshot is that, for the instrumental
argument for overall equality to succeed, it is not enough merely that
there be an end to which overall equality is instrumentally valuable. The
end must be valuable in a way that is not wholly captured in the overall
well-offness of individuals. Now nothing I have said has shown this to
be impossible. Nevertheless many might consider showing anything to

---

[9] 'True egalitarians, the objection goes, care about equality in the distribution of
good. Individualistic egalitarianism may give value to equality in the distribution
of income. But surely it cannot give value to equality in the distribution of good.
Surely the good of individuals has to be determined before it can be determined
how equally it is distributed. Consequently equality in the distribution of
individual good cannot itself be part of individual good. . . . Surprisingly perhaps,
there is actually no difficulty about making equality of individual good itself an
individual good. It is only a matter of setting up some simultaneous equations.'
(Broome, 1991, p. 181.)

be valuable in this way a tall order; hence, to that extent, the present argument makes showing overall equality instrumentally valuable a taller order than it would otherwise be.

There can be little doubt that specific inequalities — such as inequalities of institutional concern, of power or wealth — can be instrumentally harmful. It is, however, much less clear that this is true of overall inequalities. There are problems, both in showing that overall *equality* is instrumental to a valuable end, and in showing that an end to which equality might be instrumental is valuable in the right kind of way. I do not say that the points I have made constitute a knockdown argument against the claim that overall equality is an instrumental value. Nevertheless, taken together, these difficulties might be thought to provide reasonable grounds for scepticism.

Equality as an Independent Value

The second way equality might be valuable is as valuable in itself — valuable not by virtue of connections with anything else, but as a 'stand-alone' or independent value. If equality is valuable in this way — independently of connections or consequences — its value is a consequence of its intrinsic nature, and we may say, therefore, that it is an intrinsic value.

To hold that equality is an independent value is not, of course, to deny that in some circumstances we should not pursue equality. Even if equality is a value it is not the only value: whether equality should be pursued will depend on how the value of equality is to be set off against other values. Clashes between independent values will, presumably, need to be resolved by 'weighing' one value against another. (Given independence it is hard to see any basis for a lexical ordering or an algorithm.)[10]

Holding that equality is an independent value does not, then, exclude the possibility of sacrificing equality for other values. But what is excluded is the value equality has by virtue of being an independent value being affected by circumstance. To the extent that equality is an independent, intrinsic value its value depends on nothing outside itself.

---

[10] How could there be a lexical ordering of two things that are wholly unrelated? Words (in dictionaries) can be lexically ordered because letters are related (ordered). A card of the trump suit can triumph over any non-trump suit card because the trump and non-trump suits are (temporarily) ordered. For the same reason one gold medal can count for more than any number of silver medals. But if there is no connection between equality and the other value — if, that is, they are independent values — what would be the basis of a lexical relation? More generally it seems there can be no basis for an algorithm ordering wholly independent values. In ordering unrelated intrinsic values there seems no alternative to a trade off based on judgement or intuition.

This value being unaffected by circumstance, we may say that, for any two states of affairs, if one contains more equality than the other, the one that contains more equality is in one way better. We may say this because greater equality makes a state of affairs better (in one way) irrespective of what else is true about that state of affairs. Conversely, if we claim that a situation is in one way (non-instrumentally) better simply by virtue of there being less inequality, and no matter what else is true of that situation, we are taking equality to be an independent value.

Is it plausible to suppose that equality is an independent value? It is never easy to show that something is valuable as an end, and it would be unreasonable to expect a rigorous proof. Nevertheless some defence or support might be provided by use of analysis and comparison. For example, if we wanted to support the claim that knowledge is valuable as an end we might begin by analysing knowledge — identifying and describing one or more of its constitutive features. This might turn up something that it seems intuitively reasonable to say has value in itself — and thus suggest some reason for thinking knowledge valuable simply by virtue of its nature. If this fails we might try analysing something else that we believe has intrinsic value — happiness, say — and compare our analysis of happiness with our analysis of knowledge. If we find that knowledge and happiness have similarities, we might argue from those similarities, together with the claim that happiness is valuable as an end, for the claim that knowledge is too.

Can this strategy be used to support the claim that equality is an independent value? Do any of the features of equality seem to make equality valuable in itself? What are the features of equality? Equality is a state embodying a certain uniformity. There are, perhaps, certain affinities between uniformity and neatness. But these are relatively trivial considerations at best. To try to defend equality in these terms is to invite the mockery of those who portray egalitarians as — like Procrustes — driven by an obsessive intolerance for untidiness and variation. Does equality share common features with what are sometimes accepted as values — life, happiness, knowledge, say? There seem no obvious similarities here. Indeed equality, being a relation, seems quite different.

Is there any reason to think that equality is *not* an independent value? We have noted already the problem posed by the question: Valuable for whom? This problem might be thought particularly pressing if we assert that equality is an independent value — for independence may seem to leave few resources with which to deal with the problem. But we face another problem if we claim that equality is an *independent* value. As we have seen, if equality is an independent value, then its value derives from what is intrinsic to it — that is, simply on account of its nature. This nature being unchanging, unaffected by circumstances or anything external to it, equality's value as such a value is also unchanging. In particular, it never disappears: if equality ever has value as an independent value, then it always has it. So if equality were an independent value, equality would always be valuable. But is this plausible? To approach this question, consider the relationships between equality and desert, and between equality and freedom. What connections are there between equality, desert, and freedom?

One 'connection', of course, is that those who are sympathetic to the importance of equality are often sceptical about the truth of claims of desert and freedom. Egalitarians often question whether choices are genuinely free, and whether those who are said to deserve do truly deserve. These doubts are often raised together — as when it is questioned whether we can genuinely deserve if we are not truly free and responsible. But the issue we need to focus on here is not whether there is genuine desert and freedom, but what impact (genuine) desert and (genuine) freedom would have on the (non-instrumental) value of equality.

Consider first desert and equality. Suppose that what Alan genuinely deserves is not more than X and that what Beth genuinely deserves is not less than Y, and that X is less than Y. Now if we believe that equality is an independent value, we will hold that, even if we leave aside all instrumental considerations for equality, it would still be in one way better if Alan and Beth were to receive outcomes that are more equal than the unequal outcomes that they genuinely deserve. How great a departure from the deserved outcome in the direction of greater equality we think would be best will depend on the relative weights we attach to desert and equality.

Next consider freedom and equality. Suppose Alan and Beth have similar talents, resources, and opportunities, and that their lives have gone equally well, and would carry on going equally well were it not for the choices they are about to make. Let us also assume that all choices are genuine: Alan and Beth are competent, their choices are informed, and neither is manipulated or coerced.

Suppose Alan and Beth each have the choice of being in situation A or situation B. Suppose that Alan chooses A, Beth chooses B, and that A and B are unequal according to our way of measuring how well off people are. Or suppose that Alan and Beth choose to take part in a fair zero-sum gamble — for example, to bet on the toss of a coin. If we value freedom, we will hold that it is (in one way) better if Alan and Beth are free to choose between A and B, or to gamble if they wish. But if we hold also that equality is an independent value, we will hold that, even if instrumental considerations are left aside, it would be in one way better if the outcomes were more equal than the outcomes that are the consequence of free and informed choice. How far we think it best that choices are constrained in order that greater equality is achieved will reflect the relative weights we attach to the values of equality and freedom.

But these views seem implausible. If some inequality is genuinely deserved, there seems no reason to temper that inequality on the basis of the (non-instrumental) value of equality. And it is not that desert is somehow much more important than (non-instrumental) equality so that equality is always outweighed. If the inequality is deserved, it seems that greater equality would have *no* value — again leaving instrumental considerations aside.[11] And it seems plausible to take the same view with respect to freedom. If an inequality is wholly the outcome of a genuine choice, and freedom is a value, why, if we leave instrumental considerations aside, should we think that less inequality would be valuable?[12]

To accept either of these arguments is to accept that equality can cease to have (non-instrumental) value — either where the inequality is genuinely deserved, or where the inequality is wholly the consequence of genuine choice. Thus to accept either argument (or both, of course) is to reject the claim that equality is an independent value. *Setting equality off* against desert or choice is entirely consistent with equality being an independent value; but the (non-instrumental) value of equality being *extinguished* when the inequality is deserved, or is the consequence of choice, is not. If equality has no (non-instrumental) value in either of these cases, equality is not an independent value.

Once again this is not a knockdown argument against the claim that equality is an independent value. We may, if we wish, try to argue that even where an inequality is fully and genuinely deserved there would be (non-instrumental) value in equality — a value, perhaps, to be somehow set against desert. But that is, surely, an odd view to take. There seem, then, to be good grounds to reject the view that equality is an independent value.

---

[11] Even someone firmly committed to the value of equality may take this view. Thus Temkin — who writes: 'I, for one, believe that inequality is bad. But do I *really* think there is some respect in which a world where only some are blind is worse than one where all are? Yes,' — also holds that desert extinguishes the value of equality: 'In fact, I think that deserved inequalities are not bad *at all*.' (Temkin, 1993, pp. 282 and 17 original emphasis).

[12] I am not claiming that an arrangement being acceptable to those involved is a sufficient reason to think it unobjectionable. There is good reason to regard some arrangements — slavery for example — as unjust, even if they have been agreed to by the parties involved. The point here concerns only the non-instrumental value of equality. The issue is: Do we wish to claim that an inequality that has been genuinely chosen by the parties involved has disvalue when instrumental considerations are left aside?

Equality as a Connected Value

The third way for equality to be valuable is as a connected value. To be valuable in this way is to be valuable by virtue of connections to other values, those connections not being merely instrumental, but going deeper and linking equality in a conceptual relationship with other values. (Given such interconnections there is the possibility of algorithms, including lexical orderings, that determine when different values are to be pursued.)

The value of a connected value does not depend only on its nature: it may be affected by the other values with which it forms a network. (Such values not being valuable solely by virtue of their intrinsic natures we might hesitate to call them intrinsic values in the fullest sense.) The value of a connected value need not be constant — unaffected by circumstance — and on some occasions such a (putative) value may not be valuable at all. Thus to believe that equality is (non-instrumentally) valuable only in this way is to believe that, although equality may sometimes have (non-instrumental) value, it need not always do so.

Is it plausible to suppose that equality is a connected value? Equality's losing its (non-instrumental) value in the face of genuine desert or choice sinks the claim that equality is an independent value; but it is entirely consistent with equality's being a connected value. And if desert and freedom (or whatever) do not outweigh or override the disvalue of the inequality with which they conflict, but rather exclude the possibility of that inequality having disvalue, then it seems that it is desert or freedom that equality is connected with. If there were no connection between desert and equality, say, why should desert preclude equality's having value?

The idea that desert and equality are related may be surprising. At a practical level desert and equality are often used to express opposing conclusions and recommendations — with egalitarians urging equality and those who appeal to desert defending inequalities. It might be thought from this that desert and equality are opposed and unconnected — perhaps that they reflect radically different views that simply clash. But there is good reason to think that such a view must be mistaken. If equality is to be a (non-instrumental) value at all, while genuinely deserved inequalities are in no way bad, then it follows that there must be a deep connection between equality and desert; and those who believe in equality may need to consider whether they are not thereby committed to the value of desert, and vice versa.

It seems clear that equality and desert are connected. But we should not make the mistake of thinking that they are connected simply by being two sides of the same coin: lack of desert does not in itself entail that equality is required. To see this consider possible responses to the distribution of natural talents. This distribution is, let us suppose, both unequal and undeserved. The egalitarian position is that these inequalities — or at least the effects of them on overall inequalities — are to be nullified, thereby producing (greater) equality. The egalitarian agrees (let us say) that, were the inequalities deserved, they should stand. But being undeserved (and unchosen) they should be undone.

But why should the absence of desert be thought to provide any reason for equalizing? To be sure, the egalitarian's opponent can respond, if the better endowed deserved not to have more than others, then there would be reason to equalize. If the better endowed had done something so that they deserved to lose their advantaged position, equality would be required. But this is not the case — or so let us assume. It is not that the more fortunate deserve not to have their extra talents (and the benefits that flow there from); they merely do not deserve them. But if they are merely undeserved, where is the argument for equality? The problem would be solved if we could infer from our not deserving something that we deserve not to have it. But it does not follow from our not deserving something that we deserve not to have it.

The mere fact that inequalities are undeserved does not, by itself, entail that equality would have value. What is required is an account of why equality is valuable that explains why equality is not valuable when it conflicts with desert or freedom. Such an account will expose connections between equality, desert, and freedom, and seems likely to link those values with justice, fairness, and the avoidance of arbitrariness. But the details of such an argument must be left for another occasion.[13]

---

[13] This paper forms part of a larger project on which I began work while holding a Charter Fellowship at Wolfson College, Oxford; I am grateful to the Governing Body of the College for electing me to this fellowship. Material in this paper formed part of papers given at a conference in Pittsburgh of St Andrews' fellowship holders; at the Fourth European Congress for Analytical Philosophy at Lund; and at the Universities of Lancaster and Waikato. I am very grateful to the many people who commented on these occasions. I am particularly grateful to Peter Morriss who provided me with extensive written comments.

Bart Gruzalski

Mitigating the Consumption of the US Living Standard

Aristotle thought that we reach a point of negative returns: after a certain 'limit,' wealth becomes counter productive, a distraction from the things that matter (Nussbaum, 2000, p. 86).

Introduction

A significant amount of consumption in the United States is the consumption of commodities that are fashionable or technologically innovative. If Adam Smith's 'invisible hand'[1] applied, the individual choices expressed by this consumption would promote a collective good. Theorists following Adam Smith try to justify the pace of US consumption with the claim that it raises the standard of living. In contrast, I show that individuals, by pursuing their own interest through the purchase of many ultrafashionable and innovative technological goods, plausibly cause themselves collective stress and strain, as if their actions tighten an 'invisible ratchet' that makes life collectively worse. Because of this Ratchet Effect,[2] US consumers, through increased accumulations of some goods ultrafashionable and technologically innovative (hereafter, 'gufties'), plausibly lower the US standard of living.

---

[1] In *The Wealth of Nations* Smith writes: '. . . he intends only his own gain, and he is in this, as in many other cases, led by an invisible hand to promote an end which was no part of his intention . . . that of society' (Smith, 1776/1976, Vol. 1, p. 477).

[2] Economist John Kenneth Galbraith names this the 'Dependence Effect' or the 'Squirrel Wheel' (Galbraith, 1984, pp. 124–5). The term 'Ratchet Effect' more clearly expresses the idea that our consumption 'ratchets up' costs and burdens, as well as creating stress.

Being Worse off Because of Acquisitions

I begin with the acquisitions of technologically innovative goods. On the face of it the lives of consumers are better because of the purchase of these goods that only a few decades ago were thought to be luxuries or even science fiction fantasies. Yet even with these devices, US consumers do not seem to be less busy, less harried, or have more time for family, for relaxation, for visiting, or for leisured pursuits. Despite the aid of modern technologies, these consumers seem collectively more stressed and more anxious and their lives do not seem of a better quality than the lives of those who live with less technology and at a slower pace. Since we believe technologically innovative devices are helpers and time-savers, this unorthodox assessment requires explanation. One explanation of why the lives of consumers are more harried due to the consumption of gufties is that these new accumulations tend only to allow consumer to maintain a status quo relative to friends, neighbours and competitors, while adding costs that require the consumer to work longer hours. The following example illustrates one way in which this happens.

Before the telegraph, New York merchants who dealt in international commerce received updates from foreign associates once or twice a month, while those involved in national trade were visited by their customers once or twice a year. The introduction of the telegraph radically changed the pace of the merchants' activities. 'Reports of the principle markets of the world are published every day, and our customers are continually posted by telegram,' reported New York businessman W.E. Dodge in a 1868 speech. 'Instead of making a few large shipments in a year, the merchant must keep up constant action.' This constant action even invaded the home life of these merchants. Dodge continues

> The merchant goes home after a day of hard work and excitement to a late dinner, trying amid the family circle to forget business, when he is interrupted by a telegram from London . . . and the poor man must dispatch his dinner as hurriedly as possible in order to send off his message to California. The businessman of the present day must be continually on the jump . . . and the poor merchant has no other way to work to secure a living for his family. He *must* use the telegraph (Standage, 1998, pp. 165–6).

This example illustrates two typical aspects of the Ratchet Effect. First, consumers must use a new technology to maintain the competitive status quo. Second, the result of using the new technology plausibly requires that consumers work more work hours to pay for it, to learn to use it, and to maintain it. In our example, the introduction of the telegraph forced the merchants to suffer the stress of a faster pace only to maintain a status quo among themselves.

A more contemporary example illustrates the same point. Imagine Mary owns a heating and air-conditioning installation firm. Suppose her competitors begin accepting credit card payments. If Mary fails to do the same, some of her customers or potential customers will likely turn to a competitor. For this reason Mary, just in order to keep attracting customers and to maintain her status quo relative to her competitors, has to increase her expenditures of time and money because of a new technology. Collectively, the proprietors in Mary's situation are worse off once they all accept credit card payments for their services. Everyone accepting credit card payments raises the ante without improving anyone's business and thereby causes a decrease of collective overall well-being.[3]

The Ratchet Effect also occurs in the consumption of ultrafashionable goods. Suppose Betty wants to impress upper management that she is an up-and-coming professional in her field. In order to do this she incurs a maximum amount of debt to purchase a fancy condominium, to buy a new wardrobe, and to lease a new vehicle. Other ambitious up-and-coming professionals in her field may feel equally compelled to purchase similar gufties. Once everyone has similar gufties to impress upper management, no one has any advantage but, collectively, all are additionally saddled with significant debt.

Consumers, in their attempts to 'keep up with the Joneses', purchase bigger houses, fancier automobiles, the newest styles of clothing, better video equipment, and more fashionable furniture. They may try to 'get ahead of the Joneses' by purchasing the most impressive house, appearing the best dressed, or making the most money. In each case the Ratchet Effect may occur as consumers acquire more debt, experience stress, and bear the burden of additional transaction and opportunity costs without being any better off collectively.

I am not arguing that the purchase of gufties always leads to the Ratchet Effect. But because the purchases of gufties often leads to a Ratchet Effect, this brings into question the standard-of-living justifications of consumption. In what follows, I will raise this question using the capability approach to the standard of living.

The Capability Approach and the Standard of Living

According to the capability approach, writes Amaryta Sen, 'what is valued is the *capability* to live well and in the specific economic context of standard of living, it values the capabilities associated with economic matters' (Sen, 1984, p. 78). On this approach the standard of living is not an indicator of wealth, not an indicator of an amount of goods, and not an indicator of a degree of satisfaction or of contentedness, but is instead

---

[3] Judith Lichtenberg points out that 'many items once thought of as high-tech luxuries — television, cable television, computers, on-line databases — are becoming increasingly necessary for the citizen in a technologically sophisticated society. Invention is the mother of necessity . . . [and not using a technology] may cost a businessperson her livelihood . . .' See Lichtenberg (1998) pp. 158–9.

an indicator of those capabilities and the exercise of those capabilities (called 'functionings') by which human beings flourish.[4] To be able to exercise the capabilities by which human beings flourish requires the relevant material basis to exercise these capabilities. Proponents of the capability approach quote the following passage from Adam Smith's *The Wealth of Nations*:

> A linen shirt, for example, is strictly speaking, not a necessary of life ... But in the present times, through the greater part of Europe, a credible day-labourer would be ashamed to appear in public without a linen shirt, the want of which would be supposed to denote that disgraceful degree of poverty which, it is presumed, no body can well fall into without extreme bad conduct. Custom, in the same manner, had rendered leather shoes a necessary of life in England. The poorest creditable person of either sex would be ashamed to appear in public without them (Smith, 1776/1976, Vol. 2, p. 399)

In his Tanner Lectures, Sen develops the relationship between capabilities needed for human flourishing and the material bases required to exercise them:

> To lead a life without shame, to be able to visit and entertain one's friends, to keep track of what is going on and what others are talking about, and so on, requires a more expensive bundle of goods and services in a society that is generally richer and in which most people have, say, means of transport, affluent clothing, radios or television sets, and so on. ... Also the level of *capabilities* that are accepted as 'minimum' may themselves be upwardly revised as the society becomes richer and more and more people achieve levels of capabilities not previously reached by many (Sen, 1987, p. 18).

Sen is mistaken in saying that the capabilities change. The capabilities are the same: to lead a life without shame, to be able to visit and entertain friends, to keep track of what is going on, and so on. What changes are not the capabilities but rather what it takes to exercise these capabilities. As the overall level of consumption in a given society increases, we need more to maintain the minimum material basis to exercise these same capabilities.

This helps to explain the rising consumption in the United States. Those who want to appear in public without shame are at the mercy of changing styles that demand more purchases. Yesterday's clothing won't do. Neither will yesterday's automobile. And for some, an automobile itself won't even work: the very rich need a limo and a driver. As the level of consumption rises, think of what might be required to host with pride, another function referred to by capability theorists (see, for example Segal, 1998, p. 361). Having a one-bathroom house and a com-

---

[4]   Sen rejects the commodity approach because a surplus of goods does not necessarily support capabilities. Sen rejects satisfaction/preference approaches because a level of satisfaction or contentedness may be incommensurable with any economic instrument (Sen, 1984, pp. 76–7).

bined kitchen/dining room may well be woefully inadequate. It might not even be adequate to have a three-bathroom house, a formal dining room, a breakfast room and a library. To host with pride might also require a maid, a cook and a butler. It depends on how high the ante is being raised and what is required to meet it.

There is no doubt that the ante is being raised in the United States. According to a recent commentary about homes in Fairfax County in Virginia, 'an average middle-class home is the equivalent of a previous century's average mansion. Upper middle-class homes . . . are palaces by the standards of any previous century' (Coleman, 1999). This is the degree of consumption that consumers take for granted. In order to maintain the status quo in their consumptive society, consumers have more expense, more debt, more to protect, more to insure, and more to maintain. Once consumers are caught in this Ratchet Effect cycle, they need to consume more to maintain a status quo position and so typically must use more income, work more hours, and so will have less time to exercise other capabilities that are essential for a decent living standard.

The Ratchet Effect and the Standard of Living

Referring to Adam Smith's example of workers needing clean linen shirts and leather shoes in order to appear in public without shame, theorists claim, on the basis of the capability approach, that higher consumption, at least in wealthier societies, is needed to improve or at least maintain the standard of living. David Crocker illustrates the degree to which the level of consumption might rise. In his discussion of the view that the functioning 'living without shame' is upwardly revised as our society becomes more affluent, Crocker writes:

> If being able to appear in public without shame is a component of well-being and we accept that it takes more to live without shame in an affluent society than in a poor one, then there seems to be no basis for criticizing the millionaire bond trader Sherman McCoy and his wife, in Tom Wolfe' novel *Bonfire of the Vanities*, who must have a chauffeur and limousine in order to travel without shame to a dinner party just a few blocks away from their apartment (Crocker, 1998, pp. 382–3).

According to Crocker, although we may criticize McCoy's decision on moral grounds, there seems no way to criticize McCoy's rental of a chauffeured limo from the perspective of the capability approach. More generally, to the degree we focus on consumption as a way of improving well-being, Crocker claims that there is no criterion 'to identify or condemn overconsumption' other than showing 'that the consumption choice in question undermines some other features of the consumer's well-being'.

We cannot satisfy Crocker's criterion for identifying overconsumption by assessing the effects of the Ratchet Effect on the individual consumer. We can, and have above, shown that consumers collectively can be worse off because of the Ratchet Effect. The consumption of at least some gufties plausibly lowers the quality of life of consumers collectively and thereby plausibly lowers the standard of living generally.

One might question whether a lower standard of living follows from a lower quality of life. In particular, we might question whether the claim of a lower standard of living follows from the capability approach or follows from an assessment external to the capability approach that uses criteria imported from an account focusing on happiness, satisfaction, or welfare. In illustrating how consumers ratchet up their lives through the purchase of gufties, I have focused on stress, cost, and a lack of leisure, none of which is explicitly part of a capability approach. But when people are burdened with additional expenses, transaction costs, stress, and the need to spend more time working, their opportunities to relax, to spend time with their loved ones, even to host with pride — all are undermined. These additional burdens reduce the opportunities and the material wherewithal necessary to exercise many of the capabilities essential to a flourishing life. When the accumulation of gufties only maintains a status quo while diminishing other capabilities because of the Ratchet Effect, this accumulation plausibly leads to an overall diminishment in the standard of living on criteria explicit in the capability approach.

I am granting that an individual may need to consume more in order to preserve her status quo in a situation where others are consuming more. Nonetheless, in cases involving the Ratchet Effect, all would be better off if no one consumed the gufties in question. We might view this situation as a variant of a Prisoner's Dilemma: everyone would be better off if no one consumed more, but because others are consuming more, any particular person would be worse off if she failed to consume more. The focus in the Prisoner's Dilemma is on the rational choice of a particular prisoner. Since we are concerned about the standard of living, our focus, instead, is on the situation of consumers considered collectively. The collective case is the relevant case, for we want to assess standards of living for nations, cultures and societies in order to have a sound basis for public policy and macroeconomic decisions.

Consider, for example, the capability 'being able to host with pride'. As more people acquire the material basis for this capability, the more they raise the ante. If the capability approach justifies us in increasing the material basis for capabilities like 'being able to host with pride', then the outcome would be a lowered standard of living for all as they experience the Ratchet Effect, for the consumption of the gufties that allow people to 'host with pride' also leads to a collective worsening when viewed from the commonsense perspectives of expense, stress, time spent working, and the corresponding opportunity costs.

Where does this leave us? Relative to the capabilities in question, we as individuals are in a coercive situation. Either we fail to consume, and so lose the ability to exercise some capabilities as fully as we would be able to, or we consume and undermine other important capabilities, thereby, in effect, consuming our own standard of living. Because in these situations our standard of living will diminish whatever we do as individuals, public policy offers a better chance of successfully addressing the problems created by the Ratchet Effect.

Inflationary and Non-inflationary Capability Bundles

A plausible start to a public policy discussion involves distinguishing between inflationary and noninflationary capacities. Being able to host with pride is an *inflationary capability*: the continued attempt to exercise this capability requires additional consumption and an expanded material basis. In contrast to inflationary capabilities, *noninflationary capabilities* do not rely on an increasing material basis. Examples of noninflationary capabilities might include being able to eat nourishing food, to maintain strong family ties, to develop friendships, to participate effectively in political decisions affecting one's life, to reflect critically, to relax, to play, and to love. If, instead of developing inflationary capabilities, the people in a society developed only noninflationary ones, the result would be that people would collectively be better off because they had enhanced their capabilities while avoiding the Ratchet Effect. Since, as we have seen, an individual acting alone cannot bring about this end, this becomes a goal for public policy and collective grassroots action. What seems to be called for are public policies and collective grassroot activism that encourage the development of noninflationary capabilities while discouraging or prohibiting inflationary ones.

The distinction between inflationary and noninflationary capabilities does not live up to its initial promise. Talking about capabilities without identifying their exercise or functionings and the corresponding material bases required to exercise them is too abstract. Consider the capability of being able to relax. Some ways of exercising this capability would be noninflationary, and others would be inflationary. One might exercise the capability to relax by meditating or going for a walk, each of which would typically be noninflationary. But there are also ways of relaxing that would be inflationary: playing golf at St. Andrews or hiring a yacht and a crew for a party in Boston Harbour. To be completely clear about the economic impact of the exercise of a particular capability, we need to look at the material basis we need to exercise the capability through a particular functioning. Capabilities assessed from this perspective are not capabilities *simpliciter*, but capabilities that are bundled with a functioning and a material basis for that functioning. Such bundles we will refer to as *capability bundles*.[5] When a people exercise only noninflationary capability bundles, they do not experience the stress, fatigue, anxiety or depression brought about by a Ratchet Effect. They raise no ante through their own consumption.

Exercising noninflationary capability bundles would not require an expansion of the material bases required to exercise capabilities. Learning to meditate, for example, need not require any additional material possessions or services and so would not need to require growth of the material basis.[6] On the other hand, deciding that for relaxation one needed to rent a yacht and crew would require an expanded material basis. Switching from policies of growth that encourage inflationary capability bundles to policies of development that encourage noninflationary capability bundles seems therefore promising.[7]

This promise is short-lived because there are relatively few noninflationary capabilities: walking, watching clouds, meditating, and playing tic-tac-toe in the sand are among the capability bundles that can be

---

[5]   Nussbaum refers to 'combined capabilities, which may be defined as internal capabilities combined with suitable external conditions for the exercise of function'(Nussbaum, 2000, pp. 84–5). Her list of 'central human functional capabilities' is intended to be a list of 'combined capabilities' (p. 85). The difference between combined capabilities and capability bundles is that Nussbaum's combined capabilities are not calibrated to specific functions but are intended as a way of insisting on the 'importance of material and social circumstances' (p. 86), whereas capability bundles are a way of identifying the particular functioning and its corresponding material basis for the purposes of a more finely tuned economic assessment.

[6]   Of course, people can spend exorbitant amounts of money going to expensive retreat centres to learn meditation. The point is that this is not necessary.

[7]   Herman Daly makes this distinction: economic growth requires a 'quantitative increase in physical size by assimilation or accretion of materials'(Daly, 1996, p. 167), whereas economic development is 'development without growth beyond environmental carrying capacity, where development means qualitative improvement and growth means increase'(p. 9). In terms of this distinction between growth and development, development will be the attempt to create a higher living standard without growth. Since we are so accustomed to thinking that growth is the only way to avoid economic stagnation, it is important to be clear that development without growth can serve the same purpose. An economy and a society which was not in pursuit of a rapid increase of productivity and wealth would not stagnate but would be able to focus on progress and improvement. John Stuart Mill foresaw this possibility in his *Principles of Political Economy*: 'There would be as much scope as ever for all kinds of mental culture, and moral and social progress; as much room for improving the Art of Living, and much more likelihood of its being improved, when minds ceased to be engrossed by the art of getting on. Even the industrial arts might be as earnestly and as successfully cultivated, with this sole difference, that instead of serving no purpose but the increase of wealth, industrial improvements would produce their legitimate effect, that of abridging labour' (Mill, 1848/1965, p. 756).

noninflationary. It would be decidedly implausible for public policy to reinforce only these while inhibiting functionings that involved the use of credit cards, chess sets, computers, automobiles, telephones, and the many appliances and technological items found in today's homes and offices.

Public Policy and
Hyperinflationary Capability Bundles

We may take a step toward a more plausible policy by distinguishing between two different kinds of inflationary capabilities. *Hyperinflationary capabilities* include those capabilities that everyone cannot exercise to an equal level because these capabilities involve having a competitive edge. The material basis required to exercise hyperinflationary capabilities increases as others acquire more of the material basis to exercise the capability. Being able to host with pride is a *hyperinflationary capability*: for people to host with pride requires that they stay ahead of friends, neighbours and associates and so not everyone can have an equal material basis for the exercise of this capability. In contrast, *homeostatic inflationary capabilities* are not inflationary in this way because everyone can have the same material basis for the capability and everyone can exercise it equally. Homeostatic inflationary capabilities include our earlier examples of the telegraph and the use of credit cards.

Hyperinflationary capabilities are those that we employ to 'keep ahead of the Joneses'. It is implausible to think that consumers will reach a state of equilibrium in the exercise of hyperinflationary capabilities, for the value of being the best is embedded in the situation and others will strive to gain the material bases to exercise this capability, thereby upping the ante. Hyperinflationary capabilities plausibly include being able to host with pride, being able to provide the best education for one's children, being able to be the best dressed, and being able to be the highest paid person in one's group. By way of contrast, homeostatic inflationary capabilities include those capability bundles that allow one to 'keep up with the Joneses'. These homeostatic inflationary capabilities more easily allow for an equilibrium that does not require upping the ante once the ratchet has been tightened. Homeostatic inflationary capabilities include being able to keep abreast of one's competition and being able to appear in public without shame.

The distinction between these two kinds of inflationary capability bundles creates an opening for acceptable public policy. There is a history of public policies that inhibit, with taxation, conspicuous consumption. Inhibiting conspicuous consumption through taxation is one way of preventing the erosion of the living standard due to the exercise of hyperinflationary capability bundles.

The effects of inhibiting conspicuous consumption through taxation include reducing some consumption in the race to 'get ahead of the Jones', diminishing displays of conspicuous consumption that less wealthy consumers often try to imitate, and raising tax dollars to fund government programs. These effects, although salutary, would have only a modest impact on the Ratchet Effect's erosion of the standard of living. We must look elsewhere to find a viable way in public policy to enhance more significantly those capabilities undermined by the Ratchet Effect.

Time, Capabilities, and the Living Standard

The Ratchet Effect diminishments of the living standard typically involve the reduction of available time to exercise the other capabilities which are part of living at decent standard of living. These other capabilities involve everything from family relationships to political participation. It will be helpful to be clear about the capabilities involved and so we will briefly explore Martha Nussbaum's list of central human capabilities:[8]

1. Life: Being able to live to the end of a normal human life.

2. Bodily Health: Being able to have good health, adequate shelter, adequate nourishment.

3. Bodily Integrity: Being able to move from place to place, to be secure against assault (including sexual and domestic assault).

4. Senses, Imagination, Thought: Being able to use the senses, to imagine, think, and reason in a way informed and cultivated by education and training; to be able to express oneself in spiritual or artistic works and events; to be able to search for the ultimate meaning of life in one's own way.

5. Emotions: Being able to develop attachments, to love and grieve; to not have one's emotional development blighted by overwhelming fear, anxiety, or neglect.

6. Practical Reason: Being able to form a conception of the good and engage in critical reflection.

---

[8] The list is an abbreviated combination of two versions. One is from her esssay, 'The Good As Discipline, As Freedom' (Nussbaum, 1998, pp. 318–20,) and the other is from *Women and Human Development* (Nussabaum, 2000, pp. 78–80). In 'The Good As Discipline, As Freedom' Nussbaum writes that 'citizens should have all these capabilities, whatever else they have. Politically, we may think of this as an account of what quality of life measurements should measure' (p. 318). In *Women and Human Development* she does not make the claim about quality of life measurements but leaves this as a question to be addressed in another context (p. 77).

7. Affiliation: Being able to live with and toward others; being able to engage in various forms of social interaction; being able to be treated as a dignified being whose worth is equal to that of others. The latter entails protections against discrimination.

8. Other Species: Being able to live with concern for and in relation to animals, plants, and the world of nature.

9. Play: Being able to laugh, to play, to enjoy recreational activities.

10. Control Over One's Environment:
    A. Political: Being able to participate effectively in political choices that govern one's life.
    B. Material: Being able to hold property, not just formally but in terms of real opportunity; having property rights and the right to seek employment on an equal basis with others; having the freedom from unwarranted search and seizure.

Nussbaum claims that these capabilities are the minimum required to live a worthwhile life. Yet because of the consumption that causes the Ratchet Effect, we no longer have sufficient time to exercise some of the capabilities on Nussbaum's list:

1. Being able to use imagination and thought in connection with experiencing and producing self-expressive works.

2. Being able to search for the ultimate meaning of life in one's own way.

3. Being able to live with and toward others and to engage in various forms of social interaction.

4. Being able to laugh, to play, to enjoy recreational activities.

5. Being able to participate effectively in political choices.

To have fully any of these capabilities requires that one have adequate time away from work to exercise them. Without sufficient time away from work, the above capabilities only exist in some formal sense — which is neither what Nussbaum[9] nor Sen intends, nor what we measure when we use capabilities to assess the standard of living. A person would lack a decent living standard, measured on the capability approach, if the best job available paid so little that she had to work more than one job. Working more than one job does not allow the leisure required to create self-expressive works, to engage in socially interact with family and friends, to participate effectively in political choices, or to play and enjoy recreational activities. It follows that to have the capa-

---

[9] Nussbaum writes that 'by insisting on. . . combined capabilities, I insist on the twofold importance of material and social circumstances, both in training. . . and in letting them express themselves once trained; and . . . that the liberties and opportunities . . . [are] not . . . purely formal' (Nussbaum, 2000, p. 86).

bility bundles on Nussbaum's list one must also have work that pays a sufficient wage so that one job provides for food, clothing, housing, medical care, as well as incidentals. This is a second public policy implication of our discussion: that persons have access to jobs that pay a living wage.

I introduced the need for a living wage because such a wage is required for a worker to have the time needed to exercise those capabilities that constitute a decent standard of living. Yet this is only a step toward solving the problems raised by the Ratchet Effect. While many US workers are not paid a living wage, many US workers do make a living wage but nonetheless often feel pressed, harried, and unable to exercise the capabilities on Nussbaum's list. We need a further mechanism to address the widespread complaint from working US consumers that they do not have enough time.

This complaint by US workers about the scarcity of free time has substance. US workers in 2000 averaged 1978.3 working hours during the year. These long work hours are not needed for industrial nations to produce products that are competitive on world markets. The average hours worked per year by those in Europe is 1650, or almost nine weeks less of 40 hours per week work. In the Netherlands the average worker in 2000 worked 1365 hours. That is over fifteen fewer weeks of work per year than the average US worker spends on the job.[10] Echoing the theme of raising the standard of living by enhancing basic human capabilities, former Dutch prime minister Ruud Lubbers wrote:

> The Dutch are not aiming to maximize gross national product per capita. Rather, we are seeking to attain a high quality of life. Thus, while the Dutch economy is very efficient per working hour, the number of working hours per citizen is rather limited. . . . We like it that way. Needless to say, there is more room [time] for all those important aspects of our lives that are not part of our jobs (Lubbers, 1997, pp. 14–5).

One obvious public policy approach to the scarcity of time away from work for the US worker is to shorten the work week. This would provide more time for workers to exercise the capabilities essential to a decent standard of living. This policy change would not require that people work a shorter week, only that the shorter week becomes the new official standard and that the shorter week pays a living wage. This would permit all workers with jobs to exercise the capabilities on Nussbaum's list for which they currently do not have time and, thereby, would raise the standard of living by mitigating the consumption of the living standard.

There are strong precedents for these changes. There is currently an active living wage movement in the United States which has won impor-

---

[10] The source of these statistics is *Key Indicators of the Labour Market*, edited by International Labour Office (Routledge, 2001), Table 6b.

tant victories in a number of localities. In addition, the move to shorten the work week has a long history. In 1933, the US Senate passed a bill that would have made 30 hours the official American workweek (the bill was not acted upon in the Congress). More recently, many European nations have shortened their work weeks. Currently there is a US nationwide initiative called 'Take Back Your Time Day' to challenge the epidemic of overwork, over-scheduling and time famine that now threatens health, family, relationships, and communities (http://www. simpleliving. net/timeday/).

Shortening the work week would have another positive effect on the living standard. Many people who would like to work cannot now find a job. With a shortened work week employers would be faced with the choice of either paying extra for overtime or hiring new workers. It is not implausible to think that employers would prefer to hire new workers and that the number of people who are unemployed would diminish, especially if public policy were used to support employers who did so. For example, the tax revenues generated by taxing conspicuous consumption and tax revenues paid by the newly employed could be directed to offering tax relief to employers who hire new workers for shorter work-week jobs at a living wage. Once these policies were in place, recently unemployed people would have the resources to exercise basic capabilities in a way that many of them lacked when they were unemployed. This too would raise the US standard of living.

Summary

To the degree that consumers acquire a gufty to stay abreast of the competition or to maintain or improve their individual positions in a competitive situation, to that degree consumers collectively would be better off without this consumption because the added costs and burdens of the gufty produce no collective benefit. Since this is a problem for consumers collectively, it is one that invites a public policy response. One possibility is to use public policy to encourage only noninflationary capability bundles that produce no Ratchet Effect and to discourage inflationary capability bundles, but this is unworkable because too many inflationary capability bundles are woven into contemporary life. We can develop a more viable public policy approach by distinguishing between hyperinflationary capabilities ('being able to get ahead of the Jones') and homeostatic inflationary capabilities ('being able to keep up with the Jones'). There are precedents for using tax policy to inhibit the exercises of hyperinflationary capabilities that typically result in conspicuous consumption, but these tax policies at best would only provide a modest mitigation against the erosion of the living standard by the consumption of gufties. Hence, the question arises: can we directly enhance the capabilities that the consumption of gufties diminishes?

Many of the capabilities that constitute Nussbaum's list of what is required for a decent life require more time than the average US worker has available. The question is whether we can directly provide more time for US workers. Two policy proposals would do exactly this. The first is to raise the minimum wage so that it becomes a living wage and no one has to work more than one job. The second is to shorten the living-wage work week. Each of these policies have precedents. From the perspective of the capability approach to the standard of living, these two policies would raise the living standard of US workers and bring their living standard closer to the living standard of the average European worker. These two policies would support the creation of new jobs that would further increase the US living standard. Most importantly, enhanced by taxation on conspicuous consumption, these two public policies promoting a shorter work week at a living wage would go a long way toward mitigating the erosion of the US living standard caused by the Ratchet Effect.[11]

[11] Versions of this paper were presented at a Pacific Division APA Meeting in Berkeley; at Macalester College; at Humboldt State University; at Miami University, Ohio; and at the Conference on Philosophy and Its Public Role at Chatham College. I am much indebted to the comments and suggestions that participants have made on these occasions.

James W. Child

Globalization, Technology and the New Economy

Threats to the Nation-State:
Rethinking the Liberal Solution to Government Power

Liberal suspicion of government power goes back, at least, to Locke and the American founders, and survives to this day. All in all, it has stood us in good stead. There are, however, new forces afoot and it is time we liberals rethought our deep reflexive suspicion of, or even aversion to government power. No one would counsel throwing the baby out with the bath water. Large parts of the liberal solution to government power must be kept and carefully guarded. Unrestrained government is and always will be a danger: at best a problem, at worst a nightmare. But today we face new forces as threatening as over-powerful government and the emergence of dictatorship. There are forces of anarchy abroad, the very kind of forces that government (especially the nation-state) was originally formed to protect us from.

The sovereignty of the nation-state is under attack from a variety of directions. At least three factors are causing the weakening and decline of the nation-state. First are non–governmental organizations (NGOs) whose self-conscious intention is the destruction, or at least the weakening of certain states or of all nation-states, e.g. al Qaeda, the Cali drug cartel. Second are NGOs, largely benign and pacific, whose deleterious effects upon the institution of the nation-state and its sovereignty are not intentional or self-conscious, but are profound nonetheless, e.g. the World Bank, Amnesty International, Citicorp. Third are historical forces driving technological, economic and social change, the causes and effects of which are mostly unknown to those involved and affected, e.g. the development of the Internet, the globalization of banking, the internationalization of popular culture.

In fact, the first of these, i.e., the entities self-consciously deleterious to organized government, are not so new after all. They are often atavisms harking back to the Mediaeval and early modern periods, at least in Europe. The Middle Ages and the early Modern period were rife with forces that would destroy government as a matter of purpose or as a double-effect of their main aspirations. The means used by such 'gangs' included the razing of cities, and the wholesale killing of prisoners of war and innocents. Court conspiracies featured a bewildering variety of pretenders and/or usurpers, each supported by their personal coterie. These conspirators utilized torture, kidnapping, the poisoning of friends and relatives, and child murder among other means to advance their causes. Legal formalities either did not exist or served as the thinnest rationalization for struggles of raw political and military power. Where courts, even in name, could be found at all, trumped up charges and thoroughly corrupted officials were the norm. The contenders for power were *inter alios* a variety of clerical and monastic organizations, the nobility, independent cities, various unemployed *condottieri* and their mercenary forces and, occasionally, armies of disaffected, and usually starving, peasants. All these forces and factions plotted, clashed and struggled in a world without the rule of law and usually without any real, well ordered, centralized national government.

On a smaller scale, parties of highwayman, whole families of thieves and small bands of disaffected men at arms or deserting soldiers made travel unsafe, even for fairly large parties. Various armed bands and rogue forces often posed a greater threat to life, liberty and property than the forces of nation-states with over-powerful central governments (Davis, 1983). Indeed, states, or at least strong centralized rulers, represented greater security than the general anarchy typical of life during this period. This attitude is evident and explicit in the work of Thomas Hobbes, who greatly feared rogue forces, disorder and sectarian strife. His solution was a very strong central government somewhat insensitive to issues of the rule of law and, even more, to civil liberties. Its job was *protection*, pure and simple.

New (Old) International Threats to the Nation-State

Today, the nation-state is beset by a plethora of destructive forces and hostile agents. This compounds the effects of growing, uncontrollable weaknesses and instabilities in the national form of social organization. These weaknesses are naturally induced by technology and globalization. But we are most aware of the hostile parties who loudly threaten and occasionally impose great suffering upon citizens of nation states. Among such hostile agents are terrorists and international organized crime. Facilitating them are a variety of vaguely licit havens where taxes can be avoided, questionable banking can be done, where corporations with dubious or even flagrantly illicit purposes can be formed and can 'reside', where secret e–mail addresses can be put off-limits to authorities, where drugs, illegal arms, stolen art treasures, currency, trade secrets and other technology, pirated copyrighted material and illegal aliens are traded and shipped like wheat and machine tools. These opportunities cannot all be found in one place (except perhaps on the Internet). However, they can each be found variously in the Cayman Islands, Belize, Turkish Cyprus, Thailand, Columbia, Switzerland, the Netherlands, Finland, among many places.

Worse yet, these groups and organizations are forming across national boundaries. Both terrorism and organized crime are becoming internationalized. The modern state has no means of controlling its nationals involved in such activities abroad, or even to adequately police its own borders when it comes to such contraband. Most of all, it cannot control Internet traffic in and out of its country. This, as we shall see, is crucial and will become even more so. As Stephen Krasner says, '. . . technological change has made it very difficult, or perhaps impossible, for states to control movement across their borders . . .' (Krasner, 2001, p. 21).

As the task of controlling borders gets more difficult, those who would ignore them grow stronger and more daring. Participants in international organized crime include old stand–bys like the Italian and Sicilian Mafias and the Columbian drug cartels. But they also include some relative newcomers (at least to *international* crime) such as the Russian 'mafia', the Chinese triads, the Japanese *yakuza* and a number of hitherto parochially American groups which are now acquiring global reach. These include organizations such as the Dixie mafia, prison gangs like the Aryan Brotherhood and a variety of street gangs such as the Crips, the Bloods and the Hell's Angels. Last, but certainly the most dangerous, are overtly terrorist organizations that engage in various income-producing activities beyond their primary mission of waging war on all and sundry. These 'gainful' activities range from kidnapping and blackmail to the drug trade.

The similarities of these organizations, activities and the situations they create to the near anarchy prevailing in much of the mediaeval and early modern world is chilling. As Philip Bobbit puts it: 'Groups of bored and armed young men, quasi-mercenaries (as in Columbia) or quasi-soldiers (as in Somalia) are not so different in kind from small bands that fought the wars of the Middle Ages. . . . Bandits, robbers, guerrillas, gangs have always been part or the domestic security environment. What is new is access to mechanized weapons' (Bobbit, 2002, p. 217).

Understanding Change in the Nature of the Nation-State: The Decline of Sovereignty

The Concept of Sovereignty

The dramatic and portentous social and economic changes wrought by the Internet will force us to change our analytic framework and conceptual apparatus. Consider the vastly important and long-honored notion of sovereignty (van Creveld, 1999; Spryt, 1994; Morris, 1998; Hall, 1989). What will befall it and the states to which it pertains in the era of the Internet and its associated technologies? Contemporary information and communication technology roughly groupable under the rubric 'Internet', threatens to end sovereignty as we have known it since the rise of the nation-state.

In principle, at least, we may be facing a stateless, fully-wired world where voluntary contractual relations are the only binding forces (Dyson, 1997; Rosecrance, 1999; Strange, 1996). This sounds like a utopian answer to an anarchist prayer, and it may not be anything more likely than that, although it would no doubt be more like a Hobbesian nightmare than utopia. But, even if society never evolves to a point of pure statelessness, several questions still pertain. Will society develop in this direction and if it does can the nation-state work as a long term social model? If it does work, what valuable social functions will be lost as sovereignty and even, perhaps more broadly, political authority weaken? Before we explore these important issues, let us first review some of the basic concepts employed in the analysis of the notion of sovereignty.

Traditionally sovereignty has been defined as *a monopoly on the legitimate use of force or threat of force to conform the subject's behaviour to its mandates.* This definition, suitable adjustments being made, is due to Max Weber (Garth, 1945). When one limits the range and effectiveness of the use of force or threats of force to obtain the traditional ends of government, one limits sovereignty. As we shall see, the Internet and associated technologies impose such limits.

The notion of sovereignty and the sovereign state was born in the work of Jean Bodin and Thomas Hobbes. It received its canonical legal formulation in the work of the nineteenth-century legal thinker, John Austin. While its roots, like those of most Western political concepts, can be traced to the Greeks and to mediaeval political thought, the concept is thoroughly modern. This is because it arose concomitantly with the historical development of the nation-state and to some extent it depends logically on that history.

In theory a sovereign power has three signal features. First, it is the *highest authority* in any legal or political system. To use an oft used but handy notion, sovereign power *trumps* the power of any other institution or person in the land. In the United Kingdom the Queen in Parliament is sovereign because that (somewhat artificial) institution is, in theory, the highest decision maker and dispute settler in England. No other decision-maker or arbiter has more power in any case.

Second, it is the *final* or *ultimate* authority in the land. It would seem obvious that the highest power must also be the final authority, although in some federal systems this may not be so. Moreover it is clear that an authority can be final without being the highest authority. A true sovereign is both. Third, a true sovereign cannot be influenced, nor its decisions altered, by a foreign power or institution. A sovereign power is *independent*.

Of course, sovereignty is a formal and analytical concept. No nation-state was ever perfectly sovereign. However, there have been polities that approached closer to it and others that obviously failed even to come close. Our concern is to understand the nature of this continuum of states of sovereignty and especially how it has evolved over recent history.

The History of Sovereignty

Bodin and Hobbes formulated the classical notion of sovereignty in the seventeenth century. However, it had been at least approximated a hundred years earlier, during the era of 'absolute monarchy'. Yet, even such powerful monarchs as Henry VIII were not, in real life, quite so sovereign in their own person as Bodin's theoretical monarch or Hobbes' Leviathan. The Roman Catholic Church as an institution, specific religious orders and particular monasteries and abbots, the great noble families, and quasi-independent cities with their powerful guilds, all limited the achievement of complete sovereignty. Still this was the beginning of the high tide of near absolute sovereignty. The Treaty of Westphalia, 1648, which ended the Thirty Years War, is often identified as the official recognition of the nation-state 'system'. Subsequently the reign of Louis XIV became a paradigm of the nation-state.

In the eighteenth century, certain political developments began an erosion of the political possibility of true sovereignty. The movement toward *democracy* limited sovereignty. After all, democracy makes the people sovereign, so that a sort of circular path of authority emerges. The people are ruled (the subjects) so they occupy the bottom of any hierarchy of authority. But if they are ultimately sovereign in that they elect their own leaders, they also occupy the top of the same hierarchy.

Another limitation of sovereignty developing contemporaneously was *constitutionalism*. If a constitution is the supreme law of the land and cannot be unilaterally changed by a king or a parliament then that person or that body is not sovereign. Sometimes this fact is expressed by saying the constitution is sovereign, although this is confusing if not downright confused. However, it is clear that the existence of a true constitution prevents the ruler (or rulers) from being fully sovereign.

The most obvious limitation on sovereignty is *federalism*. 'Federalism', in this sense, is the preservation of the highest and final authority in one area of governmental concern exclusively for one 'sovereign' while another concern might be reserved to the other 'sovereign'. In the United States, a federal system, the supreme courts and legislatures of the several states are sovereign when it comes to things like tort law and the law of wills and probate, for example. The federal government is sovereign with regard to foreign policy and interstate commerce among other functions. Besides the United States federal systems include the Federal Republic of Germany and, at least in an early form, the European Union.

One would think that the most important source of erosion of sovereignty would be the dramatic growth in international trade and banking beginning in the nineteenth century and continuing until today. All of this interaction has created a great deal of *economic interdependence*. There was a so-called 'first globalization' of trade and banking, protected by the great British Fleet in the nineteenth century. It cut against the true economic independence of nation-states as required by the strict definition of the concept of sovereignty. Yet economic independence had never been a primary part of the concept of sovereignty. It has always be based more on political, legal, and military independence. Sovereignity continued to be the organizing principle, at least formally in international law and in both national and international politics until 1945 and in the most formal ways until the present.

Sovereignty and the Internet

As we have seen, the notion of absolute sovereignty was dramatically limited by the development of federalism, constitutionalism and democracy, as well as by growing economic interdependence among nations. Still the basic idea of a state that is, in principle, supreme and independent over the affairs of its subjects survives altered but recognizable. The development of the Internet (and associated technology and practices) has, however, changed this at a far deeper level than the three institutions mentioned above. So different is the international world, especially in economics, that it almost cannot be over-estimated. As Richard Rosecrance puts it:

> We are entering a world where the most important resources are the least tangible − where land is less important than an educated populace, where stockpiles of goods, capital and labor are less valuable than flows, and where parochial interests less than the international economy as a whole....But where the products of land no longer determine market and power relationships, a new form of state is being born: the virtual nation, a nation based on mobile capital, labor and information (Rosecrance, 1999, pp. 3–4).

The Internet renders a major part of communication and economic activity *invisible* to the nation-state and its government; both within and across borders. That which is invisible is beyond control. A vast area of human social and economic life, heretofore subject to the control (or at least potential control) of the nation-state, is now beyond its ken. And it was through this erstwhile control that sovereignty arose and was exercised. What cannot be practically and effectively controlled cannot be taxed, regulated, or made the subject of legal enforcement. If enough human activity thus falls outside the real physical and legal control of the alleged 'sovereign power' then anything even approximating true sovereignty disappears.

Consider a few examples of activity still subject to sovereign power, and what sorts of activity, heretofore subjected to it, now escape its control. Among the things that are still controllable are: (a) the production and transportation of 'hard products' such as food products, autos or houses. However, the manufacture of these must not involve information flows from or to another jurisdiction across borders (call this last exception regarding not crossing borders *Proviso I*); (b) the means of physical transport of people and their belongings, subject to *Proviso I*; (c) trade in hard goods, subject to *Proviso I*; (d) exclusively face to face meetings and rallies; (e) access to homes and work places. (Even in these areas delineated above, borders for people and ordinary freight are growing more and more porous, as volumes of travel and trade balloon and practical limitations of cost and efficiency grow, limiting the thoroughness of inspection.)

Of the things that are now uncontrollable are: (a) all sorts of one to one communication: personal, business, financial, political, entertainment, via e-mail and via meetings and other multi-person interactions held in cyberspace; (b) the Internet in interactive real time or recorded and broadcast later; (c) mass audience performances and speeches broadcast by streaming video in real time or recorded; (d) the production and conveyance of information products and services, e.g. insurance, banking, other corporate services (data processing, accounting, personnel management, recruiting and employment services, etc.), entertainment products (music, games), news and current events, information and research services, etc.; and (e) the information component of manufacturing hard goods, e.g. computer aided design, computer aided manufacturing, remote plant floor control, materials purchasing, inventory management, cost accounting, e -business purchases and sales, etc. This means that a wide variety of social, economic and political activities that have heretofore been, at least in principle, *public* are now *private* and at least in principle *strongly private* i.e. beyond the practically possible reach of sovereign power.

But why is this development so different from the adjustments sovereign power has had to accommodate in the development of federalism, democracy or constitutionalism? The difference is that these earlier developments, whatever limitations they impose on sovereignty, keep the basic monopoly of military and police power in the hands of the state; thus it is as ultimately powerful as ever. Democracy, constitutions and federalism are *normative* limitations on sovereignty. A determined sovereign can transgress them as easily as we can break a law. Limits are composed of various norms, primarily written constitutions, statutes, case law and legal procedures that can be contravened by naked power. Unfortunately such norms are sometimes honoured in the breach and occasionally overtly repudiated altogether. This might mean military takeover of a previously constitutional system, or just the wholesale ignoring of constitutional provisions by refractory police or prosecutorial agencies. The internet and concomitant developments, on the other hand, severely curtail the *actual effective power* of government by shrinking the practical *possibility of enforcement* over a wide area of economic, social and political activity. Any theory of sovereignty makes the maintenance of this monopoly of force at least a necessary condition. If the state cannot apply force to broad areas of behaviour, especially economic and political behaviour, or if it cannot have timely knowledge of areas where force may be needed, then sovereignty lapses. So, in theory, sovereignty fails for any fully networked society. In practice it is substantially diminished. But how does this substantial decrement in sovereign power actually come about? Geoff Mulgan tells us that, given the effects on sovereignty discussed above:

> As a consequence political power has neither the tools nor the authority to achieve the goals set forth by the public. The tools no longer work because mobile people and assets are harder to tax or to command and authority is deficient because a culture of skepticism assumes the worst before the best (Mulgan, 1998, p. 189).

The Limitations of External Control of Internet Traffic

So the very nature of both political power and Internet communications respectively make control realistically impossible. What are some of the conditions which limit the possibility of using adequate coercive force to establish sovereignty?

1)   A state cannot employ effective coercive force if it doesn't have adequate resources. Yet genuine comprehensive control of the Internet would be beyond the realistic economic capacity of even the richest nations. It would require the real time reception and analysis of *all Internet traffic*.

2)   A state cannot employ force or coercion against *parties* unknown.

3) A state cannot employ force to arrest *behaviour* that is unknown to its own agencies.

4) The vast *volume of signals* over the Internet makes the discovery, interception and use of any particular information difficult to find and access. Indeed, doing so in real time is already nearly impossible in many cases according to the Cooperative Association for Internet Data Analysis (CAIDA).

5) The fact that the Internet is *a network of autonomous networks* and not a structured hierarchical command system means that interception of specific signals at specific times is virtually impossible. To quote one authority, Patrick Foxhoven, Chief Information Officer of CentraComm Communications: 'In regard to the possibility of monitoring the Internet, *it simply cannot be done.* [Ignoring the] . . . encryption issues, the Internet is still just a collection of networks, public and private. There isn't any one governing force that oversees everything . . . traffic from one network flowing into another isn't always consistent. Traffic sent one way doesn't always return the same way. . . . This changes a countless number of times to insure quality of service. Therefore it makes prediction even where it will pass nearly impossible' (private correspondence).

6) *Interception over land lines is very difficult.* Without physically locating and obtaining access to the line eavesdropping is impossible. Such access on a very wide basis logistically and economically is implausible.

7) However, the eavesdropper is on the horns of a dilemma. For just as tapping land lines is difficult so is the alternative, *viz.* intercepting wireless Internet communications. The wireless eavesdropper faces the complications of a wide variety of wavelengths, systems that continually shift wavelengths, mobile directional broadcast and reception, and other devices. All such devices drive up the complexity, the time required to capture and process the signal, and thus the cost, of systematic and effective eavesdropping. Indeed, given the growing amount and complexity of traffic on the Internet, eavesdropping on all or even large segments of Internet traffic is becoming a practical impossibility.

8) Indeed, without sufficient information about the sender, the message and the receiver, interception will be impossible. Old-fashioned detective work, surveillance and interception of other forms of media (e.g. telephone taps, bugs, mail covers, etc.) can garner such information with much greater efficiency and at a fraction of the cost.

9)   *Ordinary encryption is in regular use now by private as well as govern-ment entities.* It is available through commercially-sold software systems which take intense attention, effort, time and resources to break. This increases the difficulty and cost of effective, systematic eavesdropping.

10)   In the '90s a revolutionary system called *two key encryption* came into use. It has all but sounded the death knell for practical, effective interception and decryption of Internet messages encrypted in the appropriate manner (Diffe, 1998, pp. 210–8; Gardiner, 1977, chap. 2 and pp. 120–4). So dramatic is this development that some authorities have predicted a new world of so-called *strong privacy* which would protect with absolute assurance ordinary people and businesses of all sizes from outside, including especially government intrusion (Friedman, 1995, pp. 264–70). Conversely, it will pose nearly insuperable limitations on governments in regard to taxing, control (or even knowledge) of funds flows, control of borders with regard to information, ordinary law enforcement, communication and coordination of all sorts of other activity. For societies that attempt to spy on political communication, it would become virtually impossible.

11)   Along with practically unbreakable encryption comes the development of the *anonymous remailer* who remails your electronic correspondence from a different address, usually in another country. After stripping any identifying marks from it he mails it from his address on to its final destination. Unless he reveals it, no one could find out the original source of the communication. This means that the intended recipient need not know its source. However, the real revolution is that anyone tapping the line, including most importantly, government agencies, cannot know the identity of the real sender. Some countries are already protecting the identity of the user of anonymous remailers like the Swiss protect bank account information. Finland especially has very tight protections of anonymous remailers and their customers. This protection would be effective even in those cases where the final destination is an e-mail address in one's own country.

Together virtually unbreakable encryption and anonymous remailers make for completely unprecedented 'strong' privacy. But of course the privacy of the individual and other private entities means dramatic new weakness for governments wishing to monitor or control citizen communication or merely to track criminals and terrorists and to perform legitimate taxing functions. Thus, it presents a fundamental weakening of the possibility of genuine *sovereignty*.

Power, Authority and its Limitations
in a Networked World

The Architecture of Power: From Hierarchy to Network

A nation-state assumes a pyramidal configuration both as regards authority and information. Information flows from bottom to top. At the peak of the organization a very few individuals shape the raw information into knowledge. On the basis of what they formulate, those at the top exert their authority downward through the organization by implementing general policies or specific orders. Control flows from top to bottom. This sort of organization and operation characterizes the United States Army's First Infantry Division, General Electric, the Anti-Trust Division of the Justice Department, the American Red Cross and virtually every other large organization.

The Internet is fundamentally different. It is a network composed of individual users, portals, search engines, commercial sites, public information sites and much more. It has no top, no bottom and no centre. It is not 'constructed' in accord with some previously formulated plan. It *evolves* (Kelly, 1994; Johnson, 2001). It is almost wholly voluntary. There are virtually no true 'orders' given on it. Instead there are advisory recommendations, hypothetical directions, information sources and a myriad of other opportunities. But virtually all are based on the voluntary consent of all parties involved.

Two of the proponents of the superiority of networks over hierarchies are Ester Dyson and Manuel Castells. Dyson says: 'The greatest structural impact of the Net is decentralization; things and people no longer depend upon the center to be connected . . .' (Dyson, 1997, p. 8). Manuel Castells, makes much the same point when he tells us: '. . . the new information technologies unleashed the power of networking and decentralization, actually undermining the centralization of one way institutions and vertical bureaucratic surveillance' (Castells, 1997, p. 30).

Network organization is more egalitarian and more inclined to encourage freedom, initiative and innovation throughout the organization. This is because each participant is far more *independent* than those involved in hierarchical organizations. Lest we appear to join the ranks of the uncritical partisans of network organization, let us balance issues by considering several things. Command (hierarchical) systems are very good at a number of things like fighting wars or planning and executing other large complex sets of rational goal directed plans, e.g. the building of the Panama Canal or carrying out the Apollo space program. It is just that the Internet is appropriately a *networked organization* without any significant hierarchy. Besides, it is not as though we have a choice. The Internet, given what it is, simply *cannot be* a top down, hierarchical system. Periodically we still hear some US congressman or Federal Com-

munications Commisioner or some policy expert claim that the
government 'must take control' of the Internet lest the heavens will fall.
But for the most part this is confused thinking or sheer ignorance that
would produce self-frustrating policies and fail in the end. It is rather
like the French trying to control changes in the French language with a
committee of language professors and other 'experts'. Languages and
internets are just not those kinds of things.

From Networks to 'Free Information'

One of the most important consequences of a networked world is that
the cost of information plummets, approaching 0 in the limit. This is true
whether we talk of transmitting information or storing it or manipulat-
ing it. These processes are a tiny fraction of their pre-Internet cost. In a
prescient article in 1998 Robert Koehane and Joseph Nye have pointed
out that:

> What is new is the virtual erasing of costs of communicating over distances as
> a result of the information revolution. Actual transmission costs have become
> negligible; hence the amount of information that can be transmitted is effec-
> tively infinite . . . the dramatic cheapening of information transmission has
> opened the field to loosely structured network organizations. . . . These NGOs
> and networks are particularly effective at penetrating states without regard
> to borders (Koehane, 1998, p. 83).

Indeed, determining the pre-Internet cost of information is often little
more than a theoretical exercise. Before technology provided us with
such powerful information conveyance and handling many tasks
involving massive information use were simply *impossible*, beyond the
ken of technical feasibility. It is rather like calculating the thousands of
horses it would take to draw the same load as a railroad locomotive. We
can simply *do things we could not do before*, including create and present
information in ways never imagined. This has so fundamentally
changed our technology and economy that to talk in popular terms
about the conveyance of quantities of information is to miss the point.
New things are possible! Kinds of knowledge in forms unknown to us
before are now available. Virtually unthinkable before the information
revolution, they are now easy to imagine, formulate, request and use in
economics, business, law, medicine and natural science and many other
disciplines. It is a *revolution* of mammoth proportions.

Internationalism and the Internet

The Internet forms a myriad of interconnections across national boundaries. But this is not unique. Telephone systems and radio and TV do
this. Even airline routes form complicated patterns of nodes and connections. However, the Internet has unique properties that make it threatening to sovereignty and the state. Gordon Graham puts it very well:

> The internationalism of the Internet lies not merely in the fact that it connects people across nations, for many human devices and activities do this. The point is rather that the use and the exploration of the Internet are wholly *indifferent* to international boundaries (Graham, 1999, p. 86).

Most of us have had the experience of researching a topic on the Internet, say the paintings of Goya, and suddenly realizing that without planning or even intending one has ended up in the Prado in Madrid (virtually at least). If it is sometimes hard to tell what country we are 'in' it is far more difficult for the government to tell 'where we are' or 'where we have been'. This is so with even modest efforts to efface the record of travels on the Internet. It makes it almost impossible for a government to *effectively forbid* travel to certain Internet sites or to *stop it*. There is always a route from 'here to there' and usually with anonymity. Efforts by some governments to control or curtail their citizens' use of the Internet have so far been largely in vain. However, if they should be effective in this effort, it will be at a terrible cost because it could only be done by drastically limiting and controlling Internet traffic between their country and other countries. The cost of this in lost commerce and the retarding of scientific and technical progress would be substantial, perhaps catastrophic. Moreover, the knowledge workers simply will not stand being isolated and kept in the dark. They will read and talk to each other and ultimately subvert information controls. In the last resort they will emigrate. Any nation that loses its very best people to emigration would be crippled even if it is 'completely sovereign'. Some tough types will brook these overwhelming injuries rather than have their sovereignty challenged. They will forbid any Internet providers or modems on pain of serious criminal penalties. They will execute those who try to emigrate. They will be as Orwellian as they need to be. North Korea will do this and maybe a few others. But most will not. The internet is deeply internationalist and it will punish most severely those nations that try to impose strict nationals controls on it.

Nefarious Forces and Anarchy

The Internet and the 'Bad Guys': Terrorists and Mafias

It is easy to think of the Internet as an unqualified boon to humankind. After all it does offer privacy, confidentiality and anonymity to those who really need it. This includes underground democratic movements in dictatorships, honest corporations protecting their hard won intellectual property against industrial espionage and technological pirates. Banking, insurance activities, accounting services and the transfer of confidential medical or technical information are all are morally innocuous and economically beneficial activities. However, they dare not use the Internet without being able to rely on strict confidentiality.

But is the Internet really so unqualifiedly good? No it is not. It affords the same privacy, confidentiality and anonymity to those who pursue malevolent ends. Terrorists, big time drug traffickers, the Mafia and other practitioners of organized crime could, and already do, avail themselves of the advantages of the Internet. All can communicate and plan with impunity. Blackmailers and kidnappers are actually directly facilitated in communication with their victims. Perverted people attempt to contact children on the Internet for the purposes of molestation or pornography. False advertising and confidence games garner protection for frauds and swindles. These and other perverse, and worse, activities are positively, if inadvertently, aided by the anonymity of the Internet.

Of all the various malevolent groups and organizations only two directly threaten the sovereignty of the state. Only two, if victorious, would issue in genuine anarchy: international terrorists and organized crime. True terrorists are nihilists engaging in revolution and violence for its own sake (Teichman, 1989, pp. 505–12; Walzer, 1977, ch. 12). They may have some vague end for which they are terrorizing and killing, although they are much clearer about whom they hate than what exactly they want.

The Michigan Militia may say it is against Jews, African–Americans, immigrants, the Federal government, taxes, the United Nations, the World Trade Organization and on and on. However, without any articulate purpose or clear long term objectives, they seem only bent on destruction and violence as an end in itself. Hamas may claim it seeks only Israel's destruction but then why does it make war against the United States, more broadly 'the West', the UN, moderate Palestinians and even, periodically, Yaser Arafat and other officials of the PLO. There are other extreme terrorist groups (the Real IRA, the Tamil Tigers of Sri Lanka and the Shining Path of Peru) however, the purest example of terrorists we have is surely al Quaeda. They seem interested in killing Americans anywhere, regardless of who they are, where they are or what they are doing. But their fury does not stop with America. Intermittently they are also interested in killing any Westerners, all Israelis, all Jews, Africans (the two embassy bombings) and even peaceful Arabs, a diverse and even incoherent set of targets. They want to kill all of these people for vague and indefinite reasons and with no specific goals beyond mayhem and murder.

A criminal conspiracy by itself does not necessarily represent a direct threat to government (Burke, 1983; Perkins, 1969, pp. 612–36). It surely does not pose an immanent threat of anarchy. A conspiracy under the law, a conspiracy to defraud a corporation, or to steal a car, for example, threatens only the immediate victims. However, the large and highly articulated criminal organizations known as 'mafias' are different. They

represent a strange sort of lawless rival government. In parts of Columbia and in Sicily until the 1980s, mafias have indeed acted like de facto
governments. But wherever they are, they arrogate to themselves key
government functions, such as taxation, expropriation and the administration of their own arbitrary and sometimes savage form of justice. Typically, the members of a mafia's leadership do whatever they want to
whomever they want without fear of interference by the state, the law, or
legal punishment. This is as true for the so called the Russian Mafia, the
Chinese triads, or the Japanese *yakuza* as it is for the original Sicilian
mafia itself. As Susan Strange has pointed out:

> What is new and of importance in the international political economy is the
> network of links being forged between organized groups in different parts of
> the world. . . . As various criminal groups . . . have expanded their activities
> outside their home territories, illegal markets within state boundaries have
> joined together horizontally to form a single world market (Strange, 1996,
> p. 111).

Thus, we now have world markets for cocaine and illegal weapons and
smuggled ancient artifacts as we have world wide markets for micro-
processors, life insurance and soybeans.

What is the effect of all this on the nation state? Manuel Castells captures the point with exactitude:

> The globalization of crime further subverts the nation state, profoundly
> transforming the process of government and actually paralyzing the state in
> many instances. . . . What is new is the *global linkage of organized crime* . . . . What
> is new is the deep penetration and eventual destabilization of national states
> in a variety of contexts under the influence of transnational crime (Castells,
> 1997, p. 259).

It may seem fanciful that such criminal organizations could destroy or
bring an end to centralized government as we know it, especially in a
powerful nation-state like the US or the UK. However, some novelists
have done a good job of picturing a future of anarchical forces and rogue
institutions without anything that resembles a sovereign, legitimate
government anywhere in sight (Gibson, 1986; Stephenson, 1992; Shirley,
2000; Updike, 1998).

Whether a complete demise of government is probable or a descent
into true anarchy is even possible in countries like the United States or
the United Kingdom is not the primary issue, although it is an interesting topic of speculation. The real question is this: will sovereignty and
therefore the legitimate powers of the state wane? More specifically, will
they wane to a point where nefarious and lawless NGOs threaten the
ability of the state to carry out its appropriate function, viz. to *govern* in
the full sense of that word. Will persons and property be reasonably
safe? Will insecurity threaten the quality of life? Will the possibility of
trade and financial transactions be severely limited as a result? Will gov-

ernments be deeply corrupted? Will a robust lawful order continue to prevail? In the face of forces that weaken governments and promote the power of terrorist organizations and various international mafias we face very real threats. We have seen governments in states like Colum- bia, Mexico and even Italy at various times that were genuinely threat- ened and one government, viz., Afghanistan, actually taken over by terrorists.

Characterizing Possible Solutions

This would certainly not be the appropriate venue to recommend spe- cific solutions to the questions set out above. However, we can arrive at some useful generalizations.

(1)   In the face of serious threats from terrorists and organized crime we cannot maintain business as usual. Our way of life will inevitably be changed. It has *already* been changed. Refusing to see it or deal with it will simply make it worse. One has only to look at the New York skyline to be reminded of this. Add to that the use of weapons of mass destruc- tion to complete the grim picture. This is deadly serious business. We must not pretend otherwise.

(2)   On the other hand, simply granting more power willy-nilly to the central governments to spy on, or to interfere with the private lives of its citizens solves nothing. It is quite possible to have both bad outcomes, i.e. a dictatorship that is plagued or even seriously weakened by terror- ism and /or international organized crime.

(3)   What is needed are measures that are carefully *defined* and care- fully *limited* that would be aimed at *specific, narrow objectives* in the fight against terrorism and organized crime and at the same time *would not violate* the core rights of individual citizens.

(4)   Examples of such measures might include the Clipper chip or backdoors designed into encryption programs (Denning, 1996, pp. 659– 63; Denning, 1994) or the computer matching of classes of individuals (Shattuck, 1996, pp. 645–51; Kusserow, 1996, pp. 652–8). However, in a constitutional system of the free lives of individuals, limited govern- ment *must be* hedged around with protections and guarantees against abuse of authority by government officials. The strongest hedge, at least in Anglo-American jurisprudence, is the requirement that any searches or other measures require warrants specific to the case and the parties as issued by an independent court of law.

This last point helps frame what is perhaps the most important issue of all. Such measures as warranted access to encryption programs and databases is merely a logical extension of what has been the norm since the founding of the American republic. Law enforcement can have law- ful access to private homes, private papers and personal communica- tions *but only if* the thing sought is discretely identified and the reason for seeking it is clearly and specifically related to a lawful purpose of government. Said object and purpose must be evaluated and ruled on by a court representing the constitutionally independent judicial branch of government.

It is the new technology including *two key encryption* and other measures that makes possible the movement toward a world of strong privacy. It is *strong privacy* that is new, not the need government has for limited and lawful access to private spaces and communications. That need has always been there and, when limited and controlled by constitution and court, it has proven consonant with free government and free people. There is no reason to believe it will not continue to be so. What would be novel would be giving private parties (including terrorists and organized crime) *unprecedented new privileges* of strong privacy over an ever-weakening central government.

It is worth mentioning just how revolutionary strong privacy is. Imagine that Alonzo and Belinda are plotting to blow up Chicago or Manchester or Winnipeg with a nuclear device. In the first case the two key encryption system that Alonzo and Belinda have been communicating with is on deposit at a special repository managed by the judicial branch of the government. It is secure from anyone else's access unless specific legal steps (resembling the obtaining of a search warrant in the United States) are taken. Access to it by the executive branch, i.e. the police or the prosecutors, is acquired only with a specific court order, granted only on probable cause by a judge acting as part of the judicial branch, a judge sworn to uphold the constitution. Presuming that probable cause exists, the judge will grant the warrant, the code will be broken and the bombing will be prevented.

In case two there is no provision for warrants and no codes on deposit. There is no access to the two key encryption keys. The government has no legal power nor does it have *the physical possibility* of breaking the code (in less than several millions of years.) There is literally nothing the powers of law enforcement can do but sit back and let the city be incinerated. Before September 11, 2001 all of this might have sounded fanciful, a hypothetical case for a philosophy or a constitutional law course perhaps. But we have lost our innocence. Today, only a fool could say that this could not happen.

Strengthening the government's powers in some *carefully defined* and *limited* areas may be necessary. However, there may be other areas, primarily old powers having to do with 'national security' in a Cold War sense, where we could actually remove government powers and strengthen civil liberties. We must strike a delicate balance. The task in hand is akin to that referred to by Yergin and Stanislaw to in their important book, *The Commanding Heights*:

This leaves government a daunting challenge: to figure out ways to reduce their intervention in some areas and to retool and refocus in others, while preserving the public trust. It is a challenge of imagination (Yergin and Stanislaw, 1998, pp. 396–7).

So the issue is not deciding *whether* we want stronger government that interferes more with our freedoms. It is rather reorganizing government so that the interferences we must have address today's dangers and not yesterday's, or worse yet both yesterday's *and* today's dangers. We do not have to choose between an unsafe but free society or a safe but one that is not free. Such thinking is facile and in the extreme simpleminded. As Yergin and Stanislaw say, it takes *imagination* to see new opportunities and new institutional designs. We must understand what we can do that is consistent with our most basic values, as well as what is literally impossible and what is possible. While what we face is not new under the sun, it is surely new to us and the institutional frameworks that we have inherited.

Conclusion

There are two horns of a dilemma embedded in the way humans govern themselves. On one horn we face the prospect of dictatorship or even, at the worst, an Orwellian totalitarian state. Furthermore, democracies can fall into dictatorships with a disconcerting ease, so the danger is there and we must not be blasé about the possibility.

But this must not be our only fear. There is another horn of the dilemma. If we look back a few centuries before the nation-state emerged, we see as the most threatening outcome not dictatorship but anarchy. Such was a very unstable and highly unpleasant world. It was one we should seek to avoid with as much urgency as we seek to avoid dictatorship. For, when compared with dictatorship in today's world, anarchy is at least equally probable, and equally unpleasant as well. We must tend to the power and effectiveness of the nation-state, for we need it more than we have in several centuries. We need the nation-state for managing and making rational the further development of technology and globalization. This is true even though the powers of the nation-state may be waning precisely because of the advance of globalization and technology. But most of all, we need the nation state for protection against violent NGOs that, for whatever reason, seem bent on bloodshed and destruction.

This has certainly not been a plea urging us to rush headlong toward overly strong governments and the denial of democratic and constitutional safeguards. It is meant only to raise the very real possibility that, given the economic and social forces abroad today, the similarly unappealing prospect of anarchy may be at least as probable as dictatorship. At least, it urgently requires our attention and our concern.

Richard Brook[1]

Statistical and
Identifiable Deaths

> The concept of probability is an unusually slippery and puzzling one. For one
> thing it seems to hover uncertainly between objectivity and subjectivity. Talk
> about something being probable or likely seems to reflect some knowledge
> and ignorance — if there were an omniscient God, it is hard to imagine that he
> would regard anything as merely probable — and yet most of our probability
> statements seem to claim some objective or at least inter-personal validity . . .
> (J.L. Mackie, 1973, p. 154).

A nuclear plant is under consideration. I assume, for the purposes of
exposition, that when on line one person in a group of ten thousand at
risk will die from the reactor's radiation who would not have died
because the plant wasn't built. However, the risk to each, given incomplete available evidence, is assumed to be one in ten thousand. (This is
an idealization I make use of. In practice it's extremely difficult to establish each person at risk is relevantly the same; see Shrader-Frechette,
1991, esp. pp. 89–100.) To take a real example the Environmental Protection Agency has calculated in the past that air toxics cause more than
2000 cases of cancer every year. Given that we have no special evidence
who will die we convert the relative frequency to a risk of 1 in 2000 for
each individual. Again we presume no one of the 2000 would have
developed cancer due to those pollutants not being introduced. We
accept as well that there will be significant benefits from the plant for
those at risk. Benefits that include, for example, cheaper electricity and a
significant increase in well being for rate payers.

  We put some further constraints on the problem. The prospective
builder has some significant biological and statistical information (e.g.,
effects of radiation on animal and human populations, relative frequency of accidents etc.) but not enough to identify which person will
die, only a justified belief that one will. We have what's called a 'statisti-

---

[1]   I thank the members of the Conference on Philosophy and its Public Role as well
      as my colleagues Steven Hales and Kurt Smith for comments on earlier drafts.

cal' rather than an 'identifiable' death (Keeney, 1986). Moreover, she can't acquire additional information before she builds. An additional assumption, used now for the sake of argument, is that the builder believes it would be wrong to build if she knew who would die were the plant placed in operation. Suppose she would be able to witness on a special monitor the causal consequences of building the plant. She might see Smith getting cancer and painfully dying in the hospital. Of course she might then warn Smith, and even pay him to leave. To keep my problem in focus, however, assume she won't be able to warn Smith. In that case she would not build the plant. It's not, she insists, a matter of squeamishness. She argues that if she knew the plant would cause Smith's death, then from her point of view the risk to Smith is not slight. He has nothing to gain, and everything to lose. As it is, she truthfully says the measure of the risk to Smith, as to anyone at risk, appears minimal, 1 in 10,000. She claims there is, *ceteris paribus*, a moral distinction between acting in a way that knowingly kills Smith, and acting in a way that, though causing Smith's death, appears to impose on him a slight risk. Ralph Keeney remarked in a letter, 'Many individuals feel that the value of an identifiable life should be greater than a statistical life' (see also Keeney, 1984). An EPA scientist claimed in a phone conversation, 'if one knew who would die by introducing a pesticide or power plant it would be tantamount to murder'. Certainly that overstates the case, although it expresses, I think, a popular view.

Against this view I argue that, with one significant exception, identifiable deaths are no worse than statistical deaths. If I am correct there are salient consequences with respect both to the importance of consent in imposing risk, and to what counts as fairness in distributing risk.

I make some assumptions about probability. (1) The risk of death for a person 'is simply the probability of death for that person' (Shrader-Frechette, 1991, p. 90). (2) Causal determinism is true in the areas considered by risk assessors. Thus the objective probability of those at risk is 1 or 0. Some deny that if any putative event must or must not happen then the concept of objective probability gains no hold since there are no allowable measures between 1 or 0. I don't think anything in the paper hinges on usage here; however, if it's preferable, calling probabilities '1 or 0' will mean respectively 'the event necessarily occurs,' and the 'event necessarily doesn't occur'.[2]

[2] Two accounts of objective probability not relevant to my discussion are (1) the relative frequency interpretation, i.e., the limit of the ratio of As to Bs as the number of Bs approaches infinity, and (2) propensity accounts which take probability to be the propensity of a certain chance set up (flipping a coin) to distribute a certain result, (heads). The first is obviously impractical in risk assessment, the second assumes indeterminism. Hugh Mellor writes: 'In a

Although I offer no defence of determinism its assumption might not, I believe, be contentious for those who impose risks. Indeterminism (based, perhaps on quantum phenomena like radioactive decay), as far as I can ascertain, is not offered in the literature on risk to explain the uncertainty underlying statistical deaths.

Those in the business of estimating risk use finite relative frequencies, for example, the number of deaths in a population subject to air toxics, as a ratio projectible to future populations. Those frequencies are in general, though not invariably, converted to risk estimates for individuals. For example, a health risk site on the World Wide Web states, as preamble, 'individual risk reports are based on statistics for the population group that matches the individual's surveyed characteristics' (see site http://www.you first.com/about.asp). Here risk assessment applies to individuals, the assumption being that each in the risk pool is relevantly the same as those in the population from which the relative frequency was gained. Or, in estimating cancer risks from particulate exposure in Sweden, Margareta Tornquist and L. Ehrenberg, after considering various factors relevant to risk say, 'The risks amount to 50 deaths per 100,000' (Tornquist and L. Ehrenberg, 1994). This is risk to a population, and although a useful statistic for some purposes, (reducing the total number of cancer cases) it is useless for individuals unless converted to estimates of individual risk. These conversions, although controversial, are necessary for people to compare risks of flying vs. driving, wearing or not wearing a seat belt, smoking or not, etc. It is the nature of prudence facing uncertainty that people convert relative frequency data to measures of risk to themselves. Suppose I consider having a heart catheterization where the relative frequency of death from the procedure is 1 out of 350 patients. If, given the best evidence available, I consider myself relevantly the same as those who've had the procedure I will think the chance of my death is 1 in 350. However, it conflates epistemic and ontological considerations to argue that since, given the evidence, I credibly believe I am as unlikely to die from the procedure as anyone else, I am therefore unlikely to die. From the credibility of a belief that one is unlikely to die it can't follow deductively that one is unlikely to die. [3] Though invalid the argument is I think often accepted. Other-

---

deterministic world there would be no propensities' Mellor (1971) quoted by Benenson (1984) p. 51.

[3]   Weatherford quotes R. Von Mises (1957, p. 377): 'The phrase, "the probability of death" when it refers to a single person has no meaning at all for us' (Weatherford, 1982, p. 161). The exception, of course, is when a person is objectively as likely as any other in the risk pool to die; that is, when the death is random. Then the conversion of relative frequency to a measure of individual risk compares to an example in classical probability, e.g., the chance of getting a three on the toss of a die whose sides are equally likely to appear.

wise we couldn't explain why people use finite relative frequencies in choosing or advocating an individual course of action. The argument is inductive, facing the special problem of the 'single case', how to go from statistical facts about populations to measures of individual risk.

In any case the measures of probabilities by the plant builder and those in the risk pool are epistemic, that is, numbers between 1 and 0 inclusive which measure the credibility of a belief about individual risk relative to incomplete background information. Not being directly about the world but rather about the credibility of a belief about the world these measures might be thought a form of subjective probability. On the other hand if 'level of credibility' is itself an objective notion then unlike subjective probability it doesn't simply measure the strength of a person's belief.[4]

With respect to determinism, there may be principled limits to what we can know if determinism is true. But for my purposes I assume the builder, knowing in general the causal effects of the plant, believes correctly that the objective probability of death is 1 for the person who dies; that whoever is killed dies from ordinary causal processes. On the other hand, the epistemic probability – the measure of the credibility of our belief given the evidence, of who in the risk pool will die – remains 1 in 10,000.

Moral questions about this kind of risk imposition can be raised about many policies, whether building a power plant, deciding to use a pesticide, increasing the speed limit, or permitting a major industrial project, assuming some workers will die, though epistemic probability that any individual will die is small. In some cases those at risk volunteer directly or indirectly (say, through a legislature) to bear the risk; in many cases the risk is imposed without consent of those at risk (see McLean in McLaen [ed], 1986). But in all cases I make the provisional assumption that the one who may impose risk believes it's wrong to do so if she would be able in advance to single out who will die.

The Argument for Not Building the Plant

The argument for not building the plant is straightforward. The objective probability of a fatality should be decisive for the builder in determining risk. And when the plant is on line that probability is 1 that whoever dies will die. The builder has agreed that if she knew who would die, she wouldn't build. Knowing the particular causal process that kills Smith she could no longer contend Smith was at slight risk. Should it matter that she lacks such knowledge? Imagine the following

---

[4]   On subjective probability see Weatherford (1982), ch. 5; Benenson, (1984), pp. 43–8; Nagel (1939), pp.60–75; and Mackie, (1973) p. 157–8. Mackie's objection to conflating epistemic with subjective probability is found on pp. 227–8.

scenarios. (1) There is a series of persons with more complete knowledge of the consequences of building the plant. In fact one person has complete knowledge and knows who will die. But neither she nor any of the other people can communicate with the builder. The builder knows the other persons have more complete knowledge. She knows that some person knows who in the risk pool will die. (2) We imagine the one who knows who will die attempts to communicate to the builder, but the message gets garbled. Perhaps the builder gets a paper on which is written the name of the person who will die. But it fell in the mud on way and is illegible. Or it's written in a language so foreign no one could translate it. Or the builder reads the name, accidentally destroys the paper and then forgets what she read. She knew but no longer knows who will die. (3) Or, in an interesting, if more implausible variant, the person in the risk pool who will die once the plant is online knows her fate, but can neither evade the death nor convince anyone that she is in danger. The builder knows that there is such a person but has no idea who it is, and no way of finding out. What the builder has is evidence that any person in the risk pool is as likely as any other to be the one who knows she will die when the plant begins operation.

These admittedly odd scenarios simply dramatise the claim that the facts about who will die exist in the world when the plant is built. If Smith is the one to die, it is as certain that he will die as that the world and its causal processes exist. Moreover, the builder will be able in a way to refer to who will die given the plant's operation. For example, while holding the paper with the garbled message she can say, 'I know with certainty that 'D' (the name she gives to the person referred to by the scribbling) will die, though I don't know who in the risk pool D is.' But why is it important that she know that? She has a kind of reference to D; '*the person referred to by the scribbling*', or '*the person she once knew would be the one to die*', or simply '*the person for whom there is a probability of 1 that she will die*'. Both the objective and epistemic probability that D will is 1.

One objection to the above is that the builder isn't actually referring to any particular person with the definite description '*the one for whom the probability is 1 that she will die* '. If we speak of reference here, it is reference by essential attribution rather than by direct acquaintance or through a more complicated causal chain that connects reference to the person referred to (see Donnellan, 1966). Reference by essential attribution requires that the referent satisfy the properties in the definite description. In the causal theory of reference that's not the case. Shakespeare might not, after all, have written Hamlet.

The foundations for essentially attributive reference might be past relative frequencies of death when such risks were introduced, extrapolations from animal experiments, say, when estimating the carcinogenic effects of pesticides (extrapolations themselves expressed as relative frequencies), or something else. For these foundations to permit successful (if indirect) reference we merely need assume that they causally entail someone will die when the plant goes on line.

The question remains whether there is any morally relevant difference between reference by direct acquaintance or more complicated causal connection, then indirect reference by essential attribution. One suggestion is that with direct reference we seem more acquainted with the victim. The paradigm example here is demonstrative reference when we say, 'That person over there will die,' pointing to the person. A paradigm example for reference by essential attribution is the convoluted definite description, '*the one for whom the probability is 1 that she will die*'. Acquaintance, however, appears irrelevant here. In either case the risk to the one who dies is not slight

The example I've given assumes those in the risk pool exist simultaneously with operating the plant. But injuries and deaths from, say, air toxics, may happen to persons who will, but do not now, exist. Does this effect the problem of reference? From the standpoint of reference by essential attribution I don't believe so. We assume some person in the future will die from causal processes connected to the plant's existence. We can't directly identify that person but that's also true in cases where those at risk exist when the plant is operating.[5]

Therefore, whether we think of those present or future as being in the risk pool the builder can simply act as if she knows who will die. She refers to the person as 'D', and when asked what the probability is that D will die, she can say '1'. If we agree (for argument's sake) that she should not build the plant if she could identify D in advance, then she should not build if it is a causal certainty that D will die. This perspective contests Annette Baier's claim that in statistical deaths no right has been violated since no one has been singled out. Yet, if I shoot into a crowded room knowing I will kill someone, but not knowing whom, I have as surely violated the right of that person as if I had aimed at him. This seems to me analogous to the builder who knows D will be killed but not who D is (see Baier, 1986, p. 55). Other considerations are, of course, relevant to whether a right has been violated, but not simply the distinction between knowing whom and knowing that you will kill someone.

A qualification is required here. Even if the process that caused death were truly random assume one person will die who would not have died because the plant wasn't built. And if it is wrong to increase the number of deaths by one she shouldn't build the plant. However, in the original case the death consequent to building would be the result of a determi-

---

[5]   Of course there is the general problem of whether we can know (as opposed to just believe) anything about the future. This discussion of future harm was motivated by some comments of John Haldane.

nate rather than random process. Therefore the builder knows at any time after the plant is built and before D's death that the objective probability that D will die is 1. She can't then use the argument that everyone in the risk pool is equally at slight risk, an argument not available if determinism is true. This makes a significant moral difference. In my view no moral problem exists if each in the risk pool seeking certain benefits chooses to bear an objectively slight risk of death in gaining them. Though there will be a death the builder can truly say each person is at slight risk.

Even absent randomness each of those at risk from the plant might still take the attitude, as suggested above, that it is prudent to bear it. Therefore they consent to construction. But it doesn't follow that the builder may impose the risk. The following propositions are compatible: (1) Everyone in the risk pool rationally decides to bear the risk, and (2) The builder should not build the plant. We can easily imagine people rationally willing to take risks based on their point of view, who should be forbidden to risk based on the perspective of those who impose it. True, in the case discussed, the builder and those at risk have the same limited information. But the builder has a compelling argument not to build, an argument not prudentially serviceable to those at risk, that there is an objective probability of 1 that D will die if she builds the plant; that the risk to D is not slight.

Yet one might not be convinced that construction should be forbidden if: (1) everyone in the risk pool wishes to bear what for him is a very slight risk, and (2) the builder was equally in the dark about who would die. Suppose, given the benefits, they insist that she build it. If she had knowledge of who would die their volunteering may be morally irrelevant. But it certainly seems germane if the builder has no more idea about who will die than anyone else does. They agree that based on the best available evidence the chance of death for any in the risk pool is minimal. Think of a reverse lottery of 10,000 people where the person selected dies an automatic and painful death, and those not selected get one million dollars. Suppose the outcome of the selection process, though apparently random, (bouncing Ping-Pong balls) was essentially deterministic, though neither lottery master nor players could predict the outcome.[6] If each of 10,000 rational adults desired to participate, why not permit the lottery?

Yet suppose the lottery master knew M. Smith will die but could not tell him or anyone else? We have assumed, then, he wouldn't hold the

[6]   I don't deny that in statistics there are tests for random (or effectively random) sequences and a notion of 'what is likely due to chance'. But this is compatible with an underlying causal determinism. A good discussion of problems in interpreting 'randomness' is in Mackie (1973), pp. 174–7.

lottery. Not permitting it is justified paternalism. But that's true as well if he knows no more about whose number is up than those who play, but justifiably believes that some person ('D') will die by a causally necessary sequence of events. Paternalism equally requires cancelling the lottery.

If these comments are on the mark it's not a sufficient argument for permitting a major industrial project, e.g., constructing a tunnel beneath the English Channel, certain to cause some worker deaths, that each worker knowing the risk, which appears slight, volunteers.[7] Or take another example. The EPA has estimated that UDMH, a by-product of Alar, confers a cancer risk of 45 in a 1,000,000 over a lifetime to a consumer of apple products (*Newsweek*, March 27, 1989). If the projection of that frequency is correct, let's assume forty-five in a million people will get cancer from eating apples sprayed with Alar.[8] Assume, as well, that the risk pool consists of one million adults who, loving apples with the colour and textural appeal Alar gives are willing to take the risk. If the producer knew which forty-five would get cancer but couldn't tell anyone she wouldn't sell the apples. Should it matter that she only knows that forty-five people are causally destined to get cancer when they eat apples sprayed with Alar? I think not. The risk to those persons is not slight (and Alar has been since taken off the market).

One objection to these reflections is that if taken seriously beneficial industrial or social changes would be rejected. All sorts of policies might, if introduced, confer a very slight epistemic risk to each of those at risk, but in addition a certain increase in deaths or injuries. Raising the speed limit ten miles an hour, for example, might confer significant economic benefits, but result in the death of some who would not have died due to the limit not being raised. For example, infants killed in automobile accidents. (Certainly consent here is lacking.) Relative to our knowledge, however, the risk to any one person is quite small. Should such policies to be forbidden?

The answer might depend — in the first case — on how many people would suffer with Alar off the market. Given some common coin for utility assessment, one might argue net utility is greater with the policy than without it. We might show, in the second example, that more people would suffer and die if the speed limit isn't raised than if it is. We even might (and do) indulge in more controversial trade-offs between diverse goods, e.g., loss of life and loss of income. These tradeoffs, though prob-

---

[7] Of course, it may not be sufficient for other reasons. Building the tunnel might cause more harm than not building it. See text.

[8] In reality no one might get cancer in a particular million Alar users, though the relative frequency in a longer run still be forty-five in a million who do. The assumption that forty-five in a particular million will get cancer is an idealization, one, of course, risk imposers use in contrasting risks.

lematical for many, are not an issue here (see Mishan 1971; Fried, 1969 and Jones, 1982). But in any event, by using them no reference need be made to individual risk. Suppose, to use a previous example, some person with sufficient knowledge of causal processes and initial conditions knew who would die from a diagnostic heart procedure that on average causes 1 death in 350 cases, but couldn't interfere or tell anyone. Should she ban the procedure if that were her only choice? Perhaps not. More people would die without the test. Risk to individuals plays no policy role here at all. Of significance is that 1 out of every 350 people is killed by the procedure and 300 or so lives may likely be saved. Note that this way of thinking withdraws the original assumption that it's necessarily wrong to institute a policy knowing who dies as a consequence. Therefore, in the original example if more good is done by building the plant than not, construction should proceed. The builder's ability to identify the victim is irrelevant.

This utilitarian defence for risky policies — that the policy does more good than forgoing it — remains steadfastly on the level of frequencies and therefore of groups and doesn't depend on any claims about risk for particular individuals. As Alan Gibbard comments, 'we forgo safety improvements because they are not worth the cost even if we know that some lives will be lost' (Gibbard, 1986, p. 97). Yet for some it appears objectionable to disallow probability judgements of individual risk. For example, an asbestos producer recently argued that the EPA's projection of two hundred people dying in the next thirteen years of asbestos related disease meant that the risk of death to any person was equivalent to the minute yearly risk of a person being hit by lightning. This was an argument for continuing production. It seemed no part of his argument that more people would be injured or die if production were banned. The significant and certain costs mentioned as a consequence of a ban were loss of jobs, more expensive replacement products, etc. Nor did he seem to be claiming that the costs of non-production were equivalent to two hundred deaths. Rather, these costs were contrasted with what he thought was the minute risk of death to any individual, given asbestos production. However, unless he assumes indeterminism in the distribution of risk the argument is misleading. With determinism the objective probability of death for each person killed is 1.

Some writers on risk, also rejecting purely utilitarian considerations, argue that a morally appropriate construction of a lower risk threshold, ('*de minimis* risk') for a policy should include both 'efficiency', i.e., the total number of fatalities the policy will cause, and 'equity', i.e., the fairness in distributing the risk of death. Jeryl Mumpower says

> While a nationwide (US) annual risk of 10^{-6} is approximately equivalent in terms of expected annual fatalities to a 10^{-2}, for a population of 2.3×10^4 (say, the population of a small town exposed to a chemical hazard), society might

plausibly exhibit a preference for first redressing the higher-level risk affecting the smaller group. In the interests of equity, society may decide that subgroups should not be exposed to disproportionately high levels of risk, and that risks should be shared among as many people as possible, all else being equal (Mumpower, 1986, p. 439).

With changed numbers we can put the point as follows. Assume no person in a population of 10,000 is more entitled to be free from risk than anyone else is. Moreover, suppose that two members of the population, Jones and Harrigan, each have a 50 percent chance of dying, with a certainty that one dies, if society doesn't nullify a threat to their lives, one that puts no one else at risk. Or society allows that risk to Jones and Harrigan and instead prevents a different threat to the entire population (including Jones and Harrigan), a threat which if not prevented subjects everyone to a 1 in 10,000 risk of death with a certainty of killing one. Can Jones rightly claim he is treated inequitably if society chose to eliminate the 'low level' risk to everyone rather than the substantial risk to himself?

The answer is 'yes' if probability assessments reflect a truly random distribution of risk. Here indeterminism makes a difference. If no person were more entitled than any other to be free of risk, then the right policy would be to subject everyone in the larger population to the same small risk. Given randomness, the probability, 1 in 10,000, represents the objective risk of death for everyone in the risk pool. What constitutes an equitable distribution is different, however, if probability assessments simply reflect ignorance of determining causal factors. 'Fairness' or 'equity' is an objective notion; it refers to an appropriate accord between desert or need and the distribution of goods or evils including risks. If society prevents the threat to Jones and Harrigan there is a probability of 1 that someone in the larger population, call her 'D', will die. Society appears equally fair whether it saves Jones or D. Of course Jones might end up being D, but his interest before the choice of policy is in the probability of his death.

Admittedly it would be difficult to convince possible victims that choice here is morally irrelevant. If, having to choose between being part of a small population where there was a 95 per cent risk of death, or part of a more inclusive population where the risk of death is 1 per cent, and assuming a death in either case, I would choose the latter. It seems prudent to do so. Yet, from the perspective of fairness, and given determinism, there appear no grounds for policy makers, given a choice, to prefer eliminating the high risk to the smaller population.

Concluding Remarks

This discussion is addressed to the person like the builder who refuses to build the plant if she could identify who would die as a result of its operation. She argues the risk to that person is not slight. My aim was to challenge the notion that identifying who will die, as opposed to knowing that someone will die, is morally important. Agreed, not knowing who will die seems to have surface relevance. The builder can say, as can all those in the risk pool, that, given the evidence, she believes the probability of death to each at risk is minimal. However, assuming determinism, she may also note that whoever dies had no chance to survive. Consistency apparently requires her not to build the plant.

These reflections have relevance to non-consequentialist issues such as the importance of consent to risk, and equity in the distribution of risk. Though all in a risk pool might consent to what for them appears a slight risk of death, the risk imposer, knowing who dies, would not (by our original assumption) impose the risk. She has knowingly killed an innocent person. Consent, though prudent for those in the risk pool, is not sufficient to override the moral prohibition against killing.

Aside from consent issues, distributing risk fairly is a non-consequentialist concern. I have argued, however, that if risk estimates merely reflect incomplete causal knowledge then no moral distinction exists between preventing a high epistemic risk of death to each member of a small population and preventing a slight epistemic risk of death to each in a more inclusive population.

The above critical points about the significance of consent and equity in risk distribution are predicated on the assumption of determinism in areas risk assessors consider. Determinism, of course, might not be true. But it doesn't seem sufficient simply to deny it. Those who estimate risk should say how indeterminism is used in assessing risk. Perhaps one could connect measures of the risk of ionizing radiation with indeterminism in radioactive decay. But even if that were accomplished, how would indeterminism play a role in the connection between air toxics from ordinary power plants and consequent fatalities?

To my knowledge those who assess risk don't consider the issue. Whether discussing imposition of risk, consent to risk, or attitudes toward risk, it's not always clear whether writers on risk think probability measures are epistemic, compatible with an underlying determinism, or presume real indeterminism in the world. The point is generally not discussed.[9] Yet whether events considered by the risk imposer are at bottom chancy or deterministic has, I've argued, consequences for morally distinguishing statistical and identifiable deaths.

---

[9] Jaeger *et al.* (2001) do claim (p. 17) 'Risk implies uncertainty.' They then add, 'if the future were . . . predetermined . . . the notion of "risk" makes no sense.' The point is mistaken. Some conceptions of risk, e.g., epistemic risk, obviously are compatible with determinism.

III
RIGHTS, LAW AND PUNISHMENT

Rex Martin

Human Rights: Constitutional and International

Introduction

Civil rights are at the core of basic rights (including those enshrined in constitutional bills of rights) and, I would argue, of human rights as well. What I have in mind with basic civil rights, sometimes called fundamental constitutional rights, is simply this. They are, paradigmatically, those civil rights (such as freedom of political speech or liberty of conscience) that have passed the double test of being enacted by legislative majorities and of being affirmed and, then, supported over the years by the checking devices (such as judicial review). And they are rights that have survived the scrutiny of time and experience and public discussion; they have been winnowed (focused, revised, affirmed) by the self-correcting character of the democratic process, and now continue to enjoy a very high level of social consensus support.[1]

Not all constitutional rights (for example, uninhibited freedom of contract or, to cite another, the right of persons to own and carry guns) will meet the standard set by the notion of basic civil rights and some rights not thought to be constitutional rights (like the right to a primary and secondary education) will in fact meet it. The standard set by basic civil rights is a normative, not a descriptive, theory of constitutional rights in a democratic system.

The thesis that I stated at the very beginning of this section is likely to be controversial. I want to lay out the case for it systematically. My argu-

---

[1] For the point about the role of the checking devices (in particular, judicial review) as fundamentally democratic in character, see Martin and Griffin (1995). Roughly this same point is made in Waldron (1990) and in Freeman (1990/91, 1992, 1994). Finally, the point about the self-correcting character of democratic procedures is taken from Thorson (1962), esp. ch. 8; also pp. 120–4.

ment, in the account that follows, is not intended as a conceptual analysis (broad or otherwise). Rather, it is an attempt to develop a constructive theory of the main constitutive elements of the contemporary conception of human rights. That conception draws on, and is informed by, a number of traditional strands in our thinking. The theory I'm proposing suggests connections between aspects of various of our ordinary ways of thinking about rights and human rights, connections that should be preserved.

Conceptions of Human Rights: Two Main Camps

The vocabulary of rights, in particular, of human rights, may actually be used at any of several steps: that of mere claim, that of entitlement (where only the claim-to element is really settled), that of fully validated claim (where we have the idea both of a justified claim to something and of a justified claim against some specific person[s] for it) and, finally, that of satisfied or enforced claim (where the appropriate measures required to support or to fulfil the claim have been given effective embodiment as well). The presence of these possible stages has introduced a degree of ambiguity into assertions that a right, in particular, a human right, exists.

Accordingly, we find a significant variety of contemporary opinion as to the point at which such assertions can most plausibly be thought to take hold. While some have said simply that rights are claims (Mayo, 1965), others say they are entitlements (McCloskey, 1965), and yet others (most notably Feinberg, 1973, 1980) say they are valid claims. Ranged against them have been those (such as Sumner, 1987) who emphasize that rights, even human rights, are basically established ways of acting or being treated. And, last of all, some (for example, Rawls, 1971, or Melden, 1988) have treated rights as legitimate expectations and, hence, have landed more or less in the middle.

For simplicity we could divide these contrasting views into two main camps: the view that such rights are justified claims and the view that they are socially recognized practices. I want to lay out the main case for each view rather briefly. But ultimately, as you will see, I come down on the side of social recognition.

The main starting point to the view that rights are (valid) claims is, I think, the common opinion that to have a right is to have a justification for acting in a certain way, or a justification for being treated in a certain way. Now, suppose that a candidate for rights status had all the rights-making features but one. Though accredited (in the sense of justified), it was not established; it lacked the social acceptance or the official recognition which it ought to have.

Why should the lack of such recognition deprive it of rights status? Clearly, a morally justified claim can be valid as a claim even though it has not been 'answered', so to speak, by governmental or by individual action; for the validity of the claim is in no way infirmed by the fact that the called-for responses have not been forthcoming. A morally valid justified claim can be purely a claim, for it is possible to conceive any such claim as one which holds in the absence of practices of acknowledgment and promotion, and yet is fully valid as a claim.

The thesis that human rights are universal morally justified claims is understood by its proponents to be a way of asserting that human rights (simply insofar as they are justified or valid claims, to ways of acting or of being treated, applicable to all people) are rights, whether responded to or not. The proposed thesis stands or falls on the point that morally justified claims, simply in virtue of being morally valid, are rights and that human rights owe their status as rights solely to the element of justified claim.

Human rights can be conceived, without loss, as morally justified or valid claims and nothing more. Thus, if we modeled the rights-making features on what was justified (what was accredited in that sense), the thing was already a right even before it was recognized, even before it became a practice. And when it was recognized it would be recognized as a right (as something that was fully justified) and would not simply become a right in being recognized.

Human rights are moral rights that are 'held to exist prior to, or independently of, any legal or institutional rules' (Feinberg, 1973, p. 84); that is, they are rights which are 'independent of any institutional rules, legal or nonlegal' (Feinberg, 1970, p. 85, n. 27). The word 'moral' seems to be doing much of the same work in this context that the word 'natural' used to do. Describing rights as natural implied that they were not conventional or artificial in the sense that legal rights are, and the same is implied here by describing human rights as morally valid claims. This way of looking at such rights is widely thought to be one of the great virtues of the idea that human rights are justified or valid moral claims.

The opposing view is that rights are socially recognized practices, and I would argue that a number of important figures in the history of political thought (for example, Jeremy Bentham and T.H. Green) as well as political thinkers working today belong in this camp. The social recognition view rests on three main contentions.

The first of these is the contention that the notions of authoritative recognition (if not explicit, then at least implicit, as evidenced by conduct) and of governmental promotion and maintenance (usually on a wide variety of occasions) are themselves part of the standard notion of a legal right, that is, when we are concerned with rights that are more than merely nominal ones.

Thus, on the social recognition view, the fatal flaw in the theory of rights as simply justified or valid claims (in any of its formulations) is the suggestion that practices of governmental recognition and enforcement in law can be dispensed with in the case of legal rights. Indeed, this is the very point at which both Dworkin and Raz, who might otherwise be taken to be sympathetic to some form of the valid claims thesis, desert that thesis for one that emphasizes the necessity of institutionally establishing ways of acting or being treated, if these are to count as legal rights (see here Dworkin, 1978, ch. 4, 1986, ch. 11, also pp. 65–8; and Raz, 1984, pp. 10–21).

The second point put forward by the social recognition view is that it is desirable to have, if possible, a single, unequivocal sense of 'rights': one that is capable of capturing both basic civil rights (as a special case of legal rights), on the one hand, and human (and other moral) rights, on the other, under a single generic heading.

Now, if the argument just sketched is to be credited, then the view of rights as justified or valid claims does not provide an adequate generalized notion of rights, one that can comfortably include both legal and human rights. We have already seen that legal rights cannot be satisfactorily accounted for under the heading of mere justified or valid claims. Thus, we must consider the contention that the notions of social recognition (of some appropriate sort) and of promotion and maintenance (usually on a wide variety of occasions) are themselves internal to the notion of any active right.

This brings us to the third point urged by the social recognition view. Here the argument is that all moral rights, as accredited moral rights, can themselves be construed as involving established practices of recognition and maintenance. The question is, why should we so regard them?

In order to answer this question we need to put a certain amount of logical pressure on the notion of a legitimate expectation or, if you will, of a justified or valid claim. When we regard rights (identifiable ways of acting or of being treated) as morally justified, we expect this standard to provide significant normative direction to the conduct of people, as regards a given right. Otherwise, were this not so, rightholders would be deprived of the very substance of what individual rights are rights to: deprived of the benefits that can reasonably be expected to accrue to the various ways of acting or being treated that have been designated as the rights they held.

Consider now, for example, a confessional state with a dominant and exclusivist religion. Here the beliefs that most people have (including their moral beliefs) could effectively block acknowledgment of something as a duty they have (for example, the duty to allow persons there the free exercise of religion).

In the case I've just described there's a disconnect between an accredited critical moral standard which might justify freedom of religion, on the one hand, and the way these people think they're supposed to act, on the other. The normative directive to act in a certain way (for example, to allow even persons of a minority religion the free exercise of their religion) is exactly what would be missing in the case at hand. It would not take hold there; it would not be effective in that setting.

It's not (let us hypothesize) that the people in the confessional state summarily deny this accredited critical moral standard or that they simply fail to comprehend how it could underwrite freedom of religion. Rather, their acceptance of this standard, concretely conceived, would be outweighed for them by another consideration, by another principle, which for them has normative precedence.

The duty enjoined by the accredited principle (if it had been given full acceptance) is thereby effectively blocked. Its acceptance is blocked here not merely by simple self-interest nor by intellectual incomprehension (nor by the claim that the principle, insofar as entertained, is not a moral principle). Rather, it is blocked here by a competing and, in this case, prevailing normative consideration. A duty that cannot be acknowledged in a given society cannot be regarded as a proper duty which could normatively bind conduct there.

A parallel argument could be developed about certain claims-to (e.g., to a specific liberty of conduct or to a specific way of being treated). When we regard rights as morally justified (as ways of acting or of being treated that are justified by some accredited critical moral standard) we expect this standard to provide a basis for someone to be able to claim or demand some specific liberty or some specific way of being treated as something they are morally entitled to. But if that standard was similarly blocked in a given society, it could give rise to no morally legitimate expectation there. Or, at least, it could not give rise to the one we're contemplating.

For example, consider many of the victims-to-be of the Aztec practice of human sacrifice. Let us suppose they were made captive by the Aztecs and that they had precisely the same belief system (cosmological, religious, moral) as their captors. Here the beliefs that most of the captives had (including their moral beliefs) would effectively block the idea (were they able to form it) that they have a claim to life (a claim not to be killed) to which the Aztec priests must, if they act properly, yield in the instance at hand.

In the case I've just described there's a disconnect between an accredited critical moral standard which might justify a specific claim not to be killed, on the one hand, and the actual claims-to (the moral entitlements) people properly think they have. The person we've just described (the Aztec captive) would not be in a normative position to enjoy the substance of the liberty or the way of being treated in question (say, a right to life) or to lay claim to it as a moral right they have.

Again, it's not (let us hypothesize) that the people in the Aztec way of life summarily deny this accredited critical moral standard or that they simply fail to comprehend how it could underwrite a general right to life. Rather, their acceptance of this standard, concretely conceived, would be blocked for them (even if they could entertain it) by another consideration, by a cosmological principle, which for them has normative precedence. The entitlement enjoined by the accredited principle (if that principle could have been given full acceptance) is thereby effectively blocked.[2]

We should not think that we in 'modern times' are exempt from the blocking phenomenon I've just described. Most people in the secular West today would give precedence to the normative claims of logic, mathematics, natural science (and, perhaps, even social science and history) — precedence in the sense that moral claims must be compatible with the claims of logic, science, etc., and would be blocked (set aside, revised, discounted) where they are not. And in some parts of our contemporary world the claims of particular religions or of world-shaping ideologies (like those of communism or capitalism) would have similar precedence and blocking power.

Imagine now a rather extreme case. Imagine an ideal foundational morality that no one was aware of. In all likelihood it was not even reflectively available to persons in the society in question. Such a morality could not be normatively effective in that place and time. It could not normatively direct conduct there, and the grounds of good conduct and of good judgment in moral matters, whatever these grounds were in that society, could not be connected to this ideal morality.

This is a matter about which one should not be dogmatic or too assured. But it does not seem implausible to believe that something like Nozick's libertarian individualism was not merely not known but was simply not reflectively available to our Neanderthal cousins (human though they were and, indeed, living in the state of nature). So the case I've asked us to imagine is not an impossible one and may even be a likely one.

This being so, no one would think such an ideal morality could justify rights (could justify ways of acting or ways of being treated) there. I mean it could not provide effective moral justification in such a case. It could not effectively underwrite claims and entitlements to given ways of acting or ways of being treated there, claims that could figure in the self-understanding of people. And, of course, it could not provide effective normative direction to the conduct of people in that society. It could

---

[2]   The relevant Aztec cosmological beliefs, besides a complicated theory of phases of cosmological history, included the idea that the perishing of the present cosmological order (and of the known human world within it) could be averted only by 'nourishing' the cosmos through the shedding of human blood. For a brief discussion, see Martin (1991) pp. 355–363. For extended discussion see, for example, Miguel León-Portilla (1963, chs. 2–3; 1964, esp. pp. 41–5).

not normatively justify duties to act in an appropriate manner toward these ways, duties that could figure in the self-understanding of people there. Our hypothetical ideal morality would be wholly normatively ineffective.

This is the big difference between the 'ideal morality' example and the earlier two we looked at (the free exercise of religion example and the Aztec captive one). With these two earlier examples, I have in fact specified cases that lie between two extremes, lie between two limiting cases. On the one hand, we have the extreme situation of our hypothetical ideal morality and, on the other, we would have the situation where established ways of acting or ways of being treated are fully connected with normatively effective justifying standards. In this middle ground (in the free exercise and in the Aztec cases, for example) the required normative effectiveness is merely contingently unavailable — rather than essentially unavailable (as it is in the 'ideal morality' example). But the point is, nonetheless, that the required normative effectiveness is quite absent in these middle cases, absent in the free exercise of religion example, as it is in the Aztec captive one.

All these examples suggest, then, that there is an inexpugnable element of 'social' acceptance (of social recognition) — and behind that, of normative soundness in the justifying standards — in the idea of moral rights. It is built into them, if we regard these justified ways of acting or ways of being treated as entities in a real social world, regard them as more than the conclusions demanded, or the practices enjoined, in an ideal critical morality.

Let me put this basic point slightly differently now. Adequate moral justification is justification that is not blocked by competing normative considerations; and it is not justification that exists only in Plato's heaven. It is moral justification that is reflectively available to the people involved. But more than this is required for rights (be they moral rights or legal rights) to gain a grip. The people must take that justification on board, internalize it. Where it is a right they all have or involves duties that all (or many) of them have, this business of 'taking on board' must be widespread. It must affect the self-understanding of the people involved (a whole lot of people) in the appropriate ways.

Now let us take this analysis one step further, from mere social recognition to maintenance. I would argue that any right would be vitiated as a right if it were not protected or promoted at all. In such a case the right would be a merely nominal one, a right that existed in name only but not in fact. Such rights do not, as some have suggested (Cranston, 1967, p. 48), constitute a special class of full-fledged rights. Rather, they constitute a defective way of exemplifying any justified and recognized right; merely nominal rights are rights only on paper and nowhere else.

Now, to be sure, nominal rights are rights. The point is, though, that we regard the complete and continuing absence of promotion and maintenance as infirming a right, as rendering it totally (or almost totally) ineffective. Nominal rights are rights in one sense only (that of formal acceptance or recognition and, presumably, of sound moral justification), but they fail to function as rights. A merely nominal right gives no normative direction to the conduct of other persons in fact; such persons act as if the right did not exist even on paper. No one of them takes the nominal existence of the right as a reason for doing, or not doing, as the right directs. The right here has in actual practice no directive force. Where normative justification and social recognition effectively count for so little, the rightholder is without any effective guarantee respecting that which has been recognized and formulated as a moral right. Any such right — when merely nominal — has failed in a crucial respect. It represents at best a marginal and precarious example of a moral right.

Here we have, then, the main arguments for the social recognition view that opposes the contention that rights are essentially justified or valid claims. And we reach the conclusion that the notions of acceptance or recognition (of some appropriate sort) and of promotion and maintenance (usually on a wide variety of occasions) are themselves internal to the notion of any active right, be it a legal right or a moral right or a social right.

The Role of Government in Human Rights

We are concerned in this paper with human rights. On the assumption that any right under serious discussion is not merely nominal, then, for any particular moral right (a human right included), there would have to be certain appropriate practices of identification, promotion, protection, enforcement, and so forth, in place on the part of society, and at least forbearance by (other) private persons. The determination of what is appropriate for a moral right — and here I have particularly in mind human rights (sometimes called natural rights) — then becomes the exact point at issue.

The great natural- and human-rights manifestoes were intended to impose restraints upon governments. Individuals were involved as beneficiaries of these restraints but, for the most part, were not the parties to whom the manifestoes were addressed. Or, at least, the class of all living individuals, taken one by one, was never the sole addressee of such manifestoes, nor was it the primary one. The right to a fair trial, which is often given as an example of a human right (see Cranston, 1967, p. 43) is a right that one has against governments in particular, especially one's own.

The example is by no means atypical. The right to travel (found in the UN Universal Declaration of Human Rights, 1948, article 13) certainly contemplates the absence of restraints imposed by governments; indeed insofar as the issue is the liberty to travel, as distinct from the where-withal to do so, it is primarily government that is addressed. And the right to freedom from the injury of torture is peculiarly held against governments; this is clear from the context — court proceedings and, in particular, punishment — in which the right is set (article 5). The same pattern holds with rights to the provision of a service. The duty of providing social security is explicitly enjoined on governments (articles 22, 25), and the duty to provide for elementary education, which 'shall be compulsory' (article 26), is clearly addressed, in this crucial detail at least, to states in particular.

It seems, then, that government's being an intended addressee of human rights norms is too deeply embedded to be erased. Whether we look at details of specific rights, as we find them in the great declarations of rights, or at the theory of human rights/natural rights (including its actual history), we find that government is in fact an addressee, often the principal addressee.[3] So a consideration of the relevant governmental practices is never a dispensable or even a negligible matter as regards the human rights status of these moral norms. This is not to deny, of course, that individuals are often addressed as well (the crucial prohibition invoked in the right not to be killed is addressed both to governments and to individual persons, for example).

It may be, though, I would add, that for some universal moral rights the role of government is incidental or even nonexistent. These rights hold strictly between persons. The moral right to be told the truth (or at least not lied to), the moral right to gratitude for benefits provided, and, perhaps, the moral right to have promises kept are examples. Such rights differ from, say, the right not to be killed — even when we're talking about the latter right as held against individuals — in being rights maintained exclusively, or almost exclusively, by conscience. They are moral rights merely and in no way claims against the government. Interestingly, though, it is often in these very cases that, while we are willing to call such rights moral rights, we would tend to withhold from them the name of human (or natural) right.

There is a sound basis for saying, then, that human rights norms (that is, morally justifiable claims) are addressed to governments in particular, often to governments primarily. And natural or human rights can be distinguished from other universal moral rights in this very circumstance. Where human rights (as a special case of moral rights) are thought to be addressed to governments primarily and in particular

---

[3] The US Declaration of Independence (1776) begins its famous second paragraph with the words 'We hold these truths to be self-evident, that all men are created equal, that they are endowed by their Creator with certain unalienable rights, that among these are Life, Liberty, and the pursuit of happiness. That to secure these rights, Governments are instituted among Men . . .'.

(though not exclusively), we must regard practices of governmental recognition and promotion as being the main form for such recognition and maintenance to take for these rights.

A Conception of Human Rights:
Summary and Application

Let me conclude this paper by first applying my overall account to the case of human rights as that notion is understood today (as exhibited, for example, by those rights found in the UN's Universal Declaration of Human Rights, 1948, or in the European Convention on Human Rights, 1954). Here I want not so much to expand on the model analysis as to reflect on and to appraise it. Then I want to say a brief, final word about international human rights.

In the account I've been giving, an active human right, understood simply as a moral right is morally justified by accredited standards. More particularly, I would like to suggest that in this account a human right is justified by the standard of mutual and general benefit (the benefit of each and all). There may be other standards of justification that are useful and that would be normatively sound; but the standard of mutual and general benefit is, nonetheless, perhaps worth singling out. It would be hard to say, convincingly, that something was a justified human right that quite clearly failed to meet the standard of mutual and general benefit. It would be hard, that is, if we adhered to the supposition that all rights are beneficial, in some way, to the rightholder.

Where the right in question is a human right, then the specific way of acting or way of being treated it identifies should (at a minimum) be a matter of benefit to each and all of a vast number of human beings alive now (and for the foreseeable future). A specific way of acting or way of being treated that did not meet even this somewhat relaxed standard could not be justified as a human right.[4]

Let me enlarge upon the point just made. Sound or credible moral justification is a necessary condition of any right's counting as a human right. I have argued that unless the standard of the benefit of each and all (perceived benefit) is satisfied (or can reasonably be expected to be satisfied) then we do not have an adequate moral justification in the case at hand.

How is this standard to be met? I have something fairly simple in mind. Each person is presumed to be able to reflect and to think reasonably carefully about important matters. Each is here presumed, then, to focus and to reflect on a single consideration: whether this particular

---

[4]   For the point made about rights as beneficial, see my *A System of Rights* (1993), chs. 2, 5, and 10. It is important, though, to distinguish between conditions of constitution or justification for moral rights and criteria for their possession.

way of acting or this particular way of being treated (if it were in effect for all) would on the whole (a) be beneficial for that person (as beneficial in itself or as a reliable means to some other good thing) and (b) that person can see how it would be beneficial to others as well, now and in the foreseeable future. If everyone could say, upon reflection, that this is so in their view, then the standard is satisfied. The standard is both minimal and abstract

The test probably cannot be satisfied for literally all people. Some people simply cannot or will not think straight. And others don't seem able to get the hang of engaging in moral reasoning, at any level. This is why I specified that the test could be satisfied if (arguably) the matter under consideration could be of benefit to each and all of a vast number of human beings alive now (and for the foreseeable future).

Also, there's some question whether the standard in question is a moral standard. Now, it clearly is a moral standard of conventional morality — or, at least, is a standard compatible with many different conventional moralities. Accordingly, I am satisfied that, even in the relaxed form I have just provided, it is a moral standard of sorts. And this is enough said, in my view. But this may not be enough for some normative moral theorists. They may want to enlarge the scope of those who can be regarded as perceiving the matter as beneficial so as to make it truly universal and to connect that perception with some accredited critical moral principle or with some accredited standard of practical moral reasoning.

Thus, a utilitarian, assuming certain conditions and certain matters of fact, might come up with some ideal moral rule (embracing all people, now and in the foreseeable future) which could itself be justified by the utilitarian general happiness principle. Or a contractarian (or 'contractualist') theorist might specify that no reasonable person could deny or reject the prima facie standard in question (Scanlon, 1998, p. 4) or specify that all reasonable people would accept or endorse it (Rawls, 1996, pp. 137, 217, 226, 241, and 393). My formulation requires neither of these two lines of attack to complete it. But it is compatible with both, while being neutral between them.

In sum then, the notion of a justified human right (understood as a kind of moral right) has three main features in the view I am proposing. (1) It is a way of acting or way of being treated that is justified, for all human beings, by the standard of benefit for each and all, and perhaps by other moral standards as well. (2) That accredited way of acting or of being treated has some sort of authoritative institutional recognition (in the typical case, through recognition in law and in the action of courts). (3) It is maintained by conforming conduct and, where need be, enforced by governments.

It could fail at some of these points and still have substance as a human right. Though if it failed on the point of justification (by the standard of the benefit of each and all), then it would, I think, have reached a vanishing point. But a fully functioning human right (understood as a moral right) satisfies all these points. The fulfilment or realization, at a suitable level, of these three elements is essential to any robust and non-defective human right (understood as a moral right). Their realization allows human rights to be, as they've always been thought to be, both practical and critical in character. The three features identified — sound justification, effective recognition, maintenance — are all linked elements in a procedure for constructing or constituting morally accredited human rights, functioning at full capacity.

The UN's Universal Declaration of Human Rights

The norms of the Universal Declaration in order to be active human rights — active as constitutional rights or as international basic rights — and to be morally justifiable as human rights must satisfy these three points. And, beyond that, we would require of them, as of any given right, some specification of content, some setting of scope (with provision for making scope adjustments), some competitive weightings in cases of conflict, some institutional devices for the on-site resolution of conflicts, and so on. For, otherwise, such rights will conflict with one another and collapse into an incoherent set.

Some may find extremely unattractive the notion that moral rights can be tinkered with, that new ones can be added to the list, existing ones revised, some even overturned. It is perhaps worth adding, then, that we are here principally concerned with the implementation of such rights and not their abstract formulation. Nonetheless, we should face up to the fact that changes such as these can occur even in our normative justifications. For one thing, many people believe (or hope) that by thinking more carefully about moral matters, bringing in new paradigms and perspectives, we can thereby improve our own formulations and understandings. In any event, moral norms gain or lose social support, so that they take on radically differing formulations at widely separated times in history (witness the sharply differing idea of the cardinal virtues held by the ancient Greeks in contrast to that of, say, mediaeval Christian culture). And blocking by competing normative considerations can be added or removed over time, or in different places on the cultural map coexisting at the same time. Such changes in normative justifications and their formulation can happen and, I think, do happen.

If all this is so, we cannot think adequately about human rights (where they are thought to be active rights, as distinct from mere norms) by dispensing with the institutional arrangements — scope adjustment, competitive weighting, promotion and maintenance — just emphasized.

Features such as these are part of the mechanism of normative change (of helping it along or registering it) and, more to the point, are necessary to making moral norms into active human rights, functioning at full capacity.

The proper focus here, I am suggesting, should not be on the 'manifesto' element of the UN's Declaration but, rather, on the embodiment of those norms as active civil rights within states, where such rights (presumably appropriately justified morally) could be and were authoritatively recognized, harmonized, and maintained.[5]

Some might argue that I've focused too often in my argument on the great rights manifestoes and have ignored another tradition in human rights discourse — the tradition that sees moral rights as justified claims and standards for criticizing existing political or social arrangements, whether or not these claims are recognized and enforced at all. Though it's hardly fair to say that I've ignored this tradition (since I criticized it at length earlier), let us leave that caveat aside for now.

I readily grant that others would regard such justified claims as human rights, and I see no problem in their doing so. It is not part of my project to deny human rights status to such claims or to legislate how people should be talking about human rights. So long as the three-element procedure for constituting human rights is kept on the table as essential to the big picture, I have no quarrel with the view at hand.[6]

The essentials of the three-element procedure for constituting human rights are present in the UN Declaration. Thus, human rights can be regarded here as constitutional rights within individual states. This is, in

---

[5]   The Universal Declaration avowedly has a 'manifesto' element: it speaks in its preamble of 'proclaiming' a 'common standard' and calls itself a 'declaration'. Clearly, then, it lays out a set of aspirations; but it does not stop there. Repeatedly there, the idea of the recognition of the rights proclaimed and their observation is invoked.

[6]   I would tend to call a human right that had only the one element, the element of morally valid claim (that and nothing else), *a human rights norm*. This seems apt because the phrase recognizes that we don't have a fully constituted right here while at the same time affirming that a mere morally valid claim does have status as a human right even when only the first of the constituting conditions, the condition of sound normative justification, is fully satisfied.

A good example of the alternative way of talking, with which I find no problem, is provided by Henry Shue. In Shue (1996) he begins by characterizing human rights as morally justified demands (pp. 13–15), but he immediately goes on to emphasize the importance of such rights being 'socially guaranteed' (pp. 15–18). In later chapters this particular feature is emphasized and it becomes clear that such guarantees necessarily involve the elements of social recognition and maintenance, by both private persons and governments (see esp. chs. 2 and 5 and the Afterword). For a good summary of his views, in which all the components just identified figure, see Shue (1996).

fact, the case primarily contemplated in the UN's Universal Declaration.[7]

International Human Rights

Let me hasten to add that a focus on constitutional rights within individual states is not the only option available to the resources of the present account. We are not — or need not be — limited exclusively to what might be called 'nation states' and their particular arrangements. Others, of course, using arguments like some of the ones I have employed, have alleged otherwise. Michael Walzer, for instance, says:

> Individual rights may well derive, as I am inclined to think, from our ideas about personality and moral agency, without reference to political processes and social circumstances. But the enforcement of rights is another matter. . . . Rights are only enforceable within political communities where they have been collectively recognized, and the process by which they come to be recognized is a political process which requires a political community. The globe is not, or not yet, such an arena (Walzer, 1980, p. 226, also 227–8).

To the contrary, I would want to claim that the account I have presented could allow for the notion of basic rights in an emerging supranational entity or, better, a fairly unified confederation of states (like the nascent European Union, and within it the European Convention of Human Rights). Indeed, to think clearly about human rights in the present day one would have to allow for such cases.

One of the really difficult questions about human rights emerges, though, when we contemplate even looser international federations or, sometimes, coalitions (even temporary coalitions) of states, engaged in formulating or enforcing human rights norms (in a situation where such rights are not being recognized or not being maintained in some countries). These looser federations or coalitions pose a number of problems.

In the favoured case (not always met, of course, in fact), such a federation (or such a coalition) would have to have the continuing support and cooperation of a wide variety of states; it would have to be, in effect, an agreed-upon international agency for identifying, formulating, and overseeing the understanding and the maintenance and enforcement of human rights. Such a federation, if it were international or cosmopolitan in the widest sense, would require the support of many states that were not democratic.

Perhaps only the UN or possibly the World Court system (and within that framework the UN Declaration, the two main Covenants on Human

---

[7]   The preamble to the UN Declaration begins with the assertion that the 'Member States' are intent on achieving not only the 'promotion of universal respect' for human rights and 'fundamental freedoms' but also their 'observance'. The preamble ends with a commitment to secure for these rights and liberties 'their universal and effective recognition and observance, both among the peoples of the Member States themselves and among the peoples or territories under their jurisdiction'.

Rights, and various other relevant international treaties, such as the treaty outlawing genocide) has that status worldwide, at present.[8] If it does, there is no barrier in principle to the UN's being the kind of political entity we've been describing in our account of human rights. Or, perhaps, a coalition of states acting under UN or EU auspices and authorization could be such an entity. In either of these two cases we would have a confederation of nation states, states working to a common purpose, to carry out the job of the international formulation and the maintenance and enforcement of certain basic rights.

Of course, it could be contended that, though there are many conceivable justifying arguments for human rights, none of them are currently accepted or put into practice at an acceptable level by literally all peoples. Not even the justification provided by mutual and general benefit, as it applies to specific cases or to specific lines of conduct, is uniformly accepted. Even it is not accepted in the concrete, in some given 'crux' cases; in that sense it is not accepted everywhere, not by all peoples or all governments.

Moreover, whether any of these justifying arguments offer suitable grounds for intervention, in particular, forcible intervention, against societies (against peoples) that do not accept these justifications and, especially, against societies who engage regularly and unamendably in practices that are seriously unacceptable in the light of these arguments is a difficult question.

Consider here (as examples of serious violations of human rights) genocide, slavery, and warlord-induced famine and starvation, all of them cases from our own day. Consensus might exist on the justifiability of forcible intervention in such cases. But there is far less consensus on such issues as the treatment of women, capital punishment, and legal limitations on 'hate' speech (speech much of which occurs under the heading of religious education).

The kind of justification we are talking about in all these cases would have to rely on standards considerably stronger than mutual and general benefit. For we are talking here not merely about what justifies any

---

[8]   It could plausibly be argued that democratic institutions can, acting as a set (and on a majority electoral base), effectively perform the job of creating and maintaining basic civil rights. This could be claimed because democratic procedures are a stable and relatively reliable way of identifying, and then implementing, laws and policies that serve interests common to the voters or to a large number of them, presumably at least a majority.

I would not, however, want to argue that the operation of democratic institutions and norms is a necessary condition for the creation of basic civil rights. Thus, the UN, which is made up of a good many nondemocratic (even anti-democratic) states and is not itself a democratic body, is not ruled out as a venue for the formulation and maintenance of rights that can be justified by the standard of the benefit of each and all individuals.

given human right but more especially about when, if ever, a particular human right should be forcibly enforced internationally.[9]

This takes us to yet another deep concern. Clearly, one of the most pressing problems for the international recognition and protection of human rights is that the UN by and large lacks enforcement mechanisms of its own. Accordingly, the UN must rely on existing nation states for the foreseeable future. It may well be, right now, that the problem of the international recognition and protection of human rights can be most effectively dealt with regionally rather than globally.[10]

Of course, there is (we hope) a future beyond the foreseeable future, and things may be different then. A genuinely universal international order, or a family of strong but benign transnational regional orders, may well have emerged. But our account must end at this point, with where we are now.

In any event, we have made some progress on the present project, the project of linking our model theory with human rights as currently understood. We can see a clear and coherent shape that the notion of human rights is taking in the domestic law of many countries today, in Britain and other countries in Europe, in Canada and the US. And we can see the outlines of an international order for human rights as well — most clearly in the case of the European Convention and the evolution of the EU, less clearly but not to the point of vanishing in the UN. These are the main shapes that the notion of human rights has in the world today.[11]

---

[9] I have in mind (just to cite one instance) criteria of the sort John Rawls urges (see Rawls, 1999, pp. 67, 79, 81). It should be noted that the standard of perceived benefit would probably hold in the three severe and urgent cases (genocide, slavery, etc.). All persons (including those in the affected country) could reflectively decide that the avoidance of these particular injuries was beneficial to them. It is not so clear that it could be met in the second-tier cases (treatment of women, soul-curdling religious intolerance and invective, etc.) in every single case. It might be, but again it might not be. It is the latter cases (cases where it is not met) that forcible international intervention becomes especially problematic.

[10] Some, indeed, have argued the virtues, in extreme cases, of unilateral intervention (of forcible intervention by one nation in another to prevent or stop grave violations of human rights). For one example of such advocacy see Walzer (2000), preface to the third edition, esp. pp. xiii– xvi, and ch. 6, esp. pp. 105–8; and Walzer (2002), esp. pp. 31–3.

[11] My first serious attempt at developing a theory of human rights was Martin (1980). I quickly became dissatisfied with the argument of this paper, but it took me some time to rework it into a more satisfactory form. This I did in ch. 4 of Martin (1993), wherein my main account (before now) of human rights can be found. Perhaps the simplest way to view the present paper is to see it as an attempt to improve upon — to further clarify and correct and then extend — the argument of Martin (1993).

In the writing of the present paper I have drawn on Martin (1985, 1993, 1998).

Lisa Portmess

Military Tribunals

Procedural Justice and the Problem of Evidence

Introduction

Military tribunals have long dispensed suspect justice even when defendants are guaranteed limited due process rights. China, Egypt, Nigeria, Peru, Burma, Russia, and the Sudan, among other nations, have been subject to persistent criticism by the international community, by human rights organizations and by the US State Department for their failure to guarantee defendants the right to a fair trial. US trials of Axis war criminals by military tribunals during and after World War II remain significant objects of legal scrutiny today, influential in judgments now being made about terrorist suspects (see *Ex Parte Quirin*, 1942, 317 US 1 and *In Re Yamashita*, 1946, 327 US 1). Arguments in defense of military tribunals based on national security interests and the urgent desire for justice carry unusual moral weight and diminish regard for the presumption of innocence, high standards of evidence, and other due process protections. Yet military tribunals have the appeal of achieving swift justice, and the advantage of protecting civilian courts from exploitation by enemies of the state, though they remain vulnerable to greater risks of wrongful conviction from lower evidentiary standards and fewer due process protections for the accused.

This paper will focus on philosophical questions of evidence as they arise from consideration of the November, 2001 US executive order and subsequent revisions authorizing use of military commissions for suspected terrorists and war criminals. Evidence has long been at the centre of philosophical questions about legal fact-finding and the nature of proof. The debate over the use of military tribunals for Guantanamo Bay captives provides vivid illustration of the practical implications of this theoretical debate. In the military commissions outlined by the order, forms of evidence barred from civilian courts, such as hearsay evidence, secret evidence, and evidence gathered without a secure chain of custody, are admissible before the court. In cases where evidence fails to convict, defendants may nonetheless be detained if they are judged to be dangerous. In this diminished context for evidence, contemporary scepticism in evidence scholarship, which challenges the fact-finding role of evidence in legal proceedings, seems borne out. Such scepticism emphasizes the subordination of law to power, and the dependence rather than independence of evidence in judicial decisions. As evidence sceptics see it, military tribunals reveal what is characteristic of legal systems everywhere — that the truth-finding role of evidence is always subordinate to extrajudicial priorities. In the case of military tribunals, evidence is seen as subordinate to the desire for expedited conviction; in the case of indefinite detentions it is seen as subordinate to the desire for access to intelligence and the containment of those believed to be dangerous.

Whether the diminished role for evidence in military tribunals reveals an inherent yet tolerable tension between evidence and other judicial values, present in all judicial systems and manifest in exclusionary rules in civilian justice systems, or a deeper vulnerability of judicial process to executive power merits philosophical scrutiny. If law is indeed silent in times of war, or if law everywhere is the masquerade of power, then the struggle against diminished civil liberties is for naught. A philosophical foundation for the effort to realize humanitarian law and ensure due process even for one's enemies cannot be derived from prevailing realist or sceptical challenges to the truth-finding role of evidence.

If in defence of military tribunals high evidentiary standards are understood to be one among various judicial values, highly dependent on circumstance, then diminished standards of evidence may not necessarily be seen to undermine efforts at achieving justice. Instead they might reflect, with the guarantee of a right to civilian appeal and the absence of a death penalty, a defensible balance of national security interests and due process rights. Such at least is the argument of those who defend military tribunals against sceptical challenges.

From the perspective of tribunal advocates, the indefinite detention of captives, denied even the most fundamental legal rights and access to evidence, becomes an even more serious abrogation of due process protections. In that light military tribunals, even with compromised due process guarantees, become a preferred resolution. For detainees held indefinitely without judicial review, evidence ceases to matter at all and executive determination prevails without restraint over judicial process.

In his book defending war crimes tribunals, *Stay the Hand of Vengeance*, Gary Jonathan Bass resists neorealist claims that 'a war crimes tribunal is simply something that the countries that decisively win a war inflict on the helpless country that loses it. It is punishment, revenge, spectacle —

anything but justice' (Bass, p. 11). He traces the notion of victors' justice through its long history from Thrasymachus in Plato's *Republic*, 'Everywhere justice is the same thing, the advantage of the stronger,' to its manifestation in post World War political dialogue. 'In the dangerous brawl of international anarchy, realists argue, idealistic and legalistic policies are a luxury that states can ill afford' (Bass, p. 9). Recognizing the force of the realist line of argument, Bass nonetheless believes that war crimes tribunals affirm a principled idea of legalist liberal states. In the treatment of defeated foes, Bass argues, liberal states seek to affirm domestic ideals of judicial process, extending the rule of law to the international sphere, with all of its risks of 'acquittal, delay and embarrassment'. In weighing alternative solution, Bass observes:

> There are easier ways to punish vanquished enemies. Victorious leaders have come up with an impressive array of nonlegalist fates for their defeated foes. One could shoot them on sight. One could round them up and shoot them en masse later. One could have a perfunctory show trial and then shoot them. One could put them in concentration camps. One could (as both Winston Churchill and Franklin Roosevelt suggested) castrate them. One could deport them to a neutral country, or perhaps a quiet island somewhere. Or one could simply ignore their sordid past and do business with them. Of all things, why bother to go to the trouble of a bona fide trial, with the possibility of acquittals, of cases being thrown out on technicalities, of embarrassing evidence and irritating delays, of uncooperative judges, of a vigorous defense? (Bass, p. 7.)

Yet Bass takes note of Kenneth Waltz's scepticism about injecting justice into international politics in his neorealist *Theory of International Politics* (1979): 'Nationally, the force of a government is exercised in the name of right and justice. Internationally, the force of a state is employed for the sake of its own protection and advantage.' Waltz goes on to observe: 'National politics is the realm of authority, of administration, and of law. International politics is the realm of power, of struggle, and of accommodation. The international realm is preeminently a political one' (Waltz, pp. 112–3). According to such neorealism, international norms and institutions are 'epiphenomenal, mere veils over state power' (Bass, p. 11). Better that might decides the resolution of conflicts, Waltz argues, so that 'bloody struggles over right can more easily be avoided'.

Neorealist scepticism about war crimes tribunals entails comparable scepticism about the role of evidence in whatever judicial or quasi-judicial review is eventually provided for defeated enemies. For neorealists, evidence will necessarily be in the service of national self-interest and security, supportive not of justice but of pragmatic decision making about a nation's captive foes and about the best way forward.

Whatever the philosophical position one takes on war crimes tribunals — victors' justice or principled commitment to the rule of law — the military tribunals proposed for Guantanamo detainees remain orphan tribunals proposed by a single nation. Lacking the greater impartiality of the international war crimes tribunals that Bass defends, the military tribunals proposed for Guantanamo Bay detainees reveal the fine line that exists between diminished judicial independence with its lesser standards of evidence and nonlegalist solutions of what a nation should do with captive enemies.

The foundation of a principled legalist defence of military tribunals and its high expectation for the role of evidence has its basis in the rationalist tradition of evidence scholarship. To a closer examination of the rationalist tradition we now turn.

Conceptions of Evidence

William Twining in *Rethinking Evidence: Exploratory Essays* delineates basic assumptions of the rationalist tradition of evidence scholarship in Anglo-American legal philosophy and his 'skepticism about some skepticisms' in contemporary philosophy of law (Twining, 1990, pp. 71–6). According to Twining the rationalist tradition in evidence scholarship, which dates to Jeremy Bentham's vast work on evidence and procedure in the early 1800s (Bentham, 1825, 1827, 1843) displays remarkable continuity: 'Hardly a whisper of doubt about the possibility of knowledge, about the validity of induction, or about human capacity to reason darkens the pages of Gilbert or Bentham or Best or Thayer or Wigmore or Cross or other, leading writers' (Twining, 1990, p. 75).

The rationalist theory of evidence embodies rational optimism about the determination of truth based upon evidence and rational methods of proof. According to rationalist theory, evidence holds a privileged place in arriving at legal judgments of past events. The independence and objectivity of relevant evidence — its power when carefully appraised to yield legal knowledge of past facts — figure centrally in rationalist theories of adjudication.

In contrast, sceptical challenges to rationalist scholarship on evidence, whether relativist or irrationalist, raise fundamental doubts about the truth-finding role of evidence and the possibility of legal knowledge. Broad challenges to notions of the rule of law, justice under the law and the power of evidence to establish knowledge of past events have come from many directions — from the twentieth century jurist, Jerome Frank, the sociologists of knowledge, Berger and Luckmann, and countless who espouse relativist or irrationalist theories of the law.[1] Particu-

---

[1]   Jerome Frank emphasized the unreachability of fact and the many impediments to achieving objective knowledge of past events in Frank (1930, 1945, 1949) among other writings. Frank explored the uncertainty of fact-finding in law and the obstacles posed to objectivity by juries, the adversarial system and exclusionary

larly challenging have been skeptical theories of evidence that emphasize the dependence of evidence on theoretical structures, particular schemas or stories that constitute the basis of our structures of knowledge and the basis of our judicial systems (see Tillers, 1988). Some recent evidence scholars have argued that evidence is not gathered as we gather discrete items of other kinds. Instead the context of evidence shapes from the start what information is considered relevant to establishing a sense of past events, based on its coherence with beliefs and assumptions brought to the investigation (for further discussion see Jackson and Doran, 1996). If evidence is dependent rather than independent, then facts and evidence and the theoretical structure of which they are a part form a coherent whole, neither able independently to validate the other.

In light of such scepticism, military tribunals with their diminished standards of evidence seem to illustrate the story-telling or mystifying ideology of legal systems more generally, no matter how high their standard of evidence or extensive their due process protections. These differences in perspective on the role of evidence in legal systems are more than theoretical. They influence the moral and political debates surrounding military tribunals, and ultimately shape judgments reached over time about the justice they dispense. Sceptical evidence theories, which tend to eclipse differences among different judicial systems in favour of unmasking facts as signs of state power, repressive ideologies or social construction, make impossible the discrimination necessary for vigorous public policy debate. Is, for example, the bar on appeals to federal appellate courts a fatal flaw in the constitution of tribunals, as Ronald Dworkin (April 2002) argues? Without rationalist assumptions about evidence, such arguments against particular characteristics of military tribunals founder, since even the most carefully protected use of evidence by civilian courts would manifest the same unreachability of fact as tribunals that admit hearsay and secret evidence. For evidence sceptics, evidence itself fails the test of objectivity and truth finding, not the diminished evidence of military tribunals. Thus fine discriminations in appraising evidence standards become difficult and more sweeping scepticism about law pervasive. Tempting as such scepticism is in the present 'War on Terrorism', which gives ample evidence of the vulnerability of law to executive power, 'skepticism about skepticism' of the sort Twining advocates is essential both for criticizing the diminished role of

---

rules. Much of his writing is polemical, describing facts as 'guesses', 'human achievements', 'just-so stories' and 'human feats'. Berger and Luckmann (1967) emphasize the relativity of belief and the imperfect claims to objectivity of many forms of evidence. Other contemporary sceptics of evidence focus on specific elements of the judicial process, such as the jury system, and critique assumptions of objectivity in favour of social constructionist or other relativist theories.

evidence in military tribunals and for denouncing the absence of any role at all for evidence in indefinite detentions. Ultimately such criticism must derive its standing from rationalist conceptions of the truth finding authority of evidence and its role in establishing legal knowledge.

Several assumptions underlie rationalist theories of evidence and proof. Twining enumerates several key beliefs of the rationalist tradition: that legal knowledge about particular past events is achievable, that establishing the truth about particular past events at issue is a necessary condition for achieving justice, that notions of evidence and proof in law are concerned with rational methods of determining questions of fact, that the establishment of the truth of alleged facts is typically a matter of probabilities that falls short of absolute certainty, that judgments about the probabilities of allegations about particular past events can and should be reached by reasoning from relevant evidence presented to the decision-maker, that the characteristic mode of reasoning appropriate to reasoning about probabilities is induction, that judgments about probabilities have, generally speaking, to be based on the available stock of knowledge about the common course of events and — of particular interest in the debate over military tribunals — that the pursuit of truth is to be given a high, but not necessarily an overriding, priority in relation to other values, such as the security of the state, the protection of family relationships or the restraint of coercive methods of interrogation (Twining, 1990, p. 73).

These rationalist assumptions at the heart of traditional faith in the rule of law leave latitude nonetheless for assessing the imperfect justice and compromised evidentiary standards of military tribunals. Though significant, truth is conceded to be only one value among others in the social systems in which courts operate. Dispute resolution is another such value, as are national security interests and the preservation of family relationships. To what extent the imperfect justice of military tribunals is best understood in light of a rationalist model, with the latitude it allows for balancing different goods, or in light of more sceptical theories of evidence and legal fact finding is the subject to which we now turn. A more detailed account of the provisions of the US tribunal order, in its original and its revised form, will be useful.

The Disputed Justice of US Military Tribunals

On November 13, 2001 US President George W. Bush signed the executive order allowing special military tribunals to try foreigners charged with terrorism. According to the order, such military commissions are justified by the nature of international terrorism, and by the impracticability of applying principles of law and rules of evidence generally recognized in criminal trials. The executive order called for a tribunal system that could deliver swift justice and would have greater flexibility in introducing evidence than in civilian trials. The military tribunal plan envisions a parallel judicial system under the power of the Executive Branch, different in structure from both civilian and military justice systems, which are bound by high evidentiary standards, independent appeals processes and other due process safeguards. Within the framework of the proposed military tribunals, neither the US Congress nor the judiciary would have any involvement in establishing rules of the proceedings or in the trials themselves. The executive order contained no provision for appeals and permitted trials to be held in secret. Death penalty sentences could be imposed without a unanimous vote, in closed proceedings, without the right to appeal to civilian courts.

By creating the option of military tribunals, the Bush Administration sought to prevent terrorist suspects from exploiting the constitutional protections of the criminal justice system, and from taking shelter in the constraints such protections place on prosecutors. The Administration also sought a process which would enable prosecutors to use evidence collected by US forces in Afghanistan, protect witnesses against retribution by terrorists and provide closed proceedings to protect classified evidence. In spite of the government's advocacy, and that of supporters such as Ruth Wedgwood, a Yale Law School professor and adviser to the Pentagon, or Harvard Law School's Laurence Tribe, both conservative and liberal critics challenged the tribunal framework for allowing verdicts based on hearsay or secret evidence, secret trials, inadequate legal representation, and the absence of an appeals process.

As a result of widespread criticism of the original order, the Bush administration issued a revised order in March, 2002 with greater due process protection. The March revision requires proof beyond a reasonable doubt as the standard of conviction, rather than the lesser standard of merely probative value to a reasonable person, and allow for an internal appeals process. The revision also mandates public trials whenever possible and unanimous judgment to impose the death penalty. Hearsay evidence and evidence gathered with less than a secure chain of custody could still be used, and proceedings could be closed for discussion of classified material.

Even with these revisions, critics argue that the revised order still gives rise to grave and perplexing issues about how the United States, or any democratic nation, should respond legally to international terrorism and prevent in doing so the erosion of democratic values and the rule of law. European nations particularly express concern about the death penalty provision as a complicating factor in extradition agreements. By sweeping aside standards of reasonable suspicion, trial process and civil rights for non-United States citizens, critics claim the tribunals result in a model of justice 'freed from the inconvenience of constitutional guarantees', and the restraint of international law, one that provides a mechanism for legal vengeance rather than impartial justice (Carne, pp. 302–3). With the core legal restraints of accountability, judicial independence and review removed, the international standing and impartiality of such tribunals is challenged most frequently in the European and American contexts by rationalist critics who argue from a framework of domestic legalism.

British Law Lord Johan Steyn, for example, in his November, 2003 F.A. Mann Lecture, 'Guantanamo Bay: The Legal Black Hole' acknowledges the dilemmas facing democracies from the threat of terrorism: 'Democracies must defend themselves. Democracies are entitled to try officers and soldiers of enemy forces for war crimes. But it is a recurring theme in history that in times of war, armed conflict, or perceived national danger, even liberal democracies adopt measures infringing human rights in ways that are wholly disproportionate to the crisis' (Steyn, p. 1). His argument draws its inspiration not from victors' justice arguments akin to Thrasymachus' that justice is the advantage of the stronger, nor from neorealist arguments sceptical of appeals to international law. Instead he denounces the excessive deference of the judiciary to the executive and the dramatic loss of liberty that results from executive abuse of power. His denunciation derives from rationalist assumptions about international law — especially his defence of the urgency of human rights protections for Guantanamo detainees.

> As matters stand at present the United States courts would refuse to hear a prisoner at Guantanamo Bay who produces credible medical evidence that he has been and is being tortured. They would refuse to hear prisoners who assert that they were not combatants at all. They would refuse to hear prisoners who assert that they were simply soldiers in the Taliban army and knew nothing about Al-Qaeda. They would refuse to examine any complaints of any individuals. The blanket presidential order deprives them all of any rights whatever (Steyn, p. 11).

Courts must assume responsibility, Lord Steyn argues, for granting judicial review and deciding the legality of detentions. 'Trials of the type contemplated by the United States government would be a stain on United States justice. The only thing that could be worse is simply to leave the prisoners in their black hole indefinitely' (Steyn, p. 12). To the question he raises in conclusion 'Ought our government to make plain publicly and unambiguously our condemnation of the utter lawlessness at Guantanamo Bay?' his answer is unequivocally yes (Steyn, 14). Recommending the creation of an ad hoc international tribunal set up through the UN Security Council, Lord Steyn affirms the spirit of an Israeli Supreme Court decision in which the court held that the violent interrogation of a suspected terrorist is not lawful even if such interrogation may save human life by preventing impending terrorist acts. Such restraint is essential, he argues, to the affirmation of democratic values and to long-range security.

The overwhelming criticism both within the United States and internationally to the military tribunal order is best understood, not in the light of sceptical views of unreachable facts, but in light of a rationalist legalism that retains hope for judicial process. The harshest critics of the tribunal order condemn national security justifications for lowering evidentiary standards, not the truth-finding power of evidence itself. Those like Dworkin who consider the refusal to permit appeals to appellate federal judges indefensible, or those who consider the use of hearsay or secret evidence damning to fairness, do so according to rationalist arguments. Were there not the assumption of better (i.e. more objective, more likely to be truthful) determinations of past events with higher standards of evidence and independent review, the moral force of such arguments would evaporate.

Indefinite Detention

On the same day as the Bush Administration issued its revised rules for military tribunals, William J. Haynes II, the Pentagon's chief lawyer, stated that the government may continue to hold accused terrorists who had been tried by a military tribunal and acquitted, if they were considered still to be dangerous (Seelye, 2002). Such indefinite detention in the context of refusing prisoner of war status to detainees is the subject of analysis by George Fletcher in his article 'On Justice and War: Contradictions in the Proposed Military Tribunals' (Fletcher, 2002). He notes the confusion we still feel about how to think about the use of military force in such contexts as Afghanistan. We are torn, he says, over using the language of justice and the very different language of war.

> Is this an attack by private individuals, a case of a single terrorist writ large? If the mass killings of September 11 are the crimes of individuals — Islamic fundamentalist versions of Timothy McVeigh — then we can think about arresting them and bring them to 'justice' (Fletcher, 2002, p. 365).

This way of speaking, he argues, has become part of the standard discourse of those who think and write about police-like interventions in other nations.

> If our goal is doing justice then we should focus on the individual culprits. If the point is to execute and win a war, then the primary concern should be our military objectives. The discourse of war suppresses the identity of particular actors in the aims of a collective military force. We were not concerned about the individual Japanese pilots who returned safely from the attack on Pearl Harbor. They were not criminals but rather agents of an enemy power. They were not personally 'guilty' for the attack, nor were their commanders, who acted in the name of the Japanese nation. Yet somehow we think things are different today. Individual soldiers cannot lose their identity in a collective

movement. They remain potentially liable to be brought to 'justice' for their actions (Fletcher, *ibid.*).

But is this a justified approach with regard to terrorists? Fletcher proposes that those who were complicit in the aggression of September 11 were guilty of war crimes and it makes sense 'to bring them to justice' before an international court or even before an American civilian court. But paradoxically, he argues, this requires that we acknowledge that the state of conflict with al-Qaeda and the Taliban is in fact a 'quasi-war'. War crimes are not the criminal acts of individuals, even of conspiracies of individuals. Thus we do best if we affirm the conflict as legally akin to a war, and al-Qaeda operatives as war criminals. In this way we join the ideas of justice and war in charging those operatives with war crimes before an international tribunal established by the United Nations. Such a tribunal would give greater credibility than a partisan in the war could claim for its own justice and would have the advantage of recognizing the multinational nature of victims killed in the September 11 attacks.

Fletcher's argument illustrates the complex debate over the status and rights of the prisoners held by the United States and the concern of many that credible justice, not just justice, be done. The solution Fletcher offers, bridging the two discourses of justice and war, advocates an international tribunal, even if such a tribunal proves more cumbersome and time-consuming than military tribunals. But his solution suggests vividly the unresolved legal issues surrounding the prosecution of suspected terrorists. In illustration of how unresolved these legal issues are, Aryeh Neier, former Human Rights Watch Director, notes in his article 'The Military Tribunals On Trial' (Neier, 2002) that President Bush's order for military commissions lumps together at least four categories of persons who have distinct sets of rights under domestic or international law: prisoners of war captured in Afghanistan, unlawful combatants arrested in Afghanistan or elsewhere in the world, illegal aliens within the US , and legal aliens within the US. Each falls within the planned jurisdiction of military tribunals. But little clarity has yet emerged over how the status of those now detained will be determined, and what evidence, if any, will be significant for their prosecution. Because their status is the result of conceptual, legal uncertainty — how detainees should be viewed — as well as inadequate evidence for prosecution and the use of detainees for the purpose of interrogation, evidence alone is not the decisive issue. If detainees were being held solely while evidence was gathered to sort out which among them were to be prosecuted, which to be repatriated, and which to be tried in their countries of origin, the limbo in which detainees now exist would be a simpler matter to resolve. But confusion over their ontological status remains, complicating their legal destiny.

The Pentagon so far has been unable to link many of the detainees held at Guantanamo to specific violations. Few have been valuable sources of information to interrogators and none as far as we know has confessed to war crimes. The US Administration has considered a new legal doctrine that would make possible prosecution without specific evidence of engagement in war crimes.[2] This new doctrine would make it an offence to be a senior member of Al-Qaeda, or officers of units that committed such offences. This doctrine would create the military equivalent of the charge of conspiracy which exists in civilian courts, a departure from the practice of the Nuremberg tribunal, where no one was ever charged on the basis alone of membership in the SS. According to the new doctrine, no evidence from witnesses would be required or documents proving the commission of war crimes. It would be enough that a detainee could be shown to be part of a group and furthered its aims. Such a legal doctrine risks creating an offence that is a status crime, which criminalizes mere group membership, an offence rejected by the Supreme Court. The new doctrine is likely to require not only membership but some identification with the aims of the group.

Such a legal doctrine is striking from an evidence perspective, since it can be seen as a legal effort by the Pentagon to justify the indefinite detention of suspects against whom no evidence exists of specific violations. Such unusual prosecutorial strategies raise difficult, if not impossible, questions of justification. In the nearly absent role of evidence in such executive strategizing, sceptical theories of evidence find their best confirmation. Such legal scepticism become especially convincing as detention stretches out indefinitely and some detainees are released without charge or repatriated for continued detention. In March 2004, after months of negotiation and more than two years of detention in Cuba, five British detainees were sent back to the UK where they were released without charge. One can only assume that no evidence existed to justify continued detention in Cuba or in London and a political rather than a legal solution to the contentious issue of their detention was sought. In a statement made upon the release of twenty-three Afghans and three Pakistanis, the Pentagon stated that the decision to release a detainee is based only upon his intelligence value to the United States and the threat he poses to security. In such language no acknowledgement is given to the judicial person.

At the time the new rules for military tribunals were announced, US Secretary of Defense Donald Rumsfeld introduced the possibility that captives from the Afghan war might not be released even if they were acquitted in a military tribunal. 'If we had a trial right this minute,' according to William Haynes I, the Pentagon's chief lawyer, 'it is con-

---

[2]   'Winging it at Guantanamo' *The New York Times*, April 23, 2002 A22

ceivable that somebody could be tried and acquitted of that charge but may not necessarily automatically be released' (Seelye, 2002). They are 'dangerous people', he observed. Don Rehkopf, co-chairman of the military law committee of the National Association of Criminal Defense Lawyers, said the detention of prisoners after acquittal showed that tribunal justice was set up for a predetermined outcome, stacked against defendants. In this 'innovative prosecutorial strategy' evidence becomes irrelevant. In conspiracy charges, evidence at least has the role of establishing that a defendant is guilty of furthering the aims of a terrorist organization. But in the detention of the acquitted, the absence of evidence has no power to win defendants release from captivity.

In 'The Trouble with Tribunals' Ronald Dworkin writes that 'even if national security requires our government to ignore traditional rights of accused criminals in pursuing and trying suspected terrorists, it must nevertheless recognize that it acts unfairly in doing so, and it must therefore violate those rights only when the violation is demonstrably essential' (Dworkin, April, 2002). The new rules, he argues, have two indefensible provisions: they allow the Secretary of Defense or the presiding officer of each tribunal to close the trial proceedings to the public and the press when either determines that this is necessary to guard the secrecy of 'classified or classifiable' information, to protect the physical safety of members of the tribunal or prosecutors or prospective witnesses, or to safeguard 'intelligence and law enforcement sources, methods, or activities' or 'other national security interest'. And they allow for the indefinite detention of acquitted terrorists if they are still thought to be dangerous. 'We have no right to roam the world arresting foreigners we think might be dangerous,' Dworkin argues, 'and keeping them in our jails when we cannot show them to have committed any crime' (Dworkin, *ibid.*).

Dworkin speaks in the language of customary respect for evidence in truth finding, in which we tolerate the acquittal even of those we have reason to believe guilty if insufficient evidence exists to convict. Such a high evidentiary standard is fundamental to the rule of law in civilian courts as well as in military courts that govern military courts-martial under the Uniform Code of Military Justice. But in the present state of flux brought on by the 'War on Terrorism', with the fact-finding role of evidence challenged both by its absence in certain cases and its irrelevance in others, military tribunals and indefinite detention have the potential to become wartime practices deeply regretted by those who inherit their legacy and who experience the scepticism they inspire about truth-finding and justice in times of war. In two significant decisions handed down in June, 2004, the US Supreme Court ruled that the executive branch does not have the authority to deprive accused members of al Qaeda or the Taliban of the right to judicial review. In Rasul v.

Bush the Court ruled that US courts have juridiction to consider challenges to the legality of the detention of foreign nationals at Guantanamo Bay. In Hamdi v. Rumsfeld, the Court affirmed that the US has the power to declare US citizens enemy combatants and detain them, but that such detention can be contested before a neutral decision maker. Though neither decision addressed the legality of the proposed military tribunals, both rulings affirmed due process and checked the power of the executive to create a parallel legal system for terrorism cases under exclusive executive control.

The struggle by any nation to maintain the rule of law as it attempts to assure national security reflects a deeper struggle, if the rationalist model is correct, over maintaining fidelity to truth and to evidence, no matter how imperfectly realized, when threats to security loom. That the compromise of due process rights might sometimes be necessary as democracies balance legal rights with other social values is reason less for scepticism about the law and the truth-finding role of evidence than proof of the rationalist foundation for 'outrage at the utter lawlessness of Guantanamo Bay'. Military tribunals may be an achievement of liberal states, but they risk failure if they are carried out in secrecy by those with a vested interest only in conviction, with death sentences looming and without the protection of civilian appeal. Then, with power masquerading as law, military tribunals become extralegal solutions to the dilemma of how to treat captive enemies.[3]

[3]   I would like to express appreciation to Timothy L. Challans, US Army Command and General Staff College, for his eloquent comments on a version of this paper presented at the Mini-Conference on Global Justice at the American Philosophical Association, Pacific Division Meeting, March, 2004.

Anthony Ellis

A Deterrence Theory
of Punishment

Introduction

I take it that punishment must be justified predominantly by reference to deterrence. I hold this for two reasons, though I shall not try to support them in detail here.

First, each of the so-called 'retributive' theories[1] is either internally incoherent or has implausible moral implications.

The most popular retributive theory, amongst non-philosophers, anyway, is probably the theory that offenders deserve to suffer simply because they have committed an offence, and that the intensity of their suffering should be in proportion to the moral gravity of their offence.[2] This does not involve the thought that their suffering will achieve some good, except in the trivial sense that, if they suffer, then what ought to be will be. Despite its popular appeal, this theory has often been thought to face insurmountable obstacles. First, the claim that offences demand suffering in return, with no further reason given, will strike some as arbitrary, or worse. More important, I think, it surely needs to be explained how it is possible for us to compare, in a suitable way, the intensity of suffering with the moral gravity of an offence. I share the view of many, that this explanation cannot be given, but I cannot argue that here.

There are, of course, other theories that may plausibly lay claim to the title 'retributive', and some might evade these particular objections.[3] But, though I cannot argue the point here, I believe that no 'retributive' theory can be shown to be both coherent and morally plausible.[4]

---

[1]   I do not in fact think that the notion of retribution is particularly useful as part of a categorisation of theories of punishment, but it will do for present purposes.

[2]   See, for instance, Moore (1987).

[3]   For a brief account of some of them, see Ellis (1995).

[4]   For a discussion of one such theory, see Ellis (1997).

Second, even if there were an otherwise acceptable retributive theory of punishment, we should have to reject it, for I believe that the use of coercive force against other rational agents[5] is justified only in self-defence against aggression, that is to say, against behaviour that violates a constraint that one has a right to uphold in self-interest. (As is usual, I include in this the defence of others' self-interest.) This requirement, of course, does not itself restrict us to a deterrent theory, for it is consistent with other possible justificatory aims. For instance, the currently popular idea that the main point of imprisonment is to remove offenders from circulation, and thus directly prevent their offences, is consistent with it; this of course, requires a suitable account of the conditions in which pre-emptive action is justified, but I assume that such an account can be given. So too, the idea that reform is the main aim of punishment is also consistent with it, because the attempt to reform offenders might be driven wholly by the demands of self-defence. But most punishments have no significant preventive effect and could not seriously be intended to have — small fines, for instance — and their beneficial reformative effect is scarcely more pronounced.

The simplest version of the deterrence theory of punishment — that we punish offenders to deter other, potential offenders — has usually been rejected for two reasons.

First, punishing one person in order to modify the behaviour of others seems to violate what may be called the Kantian Constraint: the requirement that we never use anyone merely as a means. There have been many ways of trying to avoid this. For now, I shall simply register my agreement with Tony Honoré that none of them will work.[6] I think that the objection is correct, and the only response a proponent of the theory could make would be to accept this and simply tough it out.

Second, the theory lays down no acceptable limits on punishment. Presumably, if we are concerned simply with deterring offenders then the appropriate level of punishment should be whatever is necessary to deter. And this might be, in particular cases, either too lenient or too severe. Of course, we can solve the problem by laying down independent moral constraints upon the acceptable levels of punishment.[7] But

---

[5] I am of course excluding children, the mentally ill and so on.

[6] Honoré, (1999), p. 19. Broadly, attempts to avoid the problem hold that punishing offenders to deter others does not unacceptably use them (because, for instance, they have implicitly assented in advance to this treatment, or because they deserve their punishment) or that they have forfeited the right not to be used.

[7] This the position of H.L.A. Hart (or one of his positions); see Hart (1968).

this may seem ad hoc; one might have hoped for a more unified theory, one in which the point of the institution itself generates the constraints.[8]

In this paper I shall sketch a deterrent theory which avoids these objections.

Self-Defensive Deterrence and the Kantian Constraint

The theory understands punishment as a form of self-defence. I assume that we have the right to use force in legitimate self-defence. I also assume that groups may use force in self-defence, and that a society or a nation may do so.

Do we, in addition, have the right to threaten retaliation against potential aggressors in order to deter them? It seems plausible to think that, at least sometimes, we do; all else equal, it must surely be better to try to prevent aggression rather than to have to deal with it forcefully when it occurs. Of course, all else may not be equal. Greater force may have to be used to deter aggression than would be required to deflect it once it had started. Or the methods used to deter could be intrinsically unacceptable. Or the threat may have little chance of succeeding or even constitute a perverse incentive to potential aggressors. But in the absence of such factors, threats of retaliation are surely acceptable. However, this raises a familiar question: If it is indeed permissible to *threaten* some level of retaliation to deter aggression, is it also permissible *to carry out* that retaliation if the threat fails to work? The justification for *threatening* is that it will prevent aggression (and any harm involved in a self-defensive response). If the threat does not work, however, that justification will not carry over into a justification for *carrying out* the threat, for carrying out the threat will, by hypothesis, do nothing to prevent the aggression and its attendant harms. Retaliation, then, seems unjustified (at least by the principles of self-defence).

But imagine that in addition to merely issuing the threat I somehow *bound myself* to carry it out.[9] I mean by this not just that I pledged myself to carry it out, but that I somehow made it the case that if the threat were ignored retaliation would be inevitable. We could suppose, for instance, that I constructed a booby trap surrounding my domain which, once it was constructed, I could not dismantle, and whose operation was automatic as soon as anyone crossed my border; I might then, with the intention of deterring anyone from crossing the border, announce that I had

[8]   Cf Montague (1995) p. 91; Ashworth (1995).

[9]   Warren Quinn also used this idea in a discussion of punishment (Quinn, 1985). Daniel Farrell has shown that Quinn's argument rests upon a false premise; see Farrell (1989). The idea that punishment can be justified as a form of self defence has also been defended by Phillip Montague (1995), and by Farrell (see Farrell, 1995 and 1989).

done this. If the threat of retaliation failed, the actual retaliation would be automatic.

Now when an offender is retaliated against by such an automatic system (let us just say 'punished' from now on) can he complain that he is being used? Initially, at least, it hardly seems so. That charge was based on the claim that offenders were being made to suffer in order to modify the behaviour of others, and that seems no longer true. After all, it may be known that the offender's punishment will have no such effect; how then can it be said that he is being punished in order to deter others? His punishment is simply a direct response to his own action, carrying no thought of how it may affect others.

However, the core of the worry may remain. Any particular offender's punishment may be known to have no deterrent effect, but the fact that punishments are actually administered must play some role, otherwise it would not be justified to go beyond a system in which the threat were merely a bluff. The obvious role is to make the threat credible to others. It may then seem that the actual offender is punished because the system requires that offenders in general be punished in order to maintain the general effectiveness of the system. And this may seem essentially no different from a system in which we picked a number of people and punished them as a deterrent demonstration to others, knowing that, for whatever reason, some of these punishments would not in fact serve that purpose; here, each offender could correctly say that he was being used to deter others even though, in some cases, the particular punishment would not have that effect.

But maintaining the credibility of the threat is not the only reason we could have for making it a genuine one. We could imagine that, for various reasons, a bluff might actually work — sufficiently so at least to maintain the system's effectiveness. In such circumstances, there might still be reasons to make the threat a real one. It may simply be more convenient for some reason. Or, again, a system of bluffs would require dishonesty, and we might object to that. There is, of course, an indefinite number of further possible reasons, reasons having nothing to do with the deterrent effectiveness of the system. So long as one of these is our reason, no-one is punished because the system requires that offenders be punished in order to maintain the deterrent effectiveness of the system. This should remove the last vestige of the worry that offenders are being used. It would be in no sense true that they are being punished in an attempt to modify the behaviour of others. The threat is addressed to each individually, and each is punished because he, individually, chose to ignore the threat; the others, and their potential behaviour, are now irrelevant.[10]

There are, of course, other possible problems with such retaliatory systems. One is that they may seem to involve the intention to cause harm at a point in time at which this harm may be known to have no beneficial effects. But that is a tendentious description. Less tendentiously, the system requires that at time $t1$, with the intention of preventing an evil, we set in motion an irreversible process, which, if our intention is not realised, will cause harm at $t2$. Now it is certainly impermissible to intend, *tout court*, to cause pointless harm; but it does not follow from this that it is impermissible to intend to prevent harm by setting in motion a train of events which will, if one's intention is not realised, cause harm. That will depend upon the totality of the circumstances, and in particular whether the agent has observed certain conditions which I shall outline later.[11]

A different sort of problem we may refer to as the problem of scatter: unless the system's method of detection were infallible such a threat would be triggered even by innocent people whom the system mistakenly took to be aggressors. (Who is 'innocent' is a problem to which we shall return.) But this does not by itself make such systems impermissible, for there are clearly circumstances in which it is permissible knowingly to put innocent people at risk as long as this is not our aim. Indeed, we do this constantly in our criminal justice systems, requiring only that benefits and risks be appropriately balanced. And so long as there is that appropriate balance, there is, as yet, no objection to such deterrent threats.

One way of making it easier to achieve that balance would be by making the system slightly less automatic, allowing it to be stopped when there is reason to think that an apparent aggressor is in fact innocent. I might do this by dividing the operation into different functions and placing each in the hands of a different person. One of them might be authorised to apprehend suspected aggressors, another might be authorised to decide whether they really were aggressors, and another might be authorised to administer punishment if appropriate. But

---

[10] Of course, it remains true that the offender is made to suffer in order to promote an end of mine, not of his; but this by itself could not ground the charge that I am *using* him. If it did, an act of direct self-defence would also ground the charge. (It might be different, in both cases, if my response were excessive.) And if we know that the fully-armed system has greater deterrent effectiveness than a system of bluffs, we may welcome this. This too would not ground the charge; its greater effectiveness might be a foreseen, but unintended, side-effect.

[11] There is, of course, an immense and ancient literature to which I cannot here do justice on the logic of the intentions embedded in threats. For a relevant discussion, see Farrell (1998).

no-one would have authority to deactivate his part of the system except in special circumstances. From my point of view, this system would be substantially similar to the simpler model we envisaged a moment ago. Once I have issued my threat I have nothing further to do in order for an aggressor to be punished; from my point of view it is now automatic. It can now properly be said that the aim of the system is deterrence, but that no-one is punished in order to deter others.

The Model and the Real World

It may seem that this model is too remote from reality to tell us anything about punishment in the real world. However, I shall suggest that it is a useful model of our own criminal justice system.

A criminal statute, we may say, lays down a threat, which we can think of as threat of retaliation against anyone in violation of its prohibition. And it is, in the important sense, like the threat in the model we have envisaged: once someone has transgressed, the procedure goes forward fairly automatically.[12]

It is automatic in the sense in which the system just imagined is automatic — a system which, of course, was meant to reflect the separation of powers that characterises modern democracies. The legislature issues threats, but it has no authority to decide whether those threats are acted on in particular cases. Prosecutors and police have that authority; but they in turn have no authority to decide whether a convicted person is punished.[13] Judges (and jurors) decide upon sentences, but only in accordance with previous law. Punishment is then in the hands of the executive, which, in general, has no authority not to administer due punishment. We might say: We, through the legislature, issue a threat; 'we', however, cannot revoke it. From 'our' point of view, punishment is automatic.

This may seem to ignore the discretion exercised by each branch of the penal system. The police are granted some authority not to pursue a complaint, or merely to issue a warning to an offender; a prosecutor may choose not to prosecute a case; a judge typically has some discretion in

---

[12] Legal systems differ, of course. In some, such as the German and Austrian systems, prosecution of all offences is, in principle, mandatory where there is adequate evidence to sustain a conviction. In others, such as the UK and US systems, there is broad discretion at most levels. It is enough, of course, for my present purposes that we can imagine a realistic system in which the normal, though not necessarily mandatory course, is prosecution. And, or so I shall suggest, this is the best understanding of the US and UK systems.

[13] Actually, in some jurisdictions the police can deal with fines for minor traffic offences. And in some systems prosecutors are empowered to dismiss cases if the accused is prepared to pay some compensation to the victim, or even make a payment to a charity nominated by the prosecutor.

sentencing. There are also exceptions to the general picture I have sketched, such as the power of executive clemency. And insofar as this discretion extended to the authority to take account of the deterrent effects of particular punishments it would, of course, reintroduce the original worry.

That it does so extend in our own legal systems seems clear. But we are not bound to this. Though there is much discretion in the operation of the law, none of it is arbitrary. When an offence has been committed, the default presumption is that it will be prosecuted and punished, and, at every level, if the law is not to take its normal course this should be because allowing it to do so would be against 'the public interest'. We need not now give a full account of what is meant by that phrase, but it need not be, and is not, construed in a narrowly utilitarian way − it already encompasses notions of what is just or fair, for instance. It would not, then, be an unrealistically radical step to embody in this notion the value of individuals which lays a moral constraint upon merely using them. We can plausibly say, then, that if, at any stage in a particular case, the question is raised as to whether the law should take its normal course, that question should not be answered by reference to whether doing so will deter others.[14]

We have, then, a system in which the legislature issues a threat whose execution is, from their point of view, automatic; they need, and can, do nothing further to ensure that it is carried out. Of course, those who are involved in carrying it out are granted some discretion in this. But so long as that discretion does not extend to deciding individual cases on the basis of deterrent effectiveness, it can correctly be said that the point of the penal system is to deter, but that we do not punish the offender to deter others.

The Limits of Self-Defence

Let us turn now to the limits on punishment. If deterrent threats are made in self-defence, then they are subject to the principles of self-defence, a central one of which is that it is permissible to use in self-defence only such force as is 'reasonably necessary'. What does that mean?

Imagine that I have only three possible responses to an act of aggression already under way: doing nothing, rational persuasion and counter-force. What I may permissibly do will be a matter of the likely costs and benefits, broadly construed.

---

[14] The UK Criminal Justice Act 1991 signalled a clear move away from deterrent considerations in sentencing: individual sentences were to be based primarily upon the 'seriousness' of the offence, with the possibility of incapacitative sentences for some offenders who posed a great risk to the community.

For each course of action, the primary benefit aimed at will be that the threatened harm is avoided or minimised. So we need to know both how great the threatened harm is, and how likely it is to occur given each course of action. If the threatened harm is slight and merely speculative then normally the correct course of action will be to do nothing, though in such circumstances there will usually be other alternatives than the three just mentioned. At the other extreme, a high probability of serious harm if I do not use force will often justify it. But not always: in particular, if it has in any case no chance of warding off the threat then it will be pointless violence, and cannot be justified under the principles of self-defence.

As to what count as costs there will be some dispute. Some will consider the harm to the aggressor a cost, but others will not.[15] Some may consider it a (moral) cost to oneself to indulge in violence, even if it is justified to do so, whereas others will not. But there are some costs that are clear: a forceful response to aggression may simply trigger a forceful counter-response on the part of my aggressor, for instance; or it may cause harm to innocent third parties. And on any plausible view forceful action will be in general more costly than non-forceful action.

These considerations, which we shall refer to as the Restraining Considerations, determine when it is reasonable to use force and how much force it is reasonable to use. Dispute about their precise content can be settled only by appeal to their source. That too, of course, there will be dispute about, and I can do little more here than state baldly what I believe it is.

It stems, I believe, from the general social necessity to minimise the use of violence. It is clear that we need disincentives to violence, and recognising the right to self-defence is one of the most important of them. But forceful self-defence itself needs restrictions, for it too poses dangers: it may spill over into, or be confused with, vengeance, with all of its attendant dangers; it may be used as a cloak for violence desired for other ends; it may provoke further violence from the aggressor, either in self-defence or in revenge; and it poses dangers to those who are uninvolved. On the other hand, an absolute prohibition on the use of force would obviously not be desirable, for this would remove a major disincentive to aggression. And it would not be generally adhered to; most would think that, in its encouragement to aggression, it made no sense, and they would not respect it. In any case, self-interest would ensure that people would not routinely forego the use of force when this meant a significant sacrifice to themselves.

---

[15] Most would think that the degree of the aggressor's responsibility would need to be taken account of, but not necessarily as limiting the victim's rights; it may be unkind to use force against an 'innocent threat', but it is not necessarily unjust.

So a compromise has to be found between an absolute prohibition and no restriction at all. It is impossible to say with precision just where it will be located. But the guiding principle will be that the use of force should be confined to limits that we can sensibly expect people to abide by, and force that is reasonably necessary is simply force within those limits. There will, obviously, be some disagreement about what those limits should be; but there is also considerable agreement. Virtually everyone agrees, for instance, that the victim of aggression should be required to forego self-defensive force when there is a significant disparity between the harm threatened and the amount of force required to thwart it: this is a restriction that normal people will see the point of, and will generally abide by. And, when it is reasonably necessary to use force, the restriction on the amount of force that may be used has of course the same point. Its effect is to reduce forceful counter-measures to the level that we can sensibly demand. We require, then, that victims should sometimes be prepared to sustain some loss when responding forcefully to an aggressor by choosing a less forceful measure than they might prefer. There is, of course, no way in practice of saying precisely how great a loss it is reasonable in general to require; it is no surprise, therefore, that judgements vary over this matter.

Let us turn now to *deterrent threats*. Again, imagine that I have three possible responses to a threat of aggression: I may do nothing, I may try to persuade potential aggressors not to aggress, or I may threaten them with retaliation in order to deter them.

The Restraining Considerations operate much as before: we need to know the scale and likelihood of the threatened harm, the likelihood of success of each course of action, and the costs of each course. But different factors will now become salient. For instance, since we are talking about merely potential aggression we shall need to think of how tempting is the aggression to potential aggressors: the more tempting it is, the greater harm it will be justified to threaten (other things being equal). There is also the possibility that the threat may act as a perverse incentive, or that retaliation will lead some to seek revenge. And, if we are talking of semi-automatic systems of retaliation, the possible harm to innocent third parties will loom much larger.

It may seem natural to think that it would be permissible to threaten in deterrence all and only what it would be permissible to do in direct self-defence. But this is not, of course, correct. The Restraining Considerations mentioned above generate crucial divergences.

First, we may take account of the probability that the threat itself may work, and the retaliation thus not be triggered. This will often relax the limits. Indeed, other things being equal, there would perhaps be no limit at all on what might be threatened if we could be absolutely sure that the threat would be effective.[16]

On the other side, there is the crucial question of immediacy. Potential aggressors can often be deterred by the threat of much less force than would be required to prevent their aggression once it has started. (It may be necessary to kill someone who is trying to kill you; but he might have been deterred if you had let it be known that if someone kills you, your friends will administer him a beating.) More generally, all sorts of resources that might have been available in advance will not be available in the heat of the moment.

The issue of immediacy also raises the question of scatter. If I booby-trap my house, and post a notice to this effect, the trap may still be triggered by innocent intruders who have not seen the notice. This problem is not confined to self-defensive threats, of course; it applies also to direct self-defence. But it is presumably a more serious problem in the case of automatic and semi-automatic systems of threatened retaliation than in most cases of direct self-defence, and requires a greater stringency in the restrictions governing their use.

Further complications arise when we move from *individual* self-defensive deterrence to *collective* self-defensive deterrence on the part of society against those who aggress against its members; there will then be special empirical facts, and, arguably, special normative considerations, to take account of. But the goal of reducing violence will still be appropriate. A threat of retaliation may be a successful disincentive against aggression. But even when wielded by the government, it must be hedged about with restrictions. For one thing, we are rightly reluctant to give governments more coercive power than is necessary, for its agents are ordinary people, as likely to misuse such power as others. And we are reluctant to allow government to resort to force too easily, for this is a lapse from the ideal relationship between government and citizens. And even when serious punishment is completely justified, it is likely to foster an alienation from the government on the part of at least some citizens (the family and friends of the offender, for instance). There is also the question of likely harm to innocents. As well as the wrongly convicted there are others, such as the innocent families of properly convicted offenders. And the more serious the punishment we threaten, the greater the costs we shall feel constrained to pay in the attempt to avoid miscarriages of justice. The government is required, then, not to use the threat of punishment to prevent crime if there is a reasonable, less violent alternative; and it may threaten no more than is reasonably required for deterrence.

---

[16]   But see Duff (1986) for the rejection of such threats.

So, though the principles are the same, what it is permissible for an individual to do in direct self-defence will often diverge from what it is permissible for society to threaten in self-defensive deterrence. Overlooking this may make it seem that punishment and self-defence are morally separate phenomena:

> Proportionality in punishment . . . is more rigorous than proportionality in self-defence. Using the death penalty for rape, for example, violates the principle of proportional punishment. . . . Yet if a woman is threatened by rape, she may legally resist by killing the aggressor. Even legal systems that have abolished the death penalty permit the use of deadly force in the defence of vital interests. While proportionality in punishment requires that the sentence fit the crime, clearly more is permitted in self-defence (Fletcher, 1988, p. 29).

Fletcher speaks here of a distinction between what is permissible in self-defence and what is permissible in punishment. But we could equally well think of it as a distinction between what is permissible in direct, individual self-defence and what is permissible in collective, self-defensive deterrence. A woman faced with imminent rape faces an immediate, serious threat, which there may be no way of repelling short of killing her attacker. A legislature deciding upon the sentence for rape faces a different problem. Its problem is to deter potential rapists, and a threat of death is not reasonably necessary for this end; for the most part, the threat of lesser punishment achieves it. So an individual woman may kill in order to resist rape, whereas the state may not punish rapists by killing them.

But if the threat of imprisonment works only 'for the most part', why should we not say that a threat of death, which may have greater deterrent force, is 'reasonably necessary'?

First, threats of death would be unlikely to achieve the desired result. Most of those who are not deterred by the threat of relatively heavy prison sentences would not be significantly more effectively deterred by the threat of capital punishment. In addition, juries would generally be unwilling to send rapists to their deaths, and this would decrease its deterrent value. This problem might be alleviated by restricting capital punishment to only a few types of rape; but this would increase the uncertainty attaching to the consequences of the offence and would correspondingly reduce its deterrent value again. Second, even if it did decrease the number of rapes, we should have to set against that the likely costs. They include the destruction of human life. Many people would think this justifiable to prevent an otherwise certain rape, but not justified as part of a somewhat speculative process designed to deter possible rapes. The likelihood of wrongful convictions would also strike most people as an unacceptable cost.[17] The point is illustrated in most legal systems. A woman immediately threatened with rape may kill to protect herself. But in most civilised jurisdictions she may not, in order to deter potential rapists (or even potential murderers), display a deadly weapon with intent to use it; and even those jurisdictions which allow the open carrying of firearms would balk at a woman booby-trapping her body with a bomb which would explode if she were attacked; these measures would pose an unreasonable threat to innocent people. The government, in adopting measures to deter rapists, is in the same position.

In order to explain the phenomenon remarked by Fletcher, then, we do not need principles of punishment intrinsically more restrictive than the principles of self-defence. On the other hand, if we derive the principles of punishment from the principles of self-defence then anything that is permissible in direct self-defence will indeed be permissible, in some imaginable circumstances, in deterrent threats. Imagine, for instance, a desert island inhabited by two people, one of whom is a determined rapist who can be deterred only by the genuine threat of death. Would it in those circumstances be permissible to set up a deterrent threat of automatic, deadly retaliation? In these unlikely circumstances, it might be.[18] But the legal system in the real world never finds itself in circumstances like these.

The Shape of Punishment

What would a legal system look like that followed these principles?

The range of offences that could be punished would be those alone which could plausibly be brought under the umbrella of self-defence. It would, then, be impermissible to punish behaviour merely on the ground that it was immoral. And it would be impermissible to punish behaviour which harmed only the agent.[19] The most obviously punishable behaviour would be paradigm acts of aggression, such as rape and murder. But regulatory offences, such as traffic offences, would also be covered since these, if legitimate, are constraints that we are justified in

---

[17] Since 1973 '[a]t least 96 people have been exonerated and freed from death rows in 22 states' (*The New York Times*, August 24th, 2001).

[18] It would depend in part upon the amount of violence that this threat, and its realisation, might themselves trigger, and in part upon the relative evaluation of sexual autonomy and human life. About that latter consideration the Protective-Deterrent theory has itself, like other theories of punishment, nothing to say. All that can be said is that *if* it is permissible to kill to avoid an otherwise certain rape *then* there will be some conceivable circumstance in which it would be permissible to mount a credible and genuine threat of death to deter a potential rapist.

[19] But presumably citizens could vote (unanimously?) for paternalistic measures to protect themselves against themselves?

protecting in self-interest, and that was how we spelled out the notion of self-defence.

It would have a robust and plausible requirement that the punishment should fit the crime: it would restrict punishment to what it is reasonable to threaten in order to deter the offence. Deterrent considerations, however, would play no further part in the treatment of particular cases.

A particular aspect of the idea that the punishment should fit the crime is the idea that the innocent should not be punished, and the deterrence theory can explain this. Punishment is retaliation against those who ignored a warning. The system is set up so as to be triggered by those who ignore that warning, not by others, and no acceptable self-defensive intention would be achieved by setting it up in any other way. 'Punishing' those who are innocent, then, will have no justification, for they have not failed to comply with the warning. Unless we were — unacceptably — using them in a deterrent display, there would thus be no way of bringing their punishment under the umbrella of self-defence.

We could, of course, set up the system so that innocents might suffer the 'retaliation'. We could issue threats to punish the innocent relatives of potential lawbreakers, for instance. Or we could threaten to harm entire groups when only certain members of the group transgress. But it is clear that punishment in these circumstances would be *using* people. Those who are punished would, either directly or indirectly, be made to suffer as part of an attempt to modify the behaviour of others; the deterrence theory can quite consistently object to that.

Questions of guilt and innocence, of course, refer to more than whether the defendant committed the prohibited act. First, punishment is hedged around with the requirements of mens rea, or responsibility. One is not punished at all unless one acted in an appropriate state of mind. And the severity of one's punishment may depend upon one's state of mind when one committed the offence, whether one did it deliberately or negligently, for instance. Second, the law recognises a number of excuses, such as necessity or duress, which can lead to an acquittal or mitigation of sentence. Many people will think that all of this reflects nothing of self-defence, for our right of self-defence against one who threatens us does not seem to turn upon his level of responsibility, or whether he is coerced into harming us. We are equally justified, they would think, in defending ourselves against a coerced threat as against an uncoerced one, against an insane assailant as against a sane one. Why, then, are such questions so important in the law?

Let us think first about responsibility. A requirement of responsibility enters into the limits of self-defence as soon as we move from direct self-defence to deterrent threats. The reason is simple: there is no point in issuing threats to those who cannot heed them, and any violence that such threats occasion would therefore be without justification. Anyone who suffered such violence would have been done an injustice. The law, then, may not justifiably threaten, for instance, the severely mentally ill with punishment, and so may not punish them. (It may, of course, detain them for the safety of themselves and others.) The threat of punishment is not addressed to them.

But some of the mentally ill, kleptomaniacs for example, are deterrable to some degree, and threats, though they may eventually be ignored, are not without effect. Is it then permissible to punish such people? If it would not be pointless to threaten them with punishment, then punishment, within the Restraining Considerations, would not be unjust. So they may be punished without injustice. It is a misfortune for them that they suffer this obsession; but others are not required to bear the burden of their misfortune and may use whatever force is reasonably necessary to protect themselves against its consequences. Whether carrying out punishment in such circumstances would be stupid, or callous are, of course, different questions.

Let us turn now to negligence. We seem to have the same right of self-defence against a negligent threat as against a deliberate one. But, typically, the law treats deliberate misconduct more severely than negligent misconduct. How can that be if punishment is a form of self-defence?

We do indeed have the same rights of self-defence against negligent and deliberate threats, but when we think about self-defensive deterrence, as opposed to direct self-defence, we should be more concerned about the prospect of deliberate misconduct than the prospect of negligent misconduct. Deliberate misconduct is in general more likely to cause harm than negligent misconduct: we have more reason to be concerned about someone who intends to kill than about someone who simply drives his car recklessly, for, in general, the former will pose a much more serious threat. Additionally, deliberate misconduct threatens the fabric of the social order in a way that negligence does not. Further, it is generally easier to deter negligent behaviour, which requires only more care, than deliberate misconduct, which requires abandoning a positively desired course of action. All of this, other things being equal, justifies a correspondingly less forceful measure.

Let us turn now to excuses, such as coercion. The actions of one who is severely coerced are guided by reasons, and so this is not like the case of the mentally ill. On the other hand, we can be quite sure that those who are severely coerced will not respond to threats of punishment (those who coerce them will find it easy to ensure that); so threats would again be pointless and any violence they involved unjustified. So legal threats are not addressed to those who are severely coerced; coercion is an excuse.[20]

Does what I have said so far mean that it is unjustifiable to issue threats of punishment whenever we are sure that this will not deter? And does that in turn mean that it is unjustifiable to threaten punishment to hard-core, recidivist criminals? The answer to the first question is Yes, to the second question No. 'Hard-core, recidivist criminals' may offend whatever we do, but they would commit far more offences if they had *cartes blanches* to do so. Deterrent effectiveness is always a matter of degree and one who eventually offends may nonetheless have been deterred *to some degree*, in the sense that the range of circumstances in which he would offend is restricted. The threat is thus not pointless, and the violence it involves may be justifiable.

I shall deal with one last issue, the law of attempts. An unsuccessful attempt to commit a crime may itself be a separate crime: one who tries to murder but fails may be convicted of attempted murder. This may seem odd from the point of view of the deterrence theory:

> those who set about crime intend to succeed and the law's threat has all the deterrent force it can have if it is attached to the crime; no additional effect is given to it if unsuccessful attempts are also punished.[21]

But the deterrence theory can explain why we have separate offences of attempt. If we were setting up a system of semi-automatic retaliation, we should not set it up so that the retaliation would be triggered only by the completed offence. Our first thought might be that we should set it up, if possible, so that it would be triggered *before* the offence was complete, indeed as soon as the offender had fully committed himself to his course of action. But the issue is more complicated. Given the goal of reducing violence, a rational strategy would not only be to give potential aggressors an incentive not to aggress in the first place; we should also want to give actual aggressors an incentive to desist from their actions even when they had embarked on them, and to give them such an incentive for as long as reasonably possible. However, if we set the trigger point very late, we might encourage potential offenders to embark on offences, and continue with them, at some cost to others, knowing that they could later withdraw if it seemed prudent. If, on the other hand, we set the trigger point very early — as soon as they had started planning the act, for instance — then this would deprive offenders of what might have been an effective incentive to desist once the act was under way; in

---

[20] Typically, only severe coercion is an excuse. (It does not usually excuse in murder cases. But if threats of punishment are no more likely to deter potential murderers than others, coercion should be an excuse here too, as some legal theorists have argued.)

[21] Hart, (1968) p. 128. Hart thinks that this is a 'fallacy'.

addition, enforcing this would require enormous resources, and considerable general deprivation of liberty. The challenge, then, is to find the point at which one's self-defensive strategy would be optimised within the Restraining Considerations mentioned earlier.[22]

This goal in turn makes intelligible why unsuccessful attempts are usually punished less severely than completed attempts. The emphasis on moral desert that characterises many theories of punishment makes this puzzling.[23] But from the point of view of the protective-deterrence theory moral desert, will of course not be the issue. All that will be relevant are the considerations mentioned earlier: roughly, what will be the likely costs and benefits of threatening various levels of retaliation against, say, unsuccessful attempts? We have reason to want offenders to desist from their offences even when they have already embarked upon them; given this, it would be perverse to threaten them with the full punishment as soon as they embark on the offence, for then they would have no incentive to desist as soon as the likelihood of apprehension is as great as when the offence is accomplished. A natural thought would be a sliding scale of retaliation: roughly, and other things being equal, the further along the course of his action the offender had progressed, the greater would be the retaliation. This would not, of course, be practical in the criminal law. Our best approximation is to fix a point at which an attempt, as opposed to mere preparations, really has been made and a point at which the attempt has been completed; between those two points we punish, but less severely than for the completed attempt.

Conclusion: The Role of Punishment

I have suggested that punishment, if it is to be justified, must be understood as the exercise of self-defence, and that it must work mainly through deterrent threats. If that is so, then punishment should assume a much smaller role in our response to crime than it does at the moment.

It is surely incredible that punishment has *no* deterrent effect. As I have already indicated, even the most hardened, or reckless, criminal will normally be deterred *to some extent* by the threat of punishment; the question is whether the extent of the deterrence justifies the costs involved. And, at least as far as current levels of imprisonment are concerned, virtually no-one thinks that this is now the case. The past forty

---

[22] And we find, in jurisprudential thought, just what we should expect, given this aim. But for a different approach, see *Criminal Attempts* (Duff, 1996).

[23] Antony Duff has tried to explain the puzzle in *Criminal Attempts* (Duff, 1996). I have criticised Duff's argument in Ellis (1998).

years have seen a huge increase in the number of people sent to prison,[24] and, paradoxically, a substantial increase in the average length of prison sentences. But there is no evidence that this has been tracked by a decrease in the crimes that have been targeted. It could, of course, be suggested that without these increases there would have been a corresponding increase in the amount of crime. But there is no evidence to suggest this; and it would be surprising if there were, given what we know about the workings of deterrence and the effect of imprisonment on offenders and their future opportunities. On the other side, the costs of imprisonment (financial costs not being the least important)[25] are enormous.

The drive towards more, and longer, prison sentences has, of course, not been driven merely by the thought of deterrence. It has partly been driven by the desire to 'get criminals off the streets'. This pre-emptive use of force, though more fraught with problems — both moral and epistemological — than is the deterrent use of force, is not intrinsically unacceptable. However, its acceptable use within the criminal justice system is surely very limited. For one thing, it requires that we be able to predict, with a satisfactory level of accuracy, those offenders who will offend again; and outside of a small range of cases, we cannot do this. The result is that many offenders are imprisoned without good reason; this is an injustice to them, and a considerable cost to the rest of us. We need not doubt that there are offenders whom, costs and benefits properly weighed, it is justifiable to keep in 'preventive detention'. But it would surely be a fantasy to think that this was anything other than a tiny proportion of the prison population in the UK and, especially, the US.[26]

That the effect of punishment on crime is generally exaggerated, and that the current scale of imprisonment in the US and UK cannot be justified, are, of course, beliefs common to a large body of criminological thought, and it is gratifying to be in this company. But what, in more detail, a penal system grounded solely in the demands of self-defence would look like is the topic for a different occasion.[27]

---

[24] In the US, at present, almost three-quarters of one per cent of the population is in prison.

[25] The current average cost of keeping an offender in prison in the US runs at around $25,000 per annum.

[26] Cf 'California reinvents the wheel', *New York Times*, 16th April, 2004, A20. On 'preventive detention' generally see, see Zimring and Hawkins (1995).

[27] An earlier version of the present essay appears in *The Philosophical Quarterly*, Vol. 53, July 2003, pp. 337–51 (Blackwell Publishing).

Jonathan Jacobs

Retributivism and Public Norms

Introduction

The focus of this discussion is the question of the moral legitimacy of punishing agents who do not and perhaps cannot recognize the justice of being punished. It would seem that a crucial element of the moral justification of punishment is that there should be a substantial degree of endorsement of the values that underwrite the norms governing sanction. If the values reflected in the norms are wrong or perverse, or if there is only partial or minority endorsement of those values and norms, that raises serious doubts about the legitimacy of punitive sanction. This is because when agents do not acknowledge the rightness of the law and the appropriateness of sanction, punishment will be mainly regulative, a strategy of social control without clearly being morally justified.

Of course, punishment *is* a strategy of social control, but not *only* that. Even if that is a primary function of punishment and is central to the explanation of why there is the institution of punishment at all, still, deliberately imposing harm upon members of civil society in an institutionalized way is something that requires moral justification. I will argue that punishment is a mode of address by rational agents to rational agents, and that it fundamentally involves communicative aspects concerning values. This is an important feature of the respect in which punishment is a *moral* practice. Even in a view such as Kant's, which comes as close to pure retributivism as any view, it is crucial that the offender should be able to rationally endorse the principles justifying his punishment. Granted, that is not quite the same as a communicative function, but in Kant's view, 'just deserts' views, and in others, which may not take expressive or communicative dimensions to be fundamental, punishment is regarded as a mode of addressing rational agents and not simply as something done *to* them. In what follows, I shall try to show that there is a place for retributivist considerations in the justification of punishment, even in some cases when those punished do not or cannot acknowledge the justice of the punishment.

Punishment and the Failure of Communication

In developing an account of how punishment can be morally justified, Herbert Morris has argued that the following conditions must be met.

> The first is that the norms addressed to persons are generally just and that the society is to some substantial extent one in which those who are liable to punishment have roughly equal opportunities to conform to those just norms. The second condition is equally important. The theory presupposes that there is a general commitment among persons to whom the norms apply to the values underlying them (Morris, 1995, p. 165).

Our concern here is whether there are cases in which offenders cannot be reasonably expected to endorse correct values and norms, but the reasons why they could not do so do not constitute excusing conditions or diminish their responsibility. The answer is yes. To see why this is so, we need to examine the moral psychology of the issue and how it bears on the normative issues.

We get some help from Aristotle. In the final few pages of the *Nicomachean Ethics* Aristotle makes the transition from a discussion of what is the best kind of life for a human being to the issue of legislation. We cannot live distinctively human lives and cannot flourish except in political communities, and law is crucial to political life and to creating and sustaining the conditions for human flourishing. Even if we are sceptical that there is a best kind of life for human beings, it is surely true that sound law is needed for us to live well. Norms that are recognized by most agents as reflecting values that they endorse support confidence in the institutions and authorities of the society and supply a measure of guidance to those who might otherwise act in ways harmful to others or who have not been well served by the manner in which they are habituated. Both for those who reflectively endorse the values registered in the law and for those who do not give much thought to such matters, the law substantially shapes the normative order, whether or not its purpose is moral education.

Aristotle notes that, 'people become hostile to an individual human being who opposes their impulses, even if he is correct in opposing them, whereas a law's prescription of what is decent is not burdensome' (*Nicomachean Ethics*, 1180a 22–23). Law has this power to compel, he says, because 'Law is reason that proceeds from a sort of prudence and understanding' (1180a 21). The authority of reason underwrites the compulsion that is proper to law. Sound law cannot be properly perceived as compulsion that is motivated mainly by passion or as merely expressive of volition. With respect to sound law, agents can see that there are good reasons, beyond narrowly prudential ones, for them to enact the values and norms that inform the law. Their rightness can be understood.

This emphasis on the importance of law comes in the context of Aristotle's culminating remarks about moral education. 'It is difficult, however, for someone to be trained correctly for virtue from his youth if he has not been brought up under correct laws' (1179b 32–3). Moreover,

> it is not enough if they get the correct upbringing and attention when they are young; rather, they must continue the same practices and be habituated to them when they become men. Hence we need laws concerned with these things also, and in general with all of life. For the many yield to compulsion more than to argument, and to sanctions more than to the fine (1180a 1–5).

After all, 'the many obey fear, not shame; they avoid what is base because of the penalties, not because it is disgraceful' (1179b 11–12). 'What argument, then, could reform people like these? For it is impossible, or not easy, to alter by argument what has long been absorbed as a result of one's habits' (1179b 17–8). We might be more sceptical than Aristotle that there is a uniquely best kind of life for a human being, but somewhat more optimistic than he was in regard to why people conform to the law and what sorts of considerations they are responsive to. Still, there remain questions about how to treat and regard offenders who are not invested in the norms reflected in the law.

In particular, there are agents who are rational and responsible but because of their characters they are unable to genuinely understand the wrongness of some of their acts and the justice of being punished for them. Can punishing *them* be justified as anything more than a strategy of social control? Can it still be properly understood as a mode of address between rational agents, and a mode of address intended to communicate with them concerning values and their rational authority?

In addressing these questions we will put aside one possible complexity. We will suppose that the social world in question is not one in which there are deep, numerous, and basic disagreements about values between agents who are reflective, informed, careful thinkers. The question of the legitimacy of punishment when there are deep disagreements is an important one — indeed, a very important one — but it is not the present concern. Our concern here is with certain agents who do not accept values that are widely shared and which are sound. Thus, the contexts in question are such that sound moral considerations are what I shall call *available* to agents. They are not epistemically out of the reach of rational agents and there are agents who have a grasp of them and are fluent with the relevant concepts. They govern the practice of many members of the community. On the part of many, they are not simply accepted; they are understood and endorsed.

This is an important condition because certain values, which we plausibly take to be correct, may simply not have been available to say, fourth century Celts or to tenth century Tatars. They were rational agents, but it would be implausible to morally blame them, for example, for the ways in which they treated enemies they captured. We appropriately find fault with their practices and attitudes. They were quite ghastly and inhumane. But it would be inappropriate to hold them accountable with reference to norms not effectively available to them. (In that respect, there is evidence that there really is moral progress, though it is not inevitable or irreversible.)

Voluntariness and the Acceptance of Norms

Gary Watson makes a helpful distinction in regard to this kind of matter. He distinguishes between attributability and accountability. He writes:

> The former kinds of blaming and praising judgments are independent of what I am calling the practices of moral accountability. They invoke only the attributability conditions, on which certain appraisals of the individual as an agent are grounded. Because many of these appraisals concern the agent's excellences and faults — or virtues and vices — as manifested in thought and action, I shall say that such judgments are made from the *aretaic perspective* (Watson, 1996, p. 21).

While we find some of the values and practices of certain individuals and groups *aretaically* defective, it would be unfair and inappropriate to regard them as blameworthy for what *we* know are wrong acts. Those agents were not (at least in certain respects) stubbornly resisting, flouting, or rejecting value considerations available to them that should, upon consideration, have motivated them to act differently.

The case is different however, in the recent Rwandan butchery, or with regard to the SS in the 1930s and 1940s, for example. Correct values were available to the offenders in those cases, and it is more clear (if not always entirely clear) that they were at fault and not merely aretaically defective. Even in the American South in the middle of the nineteenth century, the reasons for the wrongness of slavery were widely available, though there were numerous powerful impediments to their being recognized, accepted, and acted upon. True values were, by and large, available to those agents, though a variety of factors may have rendered them obscure to many, and it would be implausible to insist that there is no excuse for their not being accepted. But there is an important distinction between those who knew that slavery is wrong but did not oppose it, and those to whom the reasons why slavery is wrong were available but they genuinely thought that slavery was not wrong. They were for it in a considered way and had heard and rejected arguments (good arguments) against it. Those latter agents are examples of the sort that is of direct concern here. They are agents who could have known better but did not or do not know better. They are different from agents who knew better but did not act on their understanding.

My point is not to insist that because the relevant moral reasons were available, *of course* everyone could have seen and supported the moral case for abolition. It is that there is an important difference between agents who can grasp correct values (whether in fact they do or not) and those who cannot, though their inability is not exculpating. Through their endorsements and their enactments, that is, through voluntary, rational activity, agents and communities establish the contours and limits of their morally relevant abilities, modes of attention, strategies of judgment, and motivational tendencies.

Remarking on the way in which voluntary activity can determine capacities and incapacities grounded in character, Bernard Williams writes:

> We are subject to the model that what one can do sets the limits to delibera-
> tion, and that character is revealed by what one chooses within those limits,
> among the things that one can do. But character (of a person in the first
> instance; but related points apply to a group, or to a tradition) is equally
> revealed in the location of those limits, and in the very fact that one can deter-
> mine, sometimes through deliberation itself, that one cannot do certain
> things, and must do others. Incapacities can not only set limits to character
> and provide conditions of it, but can also partly constitute its substance
> (Williams, 1981, p. 130).

These inabilities are not simply the result of limits imposed by natural endowment. Some of them are established by the ways in which agents deliberate and engage in valuative judgment. Agents sometimes find out what they have in them through recognizing limits over which they have no control, but there are also limits that they set for themselves by what they determine to be necessary or impossible. Some of the limits of an agent's character are voluntary in the respect that they are established as a result of patterns of voluntary action. This is true both for virtuous agents and for vicious agents.

It is crucial to the view that agents are, in important respects, responsible for their characters. Elsewhere, I have argued more fully that typically they are (see Jacobs, 2001, esp. chs. 1 and 2). Briefly, the view is that human action generally is voluntary, though the features of voluntariness change with rational maturity and the growth of experience. A young child can move about voluntarily, but an older child or adult is also self-determining in action in ways that involve deliberation and decision and planning. The two year old and the twenty year old both behave voluntarily, though the latter has abilities for practical reasoning, foresight, and critical reflection that are not yet developed in the former. Attributions of responsibility to the twenty year old are enlarged accordingly. Habituation by others certainly shapes character, and dispositions that one acquires early on, before one is able to evaluate them, have considerable influence on how an agent is oriented in regard to values, sensibility, and motives. Still, habituation is generally not something that diminishes voluntariness. Rather, it trains and gives direction to the agent's exercise of voluntariness. It can do so in ways that educate the person to be thoughtful, aware, and careful in exercising self-determination, and it can do so in quite other ways. But, (a) even early habituation is (typically) the habituation of an individual whose behaviour is largely voluntary, and (b) much of the influence of habituation comes through how we habituate *ourselves* through making choices, acting for our own reasons. That is not to say that we 'plan' to have the characters that we eventually have, but that it is, to a large extent, voluntary activity that leads to our having our mature characters.[1] Character is formed in part by the strategies of action and motivation in which we have invested ourselves.

Suppose an agent is raised in an environment in which particularly malicious types of bigotry are the norm. The prevailing attitudes and values encourage and reinforce bigotry to the extent that some agents in that setting feel that it is right, or even obligatory to treat members of certain groups in ways that degrade and harm them. Otherwise 'those people' will ruin the community and upset the natural order of authority and privilege and so forth. These are not bigots who know better but nonetheless succumb to resentment or fear and let their bigotry get the better of them. They genuinely think that it is wrong to treat members of certain groups with respect. When they treat others in accord with their animus they do not later come to see this as a lapse from correct behaviour. They really think that their victims deserve no better and that to regard them as equal participants in civil society and as peers is an offence against true values. However, these are not fourth century Celts or tenth century Tatars. They are right here in our social world, or at least in near-relations to it. These are agents to whom correct values are available. There is no general epistemic impossibility cutting these agents off from them in such a way that it is just plain unreasonable to expect them to have been able to acquire sound values.

Thus, values may be *available* but not effectively *accessible* to agents if, on account of their established characters, they are no longer capable of the appropriate ethical cognition. (This is a distinction I have developed

---

[1]   An agent can be responsible for states of character even if he or she did not intend to acquire them. My view here is along some of the main lines of Aristotle's discussion in Bk. III of the *Nicomachean Ethics*. He writes: 'Actions and states, however, are not voluntary in the same way. For we are in control of actions from the beginning to the end, when we know the particulars. With states, however, we are in control of the beginning, but do not know, any more than with sicknesses, what the cumulative effect of particular actions will be. Nonetheless, since it was up to us to exercise a capacity either this way or another way, states are voluntary (1114b 30–1115a 3).

and discussed at some length in Jacobs, 2003.) Given their habits of valu-
ation and deliberation, dispositions of affect and response, and so forth,
they may be alienated from correct values in such a way that it is implausible to expect them to effectively engage with them. Individuals and
groups can become established in characters, in second natures, that set
real limits on what they can do, and that determine for them what is
practically necessary. Those limitations can be considerable strengths
(in the case of virtuous agents) or serious defects. The soundly virtuous
agent may be someone to whom the corrupt or unjust possibility simply
does not occur. The deeply vicious agent can be a counterpart to this,
having blinded himself to what virtue requires without having diminished his accountability. The vicious agents in question *could have*
acquired correct values in the respects that (a) they are rationally competent and not cognitively defective; (b) during the process of developing
mature and more or less fixed valuative attachments and states of character, these agents were able to have seen and done things differently; (c)
the fact that they could have is explained in part, by the fact that there is
understanding and endorsement of correct values in their social world.

Consider, for example, an official in an ethnically based political party
in the Balkans. Suppose he rose through the party's youth organizations,
was groomed by parents and mentors for this career, and was strongly
encouraged by widely shared notions of status, prestige, and success.
Among the leading ideas of this party are that members of other ethnic
groups are inferior, not to be trusted, a danger to the racial or religious
purity of the community, and so forth. He may go on to be a prominent
leader who endorses and encourages policies of ethnic cleansing and
institutionally organized bigotry, violence, and economic and social discrimination. Still, in that world, it was possible to acquire other values,
to see things differently, to critically scrutinize his direction, and so
forth. There was pressure and there was encouragement, but he was a
voluntary agent who enacted values he endorsed, and he could have
acquired other values. Other agents in his social world did. The impediments that he faces are not so coercive or so insurmountable that he is
simply cut off from what he should be taking into account. He is cut off
in the sense that he is alienated from correct values, but not because they
are unavailable to him.

However, given the role of character in practical cognition — its role
in shaping what count as valuative considerations for the agent, what is
choiceworthy and what is out of the question and so forth — it is just not
true that as long as an agent has not lost his reason he can properly
appreciate and respond to moral considerations. He may remain a voluntary, responsible agent though he is incapacitated for at least certain
kinds of moral cognition. Williams notes that, 'the fact that an agent has
come to that point, if he has, is certainly not enough to turn away blame'

(Williams, 1981, p. 130). The fact that an agent does what he must do, given his character, or that his character makes certain potentially action-guiding considerations inaccessible, does not, in its own right, diminish responsibility. As we noted above, it does not do so for the firmly virtuous agent to whom doing something base is out of the question (even if the possibility in some sense occurs to him or is suggested to him). Nor does it necessarily or automatically diminish the responsibility of the agent established in vice. It may be that the agent's own endorsements, willingness to act for certain reasons, and gratification from acting in certain ways (supplying him with a reason to carry on acting in those ways) underlie the limits on what he can do and his conception of what he must do.

Think of the murderous crime boss, wholeheartedly devoted to the values, the traditions, and the grandeur of his way of life, or the 'principled' misogynist, who has sophisticated explanations for why women ought to have subordinate status. These are not agents who understand their wrong acts as lapses from standards that they in some sense recognize. They are firmly attached to wrong values, but think that they are right. Aristotle had asked of those who have 'not even a notion of what is fine and [hence] truly pleasant, since they have had no taste of it. What argument, then, could reform people like these?' (*Nicomachean Ethics*, 1179b 15-7). We might reformulate the question as follows: In what way could punishment reach such an agent, or be a mode of communication with him, except as an imposition of force that regulates his behaviour? In what way could it be a form of address that actualizes its moral purpose?

Punishment and Ethical Disability

Punishment is a morally significant practice, a form of regard for the agent as a participant in a normative order. It does not aim simply to incapacitate or to deter. It expresses the community's commitment to certain values, its condemnation of violations of them, and it is intended to motivate the offender to recognize his wrong and reconsider his valuative attachments. Yet, the agents we are concerned with are just those whose habits and states of character alienate them from, or disable them for, that sort of appreciation.

That is to say that not all agents who offend do so by lapsing. There are some whose alienation from correct values is quite complete, at least in certain departments of judgment and action. (An agent may be vicious in certain notable regards without being altogether corrupt, though that is not to say that vices can be neatly compartmentalized. It would be surprising if one's dishonesty, for example, did not make a difference to how just or generous he is.) Succumbing to malicious resentment, for example, and having one's judgment and motivation corrupted by it, is different from genuinely thinking that members of certain groups are inferior and ought to be treated as such. The former agent is reachable by censure and sanction (though there is no guarantee that he will be reached or that he will make a genuine and effective effort at ethical self-correction). The second agent may not be reachable. Though he has not lost his reason, he lacks the relevant conceptual fluency to make correct judgments and the plasticity of his character is largely exhausted.

Something comparable can be said of the seemingly incorruptible virtuous agent. There is no *certainty* that this agent is utterly incorruptible, but those who know him well know that it is not reasonable to expect him to be corrupted in almost any realistically possible situation. Incapacities of character can be either meritorious or deplorable, but they can determine real practical necessities and impossibilities. Hume colourfully remarked:

> A prisoner who has neither money nor interest, discovers the impossibility of his escape, as well when he considers the obstinacy of the gaoler, as the walls and bars with which he is surrounded; and, in all attempts for his freedom, chooses rather to work upon the stone and iron of the one, than upon the inflexible nature of the other (Hume, 1748/1975, p. 90).

This may be because the jailer is above corruption or it may be because the jailer is heartless, indifferent, or cruel. The point is that whether the agent's character is virtuous or vicious it may be such that he is quite unmoved by certain kinds of considerations, or oblivious to them.

Accountability does not require that the agent, in the moment of action or in planning action knows and is able to do what is right, but that he has to *have been able* to have known it and to have done it. If in his social world he could have acquired correct values, then he may still be responsible, even if he cannot now recognize the wrongness of his acts. We must make allowance for considerations that do indeed diminish responsibility, such as severe abuse, damaging deprivation, coercion, or defects of mind that incapacitate the agent for understanding. However, the Balkan zealot for ethnic cleansing, for example, could have developed into a different sort of person even though as a mature agent it now may not be possible for him to see things differently. Where inaccessibility is traceable to the agent's own exercise of voluntariness, and correct values were available, he is still liable to sanction, and others may properly feel hostile indignation and resentment toward him. Punishment is what he deserves even if he does not and effectively cannot appreciate this, and because of that failure of appreciation, he will not be improved by it.

There are difficulties concerning contexts in which, for example, certain religious beliefs and doctrines strongly condition the ways in which people see the world, and agents are attached to values and ends with a special sort of fervour and uncritical, unconditional dedication. It may seem unfair to hold agents responsible for their characters if this is the only setting they have known and the setting encourages and reinforces behaviour and perspectives that are in fact, morally unsupportable. But the strength of an agent's attachment to certain values, and the lack of a habit of criticism are not on their own sufficient grounds for diminishing responsibility. Responsibility for how one sees things does not require that several different options have been presented to the agent. Being raised in a community which is strongly traditional and which regards outside influence as unwelcome and unhealthy can still be distinguished from the sort of upbringing that disables an agent for practical reasoning or an understanding of the rationale for which he acts. Agents committed to a tradition or doctrine may have quite articulate conceptions of how values figure in his conceptions of what is allowable, what is necessary, and what is out of the question. They may appeal to carefully reasoned arguments and considerations that they believe have decisive weight. These may not be agents whose minds will be changed by the presentation of factual evidence against their views, or arguments that raise questions about the very bases of their beliefs, though they are not beyond the pale of responsible agency despite the tenacity of their attachment to what are, in fact, morally unsound values and judgments.

The overall upshot of this and the other sorts of cases we have mentioned is that there are some individuals who merit the respect owed to rational agents, but who are incapacitated for certain types of appropriate responses to their own wrongdoing and the reasons that make it wrongdoing. Punishment cannot improve them, but because they are rational agents enacting values they endorse, it would be wrong to simply regard and treat them as pests. Plato, who argued that punishment aims at the health of the soul, wrote:

> Everyone who is punished, and rightly punished, ought either to be benefited and become better, or serve as an example to others that they may behold these sufferings and through fear become better.

And:

> But those who have committed the extreme of injustice, and have thus become incurable, serve as an example to others; they themselves benefit not at all, since they are incurable, yet others may do so when they observe these malefactors suffering in the greatest, the most painful, and the most fearful torments because of their sins, strung up forever in that prisonhouse of Hades, an example, a portent, and a warning to the unjust as they arrive below (Plato, *Gorgias*, 525).

In the *Statesman* he writes that with regard to those who are 'thrust forcibly away by an evil nature into godlessness, excess, and injustice it [kingship] throws out by killing them, sending them into exile, and punishing them with the most extreme forms of dishonor' (*Statesman*, 309a).

It is, according to Plato, appropriate to eliminate those who cannot be improved by punishment.

Most contemporary theorists are reluctant to agree with him. His view offends against the widely shared notion that rational agents, just as such, are owed a distinctive form of respect. That notion is a fixture of a great deal of modern moral thought, whether it is traced to theological or secular sources. Affiliated with it is the notion that just by virtue of the possession of reason an agent is capable of correctly appreciating moral considerations. On that view, the agent who acts wrongly is either someone who fails to enact an understanding of which he is capable, or is someone whose act is explainable in a way that shows diminished culpability. That, anyway, is part of a commonly held conception of wrongdoing. Yet, it is a mistake to suppose that offences always are to be explained as (1) lapses from values that in fact, the agent endorses, or (2) as resulting from reasonable disagreements over values, or (3) as the result of coercion, deprivation or victimization, such that the agent's acts are (more or less) excusable. Clearly, many if not most offences are indeed to be explained in one or another of these ways, but not all. There are agents who are rational, but on account of their dispositions and commitments, have a range of moral vision and employ an idiom of evaluation that effectively cut them off from sound ethical considerations without diminishing their responsibility as self-determining agents acting for reasons.

Ethical Disability and Moral Status

The agents of primary concern here would not present a difficulty if punishment were exclusively or primarily regulative. We can see that it is *not* in the perplexity that such agents cause us. We wonder if such agents are properly liable to punishment and if the ways in which they fail to acknowledge the justice of punishment diminish their accountability. We build into the law as into morality, as effectively as we can, distinctions concerning mental competence, mitigation, provocation, degrees of premeditation, malice, recklessness, negligence, and the like. One possible strategy for dealing with morally alienated, but rational agents would be to assign agents different statuses. Some could be regarded as full-fledged participants in the moral order, fully liable to sanction (because they can acknowledge the values that justify sanction) and others as less fully liable, because of the ways they are fixed in their commitments and characters.

That approach, however, would be morally more problematic than say, the calibration of judgments of responsibility in accord with an agent's age, for example. It might be replied that it would be no more problematic than the view supported here; in both cases the central issue is ascertaining whether an agent is rationally impaired in a way that diminishes accountability, or is morally impaired but fully accountable. The difference is that the view I am suggesting preserves the equal status of agents. There are reasons, concerning responsibility for character, to be reluctant to make adjustments in status on the basis of how firmly agents are committed to their values and beliefs. Those reasons are obstacles to regarding agents' self-determination as lesser just because they fail to accept or acknowledge what are in fact correct norms. The agents are to be addressed as equal participants in the practical order even if they are effectively beyond the reach of rational influence. They are owed respect, while they may also merit our loathing.

There is a widespread tendency to think that if the offender is so corrupt that he cannot acknowledge his wrong as wrong and has no interest in revising his values, then there *must* be some partially excusing causal story for why he is that way. The thought is that we should condemn the awful act, and perhaps even the awful disposition behind it, but the condemnation should not reach all the way down to retributive hatred of the agent. (The expression 'retributive hatred' is used by Jeffrie Murphy in Murphy, 1998, p. 90.) While this can be indicative of a generous spirit, it also sometimes reflects a failure to come to grips with the reality of the wrong done and the viciousness that led to it. It presupposes an implausibly optimistic conception of rationality's tendency to normative soundness. The exercise of reason and the agent's capacity to develop sound moral understanding depend upon how the agent is habituated (including how he habituates himself). It is not as though there is an unexhausted reservoir of sound rationality in every agent. We cannot, in the way that Kant seems to have done, count on a kind of rationalistic grace, a capacity to rationally retrieve and recompose oneself however one has so far been disposed to act.

At the same time Kant did helpfully caution against the judgment that an agent is incorrigible, drawing particular attention to our inability to know with certainty the inner disposition of an agent.[2] Even without accepting his noumenal metaphysics of agency there are both epistemic and moral reasons to be extremely cautious in 'declaring' an agent incorrigible. Still, it is unreasonable to suppose of an agent that just because he is rational, he is able to achieve correct moral understanding. Possession

[2]   See Immanuel Kant, *Religion Within the Limits of Reason Alone* (1793/1960). In the first several paragraphs of Book One Kant argues that we cannot have empirical knowledge of an agent's maxims. We cannot know that a man is evil. Kant also argues (in this work and in *Foundations of the Metaphysics of Morals*, 1785/1976) that no agent in possession of reason repudiates the moral law. Agents may do terrible things, and may not undertake to reform themselves, but they do not renounce obedience to the moral law, and they wish to be free of the inclinations that distract them from acting on it. See for example, Kant (1793/1960, pp. 16 , 31; 1785/1976, pp. 46, 73).

of reason is neither necessarily nor always an effective corrective to strongly held but morally wrong convictions and beliefs. The norms that a rational agent *should* endorse will only be endorsed *if* there is a basis in the agent's developed character, in his or her second nature, for attachment to the values reflected in them. Second nature may become so fixed that while the agent remains a rational agent, he is not effectively capable of making correct ethical acknowledgments.

Agents whose characters alienate them from sound ethical considerations especially invite our hostility. While it is crucial that our anger and indignation not become vindictive, it is also true that sympathy for the wrongdoer should be very disciplined. It can misrepresent the normative features of the situation and distract judgment from its proper focus. As Michael Moore observes, 'Sometimes the compassion for victims is not absent, but gets transferred to the person who is now about to suffer; namely, the wrongdoer'(Moore, 1995, p. 122). We are often reluctant to confront the reality of vice or evil, and our fear of confronting it, or fear of our own susceptibility to hatred or vengeance may overwhelm our willingness and determination to do justice. A criminal represents an opportunity for a lot of moral mistakes; for malice, for vengeance, for misguided sympathy, for pathos-motivated excuse-making, for consoling fictions about the good that is in people, for hypocritical denunciations of how irretrievably evil they are, and so forth. Moore writes:

> My own view is that such a transfer of concern from victim to criminal occurs in large part because of our unwillingness to face our own revulsion at what was done. . . . It allows us to look away from the horror that another person was willing to cause (p. 122).

He notes that this may indicate not only unwillingness to face evil, but also 'a narcissism that is no virtue. A criminal, after all, represents an opportunity to exercise (and display, a separate point) one's virtue' (p. 123). Still, it does seem as though there are some agents who *both* merit respect as rational agents and merit deep moral hostility, retributive hatred, because they are profoundly vicious. This sort of hatred is not simple revulsion and a desire to be rid of the offending being. It is a combination of denunciation of the wrong done with the resolve that justice should be done, and the desire that the offender should be punished even if he or she will not be corrected by it or acknowledge the justice of it.

Many agents *are* reachable and do respond to censure and sanction by acknowledging their wrong and perhaps also with a resolve not to commit wrong again. In a decent society that is the norm. They are not proper objects of hatred, and resentment that is aimed at them should end with their punishment, and they should not be stigmatized. (We often do a very bad job in those respects.) But there are agents so completely alienated from correct values that the communicative aims of punishment are nearly certain to fail on account of their unreceptivity. It is legitimate to punish them, even though some of the main moral purposes of punishment are bound to be frustrated in their cases.

The Persistence of the Difficulty

We noted above that we are reluctant to accept Plato's counsel that the incorrigible person simply be destroyed or be made an example. We also remarked early on about the widespread scepticism concerning Aristotle's conception of a human function and a unique or metaphysically and ethically privileged actualization of human nature. Contemporary liberal notions of the educative and formative role of politics and law are at some considerable distance from theirs. In addition, we are committed to more morally democratic views than Aristotle's in so far as it is widely held that all rational agents are owed a certain fundamental sort of respect and are to be regarded as equal participants in the normative order. The rationality of the law and the rationale for sanction should be intelligible by all normal, mature agents. Still, Aristotle is almost certainly right about something that is often under-acknowledged in a great deal of modern and particularly, liberal political thought; namely, that there are certain virtues that are crucial conditions for sustaining a morally decent political order.

Even if a political order is very permissive with regard to conceptions of good that people are at liberty to pursue, and even if it seeks to maximize moral independence, its survival and success will still (and perhaps especially) depend upon a commitment to certain values and norms on the part of a great majority of participants in that society. This is particularly clear in regard to justice; whatever the principles and values encoded in law, justice does not have a chance unless agents are committed to it as a matter of individual virtue. However sound the rules are by the test of some abstract exercise, they make a difference to the social world only upon the basis of agents' actual virtues. Moreover, while the law may not be regarded as an applied tool of character formation, it still registers and reflects basic commitments about what is morally permissible and what is intolerable. There will be some agents who are not committed to those values, or who self-consciously reject them.

This is disturbing but should not be shocking. These agents *could have* attached themselves to the values that inform basic norms of civil society even if *now* they cannot do so. Because they could have, and because of the role of their own voluntariness in being who they are now, doing what they do, it is morally legitimate to punish them.

Dan Farrell

Capital Punishment and Societal Self-Defence

Introduction[1]

The two most common arguments for capital punishment, at least in the United States, where capital punishment is strongly supported by a significant majority of the electorate, are the retributive argument and what we may call the societal-self-protection argument. The retributive argument, of course, holds that people who knowingly and willingly do wrongful harm to others deserve to be harmed themselves, with the most grievous harms deserving the most serious retribution, and that it is the state's job to see to it that this retribution is exacted. The societal-self-protection argument holds that capital punishment is both necessary and justified as a way of preventing (or at least reducing the incidence of) harm to the innocent, the assumption being that at least some potential capital criminals are less likely to kill innocent people if they know there is a significant likelihood that they will lose their own lives if in fact they kill an innocent individual.

Although the first of these arguments is the more popular of the two, at least in the United States, I am not going to pay much attention to it here. Personally, I think this argument is a bad argument, not because I object to the idea of negative dessert, but because I object to the idea of putting the state into the business of punishing people because of their

[1]   Earlier versions of this paper were presented at California State University at Chico, Oberlin College, the University of Illinois, Urbana/Champagne, the Moritz College of Law at the Ohio State University, and the Mershon Center for National Security Studies at the Ohio State University, and I am grateful to my audiences on those occasions for their helpful comments. I am also indebted to Brian Bix and Sigrun Svavarsdottir for extremely helpful comments on an earlier draft of this paper.

(presumed) negative dessert and, more importantly, because I object to the assumption, which is central to the retributive argument, that giving presumed wrongdoers what they deserve is sufficiently important as to justify doing it, via the institution of punishment, even though we know that in a certain number of cases we will be punishing people who, because they are innocent, do not deserve to be punished, even by the retributivist's own lights. Despite the fact, though, that these objections, especially the second of them, seem to me to be overwhelmingly compelling, my experience in public debate is that no one who already supports the retributive argument is the least bit likely to be moved by these or any other objections that might be made against the retributivist position. On this issue, it seems to me, we are, at least at present, in the unhappy position of being unable (or at least very, very unlikely) to change each others' minds: either one accepts the retributive argument, despite the best objections its critics can muster, or one does not. Until someone comes up with something new to say in this connection, change of mind, at least for the time-being, seems not to be in the air.[2]

In the case of what I have called the societal-self-protection argument, by contrast, I think there is at least some reason to believe that what we might call philosophical progress on the issue of capital punishment is possible. For with respect to this argument, as I shall show, there is indeed something new that can be said, something that has been missed by both sides in this debate and that bears very importantly on how we ought to think about this line of argument. For, apart from legitimate concerns about the empirical claim that capital punishment in fact deters capital crimes, the main moral objection to the societal-self-protection argument is that it treats the deaths of those who are executed, and thereby those individuals themselves, as a mere means to a (presumed) greater social good. And this objection, I shall argue, can be met, once we

---

[2] I should note, in fairness, that a number of supporters of the retributive argument do appear to have been moved by recent and very compelling evidence that suggests that the frequency of wrongful (or mistaken) convictions is much higher than even worriers such as I would have expected. This, though, so far as I can see, is viewed by supporters of the retributive argument not as a reason for abandoning the practice of capital punishment, or at least exploring other approaches to justifying it, but, rather, as a reason for at most a moratorium on capital punishment until such mistakes can be gotten back into an 'acceptable' range. It is perhaps worth recalling here that the response, in states that allow capital punishment, to the discovery that poor people and persons of colour are much more likely to be executed than affluent people and whites, in judicial circumstances that are otherwise exactly similar, was not to abandon the practice of capital punishment, in light of what one might reasonably suppose are inevitable injustices like these but, rather, to do whatever one thought possible to reduce the frequency of such injustices.

understand the societal-self-protection argument as it ought to be understood.

I proceed in my exposition as follows. I begin by summarizing, very briefly, a general point about deterrence-based theories of punishment that I have defended at greater length elsewhere, namely, that such arguments are best understood not as appeals to the overall social utility of a system of threats and punishments but, rather, as appeals to a fundamental right to (societal) self-defence. I then turn to the question of whether, in light of this point, which basically asks us to reconstrue the moral basis of such theories, the debate about capital punishment looks any different and, in particular, whether the standard moral objections to capital punishment, at least when it is based on arguments of this sort, have the force they are sometimes thought to have. My answer is that they do not and that seeing this is extremely important if we want to advance the moral assessment of this institution in an intelligent way.

Self-Protection and Distributive Justice

At least two things need to be established by anyone who hopes to justify the institution of punishment on the grounds that this institution will save innocent people from wrongful harm by deterring some of those who would otherwise harm them: (i) that punishment in fact deters (at least some) wrongful harms; and (ii) that, given (i), protecting the innocent by means of punishment of those fairly convicted of illegal acts is morally permissible. That the first of these claims must be established by anyone seeking to make out a defence of punishment on the grounds of its deterrent effects is of course obvious and is readily admitted by those who wish to defend punishment in this way. What is more, and just as importantly, recognition of the need to prove or at least defend this claim is a central point of attention in the work of those who are sceptical of this approach (particularly, of course, by those debating this issue in the context of capital punishment). However, with respect to the need for an argument for the second claim above, the situation is rather different, it seems to me, both as regards defenders and as regards critics of societal-self-protection arguments. For while both sides recognize the need for an argument for (ii), there is a surprising absence of discussion as to what that argument is. Both sides invariably just assume, it seems to me, that the defence of (ii) must involve an appeal to the overall social utility, given (i), of adopting an institution of punishment to protect ourselves from harms that would otherwise be inflicted on us. Certainly, the best-known attacks on (ii) make this assumption, and in fact these attacks would make no sense without it.[3] Equally clearly, though, defenders and expositors of the societal-self-protection argument make this assumption too: no textbook discussion of 'the problem of punishment', for example, and in particular of the problem of why we should not suppose we would be justified in punishing the innocent if we could thereby deter more of the potentially guilty, makes sense without the assumption that, given the truth of (i), the defence of (ii), and hence of a deterrent theory of punishment, is to be based on an appeal to the overall social utility of punishment and hence on some version, however complicated, of a purely consequentialist moral theory.[4]

But, of course, it is quite odd, when one thinks about it, that virtually everyone writing on this topic should assume that a deterrence-based answer to the problem of punishment must involve, in its fundamental moral assumptions, an appeal either to utilitarianism, specifically, or, more generally, to some form or other of consequentialism. After all, the point of the threats and enforcements that the deterrence approach wishes to justify is societal self-defence. And why should one suppose that the best, much less the only possible, explanation of a putative right to self-defence must be an appeal to some form of utilitarianism?

Utilitarianism can, of course, as can consequentialisms generally, make a place for 'rights' or 'rights' talk, and thereby make a place for a presumed right to self-defence. Clearly, though, one does not have to be a utilitarian in order to believe in a right to self-defence, and in fact neither ordinary thought nor what little literature there is on the notion of self-defence makes a right to self-defence dependent on a more general utilitarian (or consequentialist) background.[5]

Suppose, then, one wanted to take seriously the possibility that deterrence, or 'deterrent violence', as I shall call it, meaning thereby both the threats and the enforcements that deterrence is thought to require by those who believe in it, is at bottom a matter of (societal) self-defence, and suppose one wanted to be able to appeal to self-defence as a basis for deterrent violence, without embracing, in support of this, either utilitarianism or any other form of consequentialism. How might one do this? How, that is to say, might one explain or justify or otherwise 'ground' the right to societal self-defence, if not as a consequence of a commitment to utilitarianism or some other consequentialist view?

---

[3]   See Ewing (1929), for example. But see also almost any standard account of the pros and cons of 'Deterrence' as an answer to the question: What is the general justifying aim of punishment?

[4]   See especially, on the philosophical side, Rawls (1955) and Hart (1968).

[5]   For an excellent discussion of recent philosophical work on the justification of self-defence see Jeff McMahan (1994).

In attempting to answer this question, it will be useful to consider, first, the question of how one might ground a right to individual self-defence on a non-utilitarian, non-consequentialist basis. The answer to this question, it seems to me, is fairly straightforward, though certainly not without deep and interesting complications. To see this, consider the following possibility: violence in legitimate cases of direct self-defence, let us suppose, is violence that is based (and ultimately justified) on an appeal to the idea of distributive justice. Specifically, legitimate violence in direct self-defence is violence that is permitted by the following principle for the just distribution of harms in a special subclass of all those cases in which, whatever a given agent does, someone will inevitably be harmed:

P1: When someone knowingly and willingly brings it about, through his own wrongful conduct, that someone else must choose either to harm him or to be harmed herself, the latter is entitled to choose that the former shall be harmed, rather than that she shall be harmed, at least if the harm inflicted on the former is roughly proportional to the harm that would otherwise be inflicted on the latter.[6]

The basic idea here, of course, is that in circumstances of the relevant sort, an innocent defender is entitled to distribute the relevant harms in the way P1 allows, not because the consequences of doing so, or of a rule allowing her to do so, are better than the consequences of available alternatives, but because she has a right to do so that is grounded on considerations of elementary justice or fairness.[7]

A lot more would need to be said about P1, of course, if our goal were to defend it and to defend it as the proper starting-point for a tenable non-utilitarian account of the moral basis of a presumed right to individual self-defence. That is not our goal here, however. Rather, here I want to ask how P1, supposing it strikes us as plausible, might be relevant to our question above, about the possibility of a defence of a right to societal self-defence that could be used in a non-consequentialist defence of

---

[6] A principle similar to P1 is suggested by Philip Montague (1983) pp. 31–36, and my own work is indebted to this important paper. For a more careful discussion of issues related to P1 than I can offer here, see especially Farrell (1995). On the historical roots of this sort of view, see Farrell (1988).

[7] Ironically, given his reputation as an old-fashioned 'fierce' retributivist in the theory of punishment, it is Kant who is the most eloquent classical defender of a right to use coercive violence to protect oneself and one's fellow citizens from wrongful interferences with individual freedom and hence of an early non-consequentialist version of what we are calling the 'societal-self-protection argument'. See *The Metaphysics of Morals* (Kant, 1797/1996) Part I ('Metaphysical First Principles of the Doctrine of Right'), throughout, but especially pp. 388–9, where Kant concludes that '[r]ight and the authorization to use coercion mean one and the same thing'.

claim (ii) above in the standard argument for punishment as a form of societal self-defense.

At first blush, it may seem that P1 is pretty clearly not only irrelevant to that earlier issue but also irrelevant to the more general question of how deterrent violence could itself ever be justified in a non-consequentialist way, whether in cases of one-on-one interactions between individuals or in cases where a group of people is attempting to defend its members, via an institution like punishment, against potential individual offenders. After all, P1 seems to apply only to cases of (individual) direct self-defence. What could it have to do with attempts to deter aggressive violence, much less with attempts to do this in a social institution like punishment?

Appearances here are misleading, though, as I have tried to show elsewhere. For one thing, even as it stands, P1 is actually directly relevant to at least one kind of case that does not involve direct self-defence but that does involve a choice either to harm another as a way of deterring still others from doing harm to oneself or letting oneself be harmed by those others. To see this, imagine the following situation. Suppose someone wrongly attacks you, knowing that once his attack has been accomplished you will be in the following position: unless you retaliate against him for his attack, certain other, potential attackers will be much more likely to attack you themselves, in the future, than they would otherwise have been (i.e., than they would have been had he not attacked you, in full view of them, in the first place). Once this person has attacked you, in other words, you can contain the probability of similar attacks by other people to the level at which it would otherwise have remained, only by retaliating against him in a certain way (something, let us suppose, he knew would be the case, should he attack you, before he commenced his attack). Clearly, in such a situation you are in a position to appeal to P1 to justify retaliation against your attacker, and you are in a position to do so even if retaliating is not necessary for protecting yourself from further attacks by him. For you are, as a result of his attack, in a position such that you must either harm him or be harmed yourself. And you are in this position only because of an informed, wrongful decision on his part.[8]

Let us ignore for a moment the fact that it is extremely unlikely that one would ever actually be in a situation like the one described here — a situation, that is, where one knows that if one does not retaliate against a deliberate act of wrongdoing, others will be likelier to harm one than they would otherwise have been, and where one has good reasons for believing that one's attacker knew, before he attacked, that one would be in this position if he attacked. The important point, for present purposes,

[8]   For a more thorough discussion, see Farrell (1985).

is simply that such situations are in principle possible and that, in them, one could appeal to a principle like P1 in order to justify, on non-utilitarian grounds, acting against one's present antagonist in order to protect oneself against other, potential aggressors.

What, though, does this have to do with the possibility of constructing a non-utilitarian defence of the institution of punishment? The latter, after all, is not an institution in which we deal with potential aggressors by waiting until someone wrongfully aggresses against us, and then penalizing that person to whatever degree is necessary in order to keep the probability of other attacks from going beyond where it would have been had the present attack not occurred or occurred and been treated as we estimate it needs to be treated to prevent similar attacks by others in the future. Rather, punishment, at least as it interests us here, is an institution in which we try to decrease the probability of wrongful attacks by threatening potential attackers with certain penalties, should they attack, and then imposing those penalties if such attacks nonetheless occur and the alleged attackers are duly convicted in a fair trial. And what, one might reasonably ask, does the notion of distributive justice, and a principle like P1, have to do with that?

The short answer, it seems to me, is 'Quite a lot'. For suppose, following a suggestion made by Kant in *The Metaphysics of Morals*, we were to come to believe that it is reasonable to hold that as a society we face essentially two options so far as controlling wrongful interferences with individual rights and liberties are concerned: either we adopt and enforce a system of threatening potential perpetrators of such interferences with individual rights and liberties with certain harms in the event they engage in such actions, and then inflict those harms if those actions nonetheless occur and the perpetrators are duly convicted in fair trials, thereby lowering the frequency at which such interferences with individual rights and liberties occur; or we do not adopt such a system, for whatever reason, thereby foregoing the assumed decrease in attacks of the relevant sort and, therewith, the protection of the innocent that that system would have afforded us.[9] Simplifying somewhat, it seems to me we can say that, just as with P1 and the direct resistance and acts of general deterrence that it warrants, so too in circumstances of the sort we are now imagining, a certain conception of justice or fair play allows us to choose in favour of visiting the relevant harms on those who will otherwise knowingly and willingly harm the innocent, rather than allowing harm to fall on the innocent as a result of not adopting the relevant system and thereby sparing potential and actual wrongdoers from harm (both the harm of being threatened with harm if one does wrongful harm

---

[9]   Kant (1797/1996), pp. 455–6.

to others and the harm of being punished if one ignores the relevant threats and does harm to the innocent nonetheless).[10]

No doubt, much more needs to be said before the reader will be inclined to agree with this last assertion. Suppose, though, he or she could be gotten to agree. We would then have, in addition to P1, another principle for the just distribution of harm in the relevant sorts of cases — namely,

P2:   When our situation is such that either (a) we adopt and act on a plan of making and enforcing threats of a certain sort, thereby protecting ourselves from wrongful aggression on the part of those against whom those threats are addressed, or (b) we do not adopt such a strategy, thereby leaving ourselves subject to an avoidably high probability of being attacked by those individuals, we are entitled to choose the former alternative over the latter, at least if (i) our threats are within certain limits, and (ii) they are threats to harm those, and only those, whose wrongful conduct we are trying to deter (see Farrell, 1990 and 1995).

This, of course, is a principle that answers, in a non-utilitarian way, the second question we said advocates of the societal-self-protection argument for punishment must answer and that, as we noted, traditional treatments of societal-self-protection arguments invariably answer by appealing to some form of utilitarianism — namely, the question of why we should suppose that, if there is evidence that threatening and imposing a given penalty will in fact reduce the frequency of a given kind of crime, we are justified in acting on that evidence to prevent harm to the innocent by threatening and imposing the relevant penalties. The question I now want to take up is the question of whether the debate about the justifiability of capital punishment looks any different if we replace the utilitarian account ordinarily assumed by both defenders and critics of the societal-self-protection argument for capital punishment with a non-utilitarian or deontological account like the one I have just sketched.

Capital Punishment

We may note, to begin with, that nothing in what we have said touches the empirical issue that proponents of the societal-self-protection argument must address: the burden is on them to show that there is indeed evidence to support the claim that capital punishment in fact deters at least some capital crimes. To the degree that it is reasonable, given the state of our empirical knowledge, to doubt that capital punishment deters capital crimes, or to believe that in some perverse and unexpected way capital punishment may even increase the frequency of such

---

[10]   See Farrell (1995) for an extended defence of the line of argument I am merely summarizing here.

crimes, an argument based on the sorts of considerations we have brought forward will be no better off than an argument based on an appeal to social utility.[11]

As I have already indicated, though, there are other, non-empirical objections to the societal-self-protection argument that deserve our attention. One of these, in particular, is especially important, since, if it is sound, the societal-self-protection argument would have to be rejected even if it could be conclusively shown that that capital punishment does indeed deter capital crimes. This is the objection, often associated with Kant (though mistakenly, in my view, as I explain elsewhere [Farrell, 2003]), that holds that it is wrong to kill a person, regardless of the wrongs that he has done, simply as a means to protecting ourselves from others who are or might be inclined to do as he has done. This sort of objection can, of course, be made as a perfectly general objection to any harms inflicted for the purposes of what we can call general deterrence, but here I confine myself to considering its plausibility as an objection to the use of capital punishment to deter capital crimes.

Now, whatever its force as an objection to standard versions of the societal-self-protection argument, which rely on social utility as their answer to the second question that all deterrence-based defences of punishment must answer — namely, the question of what justifies us in punishing for the sake of general deterrence, assuming punishment does in fact contribute to it — it seems to me the objection we are now imagining has no force whatsoever against non-utilitarian versions of the societal-self-protection argument that, like the version suggested above, rely not on social utility to answer the relevant question but, rather, on the idea of one's right to distribute harms in a certain way when the necessity for distributing those harms is the result of a free, informed, and wrongful choice of one of the parties whose being harmed will by hypothesis spare others from being harmed. For in such cases, while it is indeed true that that person is being harmed so that others will not be harmed, it is certainly not true that that person is being harmed merely as a means to this end (i.e., because harming him will serve that end and we happen to be able to harm him for that purpose). To see this, take, first, the case of direct self-defence: it would never even occur to us, I submit, to argue that self-defence is impermissible, at least in a paradigm case, because it is in effect 'using' one person (the attacker) as a means to benefiting another person (the defender). But why is this? Surely it is because, in

---

[11]   Note that this issue is a bit more complicated than I am indicating here, since in addition to standard versions of the societal-self-protection argument, which rely on the assumption that capital punishment deters at least some capital crimes, or at any rate makes them less likely, there are other versions that assume that, while we do not know whether or not capital punishment deters capital crimes, we are well advised to try it just in case it does.

thinking of clear cases of legitimate self-defence as morally unproblematic, we are implicitly thinking of the violence used in self-defence as both based on and justified by the sorts of considerations that lie behind a principle like P1 above — that is, considerations that have to do not simply with the net effect of a defender's harming her attacker but also, and just as importantly, with the defender's right to hold her attacker responsible for the fact that someone must be harmed and, in light of this, to choose that he (the attacker) be harmed, at least all other things being equal, rather than his victim(s).

Similarly, and perhaps more interestingly, for cases of general deterrence like the one imagined above: if, even without antecedent threats or warnings, someone is responsible for the fact that either he must suffer or I must suffer, and if the actions of his that made this the case were free, informed, and wrongful actions performed with the knowledge that this would be the upshot, it can hardly be said that in deciding that he should be harmed rather than I, I am thereby 'using' him as a mere means to my own well-being. For here, as in the case of violence used in direct self-defence, my reason for choosing that he should suffer, rather than I, has to do with much more than the fact that only if he suffers will I escape harm. That is to say, here, as in the case of direct self-defence, my case for making the choice I am making has to do with his prior choices and my right to hold him responsible for the consequences of those choices.

What about the case of capital punishment, though, where harming another is part of a system of threats and punishments that exists as a result of our choices — choices that are aimed at providing protection to the innocent on the assumption that such a system will in fact protect the innocent, at least to a degree? In what sense is such an institution anything other than a system whereby we use the fact that someone has done serious wrongful harm to others as an excuse to do serious harm to him, with the aim of protecting ourselves, thereby, from similar wrongful harms from others?

My answer will not be surprising, in light of what I have already said above. For if we assume for the sake of argument that we have reason to believe that we are in a situation which is such that either we adopt the relevant system, thereby decreasing the odds that the innocent will suffer wrongful deaths, or we do not adopt that system, thereby forgoing the chance to decrease the probability of wrongful murders, we are in a position analogous to the position of the person in a standard self-defence case who reasonably believes he has to kill another in order to have at least a chance of preventing that person from wrongfully killing him. And, as we have seen, whatever one says of the view that in such a situation one is entitled to act to save the innocent (whether oneself or another) at the expense of the person who has made this situation necessary, one cannot plausibly say that, in embracing that view, one is allowing oneself to treat others as mere means to one's own (or other innocent parties') well-being. Rather, one is, rightly or wrongly, insisting that justice, or fairness, allows one to distribute harms in a certain way when one is in a situation where someone must inevitably be harmed and it is due to the free, informed, and wrongful choices of one of them that this is the case.

There are, of course, other moral objections to the societal-self-protection argument for capital punishment, and to capital punishment generally (regardless of the arguments by which it is defended), besides the objection that the societal-self-protection argument requires us to treat those whom we execute as mere means to a larger social good. And while it would be impossible to consider here the implications of the approach suggested above for all of these other objections, it will be useful, I think, to consider, very briefly, its implications for at least three especially common objections that I think are also very important objections.

One is an objection that takes many different forms but that I think can be fairly summarized by the claim that, whatever good it does, and regardless of whether or not it is a way of treating others as mere means, capital punishment is wrong because it requires us to arrogate to ourselves a right that, if it belongs to anyone, belongs only to God — namely, the right of deliberately and actively ending another person's life (that is to say, killing them). (This objection can, of course, be stated without the reference to God. The claim in that case is simply that no one has a right, under any circumstances, to actively end another person's life.)

The problem with this objection, it seems to me, is that it requires an assumption that most of us are not willing to make — namely, that, unless one is God, it is always wrong actively to end a human being's life, regardless of the circumstances. After all, most of us believe that it is sometimes permissible to kill in combat, at least as a defender in a just war, and most of us believe, as well, that, even outside of war, killing in direct self-defence, or in defence of another innocent person, is under certain circumstances morally justifiable.

To be sure, the objection we are now considering can be reformulated to take these exceptions into account. It then becomes the view that, while taking another person's life can in principle be justified under certain special circumstances, those circumstances do not include the circumstances that are thought by some to justify capital punishment. But, of course, this simply begs the question, unless we are shown why this is supposed to be so. And showing this, it seems to me, as a matter of principle, will be problematical when the argument for the in-principle justifiability of capital punishment is an argument like the one sketched above. For, whatever its flaws, one virtue of that argument is that it uses, for the in-principle justifiability of capital punishment, a premise exactly analogous to the premise that most of us would say justifies deadly violence in direct self-defence, whether in private life or in a just war.[12]

A related objection is that capital punishment is wrong, even if we can thereby save innocent lives, because it sends out the wrong message, especially to children — namely, that under certain circumstances it is morally permissible to do exactly what we are telling potential capital criminals not to do and will in fact be executing them for doing if they do it. On its face, of course, this argument, which we often hear from our students, is a bad argument — indeed, a rather charming case of a clear but superficially oblique petitio — since it assumes exactly what the critic needs to show: namely, that what we would be doing in executing capital criminals would be exactly what we want to keep capital criminals from doing (i.e., killing others wrongfully). The objection is worth noting, though, both because of its surprising popularity and because, on a charitable interpretation, it expresses, albeit obscurely, an important and quite legitimate concern — namely, that people, especially children, sometimes get, not the message we want them to get, but some other, sometimes quite different message instead. Thus, if it could be shown to be true that in societies that resort to capital punishment it generally turns out to the case that people grow up being more casual about homicide than they would otherwise be, and that this is not an accident but, rather, a consequence of the existence of that institution as young people grow up, this would, I should think, be a good reason to think twice about supporting capital punishment.[13]

Note, though, that quite apart from the fact that, thus construed, this objection rests on an empirical assumption it would be very difficult to prove or disprove, a defender of the version of the societal-self-defence argument that was sketched above is in a position to make what seems to me to be an important point in connection with the sort of concern we are supposing lies behind this objection. For if we had reason to believe that capital punishment does in fact deter some capital crimes, and were tempted to resort to it for that reason but were also concerned about the objection we are now considering (the 'misunderstood message objection' as we might call it), surely the defender of the deontological or 'distributive justice' version of the societal-self-protection argument would want to make the following point: whatever the odds of our audience

[12] I suspect that this objection is in fact always made on the assumption that the defender of capital punishment is using overall social utility, rather than distributive justice, as the key moral premise in his argument.

[13] Many opponents of capital punishment think it is obvious that it has exactly the effects we are discussing, and they may be right in thinking that it has this effect. Finding compelling evidence for this claim, though, is difficult.

misunderstanding what we are doing when we resort to capital punishment either without a clear explanation of why we are doing so or with the standard utilitarian explanation for why we are doing so, the odds of a (harmful) misunderstanding of what we are doing are surely much lower when our explanation is that in resorting to capital punishment we are, given our empirical knowledge, doing nothing more than defending ourselves, and other innocents, from wrongful harm and, moreover, thereby doing something that is no different, in principle, from what we do when we directly defend ourselves, sometimes violently, from someone who is about to assault us. The defender of our version of the societal-self-protection argument, that is to say, would be anxious to make it publicly and very widely known exactly what the proper rationale for capital punishment is, in his view, hoping thereby to reduce very significantly the likelihood that the use of capital punishment will lead the unreflective to see it as in principle no different from the kinds of conduct we are using it to deter.

It is, of course, possible that capital punishment will have the effect of diminishing some portion of a citizenry's respect for human life, and possibly even increasing the average citizen's likelihood of wrongfully taking an innocent life, regardless of how that institution is explained and defended in societies in which it is adopted. And where this is the case, members of such a society would surely have good reason to think twice about adopting that institution. My point here is simply that it seems reasonable to suppose that a defence of capital punishment that plausibly makes it out to be a matter of the relevant sort of justice-based societal self-defence is much less likely than other defences of this institution to be misinterpreted in ways that lead young people to believe that their society places less value on human life than, in their everyday moral training, they are typically led to believe.

I want to conclude by considering an objection that is not peculiar to the societal-self-protection argument but that I think everyone would agree any defence of capital punishment must face. This is the objection, raised above against the retributive argument, that rests on the fact that it is impossible to ensure that there will not be mistakes in our courtrooms that lead to the deaths (by execution) of innocent individuals. This objection, which holds that the fact just alluded to is a reason to reject this institution, has been made all the more salient, in the United States, by recent evidence, mentioned above, that such mistakes are in fact much more common than many defenders of capital punishment might have liked to suppose.[14]

---

[14] A related objection, which space does not permit me to discuss here, rests on compelling evidence that, in the United States at least, capital punishment is, or at least until quite recently was, much likelier to be imposed on poor people, and on

254 Philosophy and its Public Role

Notice, first, that someone who rejects the retributive argument because of the fact just noted is not required, logically, to reject the societal-self-protection argument for the same reason. For such a person might well believe that, while the moral value of giving wrongdoers their just desserts is insufficient to justify seeking to do this in circumstances in which one knows that in doing it one will occasionally execute innocent people, it is, despite this, an open question whether the values that are served or protected by a non-retributive system of punishment are similarly unable to justify capital punishment, given the same assumption about our inability to preclude mistakes. The utilitarian, for example, will want to weigh the presumed good effects of capital punishment, supposing there are some, against its bad effects, which of course must include the unavoidable deaths of innocent but mistakenly convicted individuals. Our question here is how the defender of the justice-based version of the societal-self-protection argument that we have sketched above will deal with the fact of institutional fallibility and whether his way of dealing with it makes his account any more or less attractive than alternative deterrence-based accounts.

We may note, to begin with, that there is an analogous or at least closely related problem in cases of individual (direct) self-defence. For in at least some such cases it will be impossible for the defender to act in self-defence without admitting to herself that there is a distinct possibility that in defending herself she will inevitably harm one or more innocent bystanders. And, of course, in some such cases, that harm will include the possibility of a bystander's being unintentionally killed. What are we to say, on the justice-based account of direct self-defence that was sketched above, about the permissibility of taking self-defensive measures in such cases?

Answering this question is, of course, a vexed issue, both in law and in morals. One thing on which nearly everyone agrees, however, is this: in circumstances of the relevant sort — i.e., in circumstances in which one cannot be certain that in acting to defend oneself from wrongful harm one will not unintentionally harm innocent bystanders — acting in

---

persons of colour, than on exactly similarly situated affluent people and whites. (Though there has been less systematic research to show this, it seems likely that this same generalization holds true for other, less severe sentences.) My own view is that this, along with the objection we are now discussing, is the most serious objection of all to the actual practice of capital punishment and that unless this particular aspect of that practice can be eliminated, at least so far as reality allows, capital punishment should not be legally (i.e., constitutionally) tolerated, even if there were compelling evidence for the assumption that this institution does in fact deter capital crimes. Notice, though, that this is not an in-principle objection to capital punishment, as such, but, rather, a very serious objection to the resort to capital punishment under circumstances in which the effects of the relevant biases cannot be eliminated.

self-defence is not always clearly impermissible. Rather, what most of us are inclined to think, and what prevailing laws generally hold, is that whether or not risking harm to the innocent is morally permissible in such cases is a complex function of just how likely it is one will be harmed (fatally) if one does not act against one's attacker, just how likely it is that innocent bystanders will be harmed by one's actions, and just how much harm to bystanders is likely if one so acts.

Clearly, our thinking here, along with most legal opinion, is analogous to our thinking about so-called 'collateral damage' in a just war. We may not intentionally harm the innocent in such a war, most of us would say, even if doing so will assist us in defending ourselves against the unjust aggressor. This, however, for most of us at any rate, does not preclude the possibility that we may sometimes intentionally perform actions, in a just war, that we know or reasonably believe will cause serious harm to the innocent. In such cases, whether or not we are justified in going forward with the potentially harmful actions is, we believe, as in the sorts of cases just discussed, a complex function of the likely amounts and probabilities of goods and harms that will likely be done.[15]

I see no reason to believe that, morally, the situation is any different with respect to the question that currently interests us — namely, the situation in which we would find ourselves if we had reason to believe that the practice of capital punishment would significantly reduce the incidence of capital crimes but in which we also knew that, despite our best efforts to avoid such effects, it would be impossible for us to eliminate entirely mistaken convictions and wrongful executions. Critics opposed to capital punishment as a matter of principle are inclined to argue that, while the inevitability of wrongful convictions (at all levels of seriousness of crimes and punishments) is not a reason to dismantle the criminal justice system as a whole, it is a reason to eliminate capital punishment, because the effects of capital punishment are so different from the results of a prison sentence, no matter how long. But since an analogous point would not, I think, induce us to agree that individual self-defence is never permissible when fatal harm to innocent bystanders is possible, or that self-defensive acts of war are never permissible when fatal but unintended harm to the innocent is possible, I see no reason to believe that the situation is any different in the case of a system of threats and punishments that is designed to protect the innocent against

[15] Note that, despite appearances, this is not a form of utilitarianism but, rather, a calculating of utilities that is, on most views, both permitted and required by a 'natural-rights' or 'justice-based' approach to these matters. Note too that I am assuming for the sake of argument that defenders of the so-called Doctrine of Double Effect are right in holding that foreseeable consequences of one's intentional actions are not always consequences that one intends. For a defence of this assumption, see Bratman (1987) pp. 139–64.

wrongful death and that is grounded not on its overall social utility but on a justice-based right on the part of the innocent to defend themselves against wrongful harm. To be sure, such a system would not be justified, any more than direct self-defence or analogous defensive acts in an otherwise just war would be justified, if the probability of wrongful harm to the innocent were unacceptably high. Our point here is simply that, while we have said nothing about what would count as an unacceptably high probability of harm to the innocent, it seems clear that most of us believe that not just any probability of (fatal) harm must count as unacceptably high.

Conclusion

I have attempted to show that the most important in-principle objection to one main argument for capital punishment is a bad objection, and I have attempted to do this by arguing that the proper moral basis for that argument is a deontological or non-consequentialist principle rather than, as is commonly thought, a utilitarian principle. I have not addressed the obvious empirical objection to this argument, which holds that we have no good reason to suppose that capital punishment in fact deters capital crimes. Nor have I discussed, at sufficient length, two very important objections that any defence of capital punishment must face — namely, that, quite apart from the question of its relative effectiveness in deterring capital crimes, capital punishment is wrong because (a) we know we cannot entirely eliminate executions based on mistaken criminal convictions, and (b) we have good reason to believe that racism and 'classism' will inevitably make the distribution of capital sentences profoundly unfair. All of these objections, it seems to me, need careful attention and may well, in the end, be sufficient to support the claim that capital punishment should be eliminated in the United States, as it has been in so many other democratic countries. Nonetheless, I think it worth knowing that, if it is unacceptable, capital punishment is unacceptable for these other reasons and not because it is, as a matter of principle, a morally unacceptable way of dealing with the problem of capital crimes.

References

Allen, G.W. (1967) *William James: A Biography* (New York: Viking Press).

American Society for Reproductive Medicine, 'Posthumous Reproduction'. Available at: www.asrm.org/Media/Ethics/ poshum.html (Accessed: March 25, 2004).

Archard, D. (1998) *Sexual Consent* (Boulder, Colo: Westview Press).

Aristotle, *Nicomachean Ethics*, Second Edition, trans. Terence Irwin (Indianapolis: Hackett Publishing Company, Inc., 1999), 1180a 22–3.

Ashworth, A. (1995) *Sentencing and Criminal Justice* (London: Butterworths, 2nd edn).

Auden, W.H. (1927, 1977) 'Get there if you can and see', in *The English Auden: Poems, Essays and dramatic Writings 1927–1939*, ed. E. Mendelson (London: Faber and Faber).

Ayer, A.J. (1968) *The Origins of Pragmatism* (San Francisco: Freeman, Cooper and Company).

Bahadur, G. (2002) 'Death and Conception', *Human Reproduction*, 17 (10).

Bantock, G.H. (1973) 'Towards a theory of popular education', in *The Curriculum: Context, Design and Development*, ed. R. Hooper (Edinburgh: Oliver and Boyd).

Barry, B. (1995) *Justice as Impartiality* (New York: Oxford University Press).

Batzer F., Hurwitz, M., Caplan, A., (2003) 'Postmortem parenthood and the need for a protocol with posthumous sperm procurement', *Fertility and Sterility*, 79 (6).

Bayne, T., Kolers, A. (2003) 'Parenthood and Procreation', *Stanford Encyclopedia of Philosophy*, http://plato.stanford.edu/entries/ parenthood. Accessed: March 8, 2004.

Benda, J. (1955) *The Betrayal of the Intellectuals* (Boston, MA: The Beacon Press).

Benenson, F.C. (1984) *Probability, Objectivity and Evidence* (London: Routledge & Kegan Paul).

Benhabib, S. (1996) 'Toward a Deliberative Model of Democratic Legitimacy', in *Democracy and Difference*, ed. S. Benhabib (Princeton, NJ: Princeton University Press).

Bentham, J. (1825) *Traité des preuves judiciares*, ed. Dumont; *A Treatise on Judicial Evidence* (London: Baldwin, Cradock & Joy).

Bentham, J. (1827) *The Rationale of Judicial Evidence, Specially Applied to English Practice*, 5 volumes, ed. J.S. Mill (London: Hunt & Clarke).

Bentham, J. (1843) *Principles of Judicial Procedure* in *The Works of Jeremy Bentham*, ed. J. Bowring, Vol. 2 (Edinburgh: Tait).

Berger, P. and Luckmann, T. (1967)   *The Social Construction of Reality* (London: Allen Lane).

Berlin, I. (1991) 'The Bent Twig', in *The Crooked Timber of Humanity: Chapters in the History of Ideas*, ed. Henry Hardy (London: John Murray).

Bobbit, P. (2002) *The Shield of Achilles* (New York: Knopf).

Bousfield, A. (1999) *The Relationship Between Liberalism and Conservatism* (Aldershot: Ashgate).

Bratman, M. (1987) *Intention, Plans, and Practical Reasoning* (Cambridge, MA: Harvard University Press).

Brecher, B. (1998) *Getting What You Want? A Critique of Liberal Morality* (London: Routledge).

Broome, J. (1991) *Weighing Goods* (Oxford: Basil Blackwell).

Burgh, R. (1982) 'Do the Guilty Deserve Punishment?', *The Journal of Philosophy*, 79.

Burke, J. and Kadish, S. (1983) 'Conspiracy', *Encyclopedia of Crime and Justice*, Vol. I, (New York: The Free Press).

CAIDA (Cooperative Association for Internet Data Analysis), http://www.caida.org

Caldwell, W. (1900) 'Pragmatism', *Mind*, 9.

Callan, E. (1997) *Creating Citizens. Political Education and Liberal Democracy* (Oxford: Oxford University Press).

Callan, E. (2000) 'Discrimination and Religious Schooling' in *Citizenship in Diverse Societies*, ed. W. Kymlicka and W. Norman (Oxford: Oxford University Press).

Carne, G. (2001) 'Military Tribunals: A Terrible Swift Sword', *Alternative Law Journal*, 26.

Carr, D. (1987) 'Freud and Sexual Ethics', *Philosophy*, 62 (241), pp. 361–73.

Carr, D (1993) 'Moral Values and the Teacher: Beyond the paternal and the permissive' *Journal of Philosophy of Education*, 27 (2) pp 193–207.

Carr, D (2000) *Professionalism and Ethics in Teaching* (London and New York: Routledge).

Carr, D. (2002a) 'Moral Education and the Perils of Developmentalism', *Journal of Moral Education*, 30 (1), pp. 5–19.

Carr, D. (2002b) 'Metaphysics, Reductivism and Spiritual Discourse', *Zygon*, 37 (2), pp. 491–509.

Castells, M. (1997) *The Information Age* (Oxford: Blackwell).

Coleman, A. (1999) 'Hurricane Thoughts: Or, what is it with wealth, anyway?', at www.fool.com.

Cranston, M. (1967) 'Human Rights, Real and Supposed', in *Political Theory and the Rights of Man*, ed. D.D. Raphael (Bloomington, IN: Indiana University Press), pp. 43–53.

Crisp, R. (1997) *Mill on Utilitarianism* (London: Routledge).

Crocker, D. (1998) 'Consumption, Well-Being, and Capability,' in *Ethics of Consumption*, ed. D.A. Crocker and T. Linden (Oxford: Rowman and Littlefield Publishers).

Cupit, G. (1996) *Justice as Fittingness* (Oxford: Oxford University Press).

Cupit, G. (2000) 'The Basis of Equality', *Philosophy*, 75.

Daly, H. (1996) *Beyond Growth* (Boston: Beacon Press).

Dancy, J. (1995) 'Why There Is Really No Such Thing as the Theory of Motivation', *Proceedings of the Aristotelian Society*, 95, pp. 1–18.

Davis, N. (1983) *The Paston Letter* (Oxford: Oxford University Press).

de Tocqueville. A. (1839/2000) *Democracy in America*, trans. Reeve, H. (New York: Bantam).

Denning, D. (1994) 'Encryption and Law Enforcement' (unpublished paper) Commission on Professionals in Science and Technology (see http://www.cpst.org).

Denning, D. (1996) 'The Clipper Chip will Reinforce Privacy', in *Computerization and Controversy* (San Diego, CA: Academic Press).

Dewey, J. (1930/1973) 'From Absolutism to Experimentalism' in *The American Hegelians*, ed. W. Goetzmann (New York: Knopf).

Diffe, W. and Landau, S. (1998) *Privacy on the Line* (Cambridge, MA: MIT Press).

Donnelan, K. (1966) 'Reference and Definite Description', *Philosophical Review*, 75.

Douglas, M. (1966) *Purity and Danger* (London: Routledge and Kegan Paul).

Douglass, A., Daniels, K. (2002) 'Posthumous Reproduction: A Consideration of the Medical, Ethical, Cultural, Psychosocial and Legal Perspectives in the New Zealand Context', *Medical Law International*, 5.

Duff, A. (1996) *Criminal Attempts* (Oxford: Oxford University Press).

Dummett, M. (2001) *On Immigration and Refugees* (London: Routledge).

Duncan, E.H. (1975) 'Eighteenth-Century Scottish Philosophy: Its Impact on the American West', *Southwestern Journal of Philosophy*, Vol. 6 (1).

Dworkin, R. (1978) *Taking Rights Seriously* (Cambridge, MA: Harvard University Press); first published 1977; important appendix added in 1978.

Dworkin, R. (1986) *Law's Empire* (Cambridge, MA: Harvard University Press).

Dworkin, R., (1989) 'The original position', in N. Daniels (ed.), *Reading Rawls: Critical Studies on Rawls' A Theory of Justice* (Stanford, CA: Stanford University Press) Second edition.

Dworkin, R. (2002) 'The Threat to Patriotism', *New York Review of Books*, February 28.

Dworkin, R. (2002) 'The Trouble with the Tribunals', *New York Review of Books*, April 25.

Dwyer, J (1998) *Religious Schools v Children's Rights* (Ithaca and London: Cornell University Press).

Dyson, E. (1997) *Release 2.0* (New York: Broadway Books)

Ellis, A.J. (1995) 'Recent Work in the Philosophy of Punishment', *Philosophical Quarterly*, 45.

Ellis, A.J. (1997) 'Punishment and the Principle of Fair Play', *Utilitas*, 15.

Ellis, A.J. (1998) 'Criminal Attempts', *Journal of Applied Philosophy*, 15.

Ewing, A. C. (1929) *The Morality of Punishment* (London: Kegan, Paul).

Farrell, D. (1985) 'The Justification of General Deterrence', *The Philosophical Review*, 94.

Farrell, D. (1988) 'Punishment without the State', *Nous*, 22.

Farrell, D. (1989) 'On Threats and Punishments', *Social Theory and Practice*, Vol. 15.

Farrell, D. (1990) 'The Justification of Deterrent Violence', *Ethics*, 100.

Farrell, D. (1995) 'Deterrence and the Just Distribution of Harm', *Philosophy and Social Policy*, 12.

Farrell, D. (1998) 'A New Paradox of Deterrence', in *Rational Commitment and Social Justice: Essays for Gregory Kavka*, ed. J.L. Coleman and C.W. Morris (Cambridge: Cambridge University Press).

Farrell, D. (2003) 'Deterrent Punishments in Kant's Ideal State', in *Ritgerdit Landa Mikael Kairlssyni*, ed. Kristjansson and Gunnarsson (Reykyavik: University of Iceland Press).

Feinberg, J. (1970) *Doing and Deserving: Essays in the Theory of Responsibility* (Princeton, NJ: Princeton University Press).

Feinberg, J. (1973) *Social Philosophy* (Englewood Cliffs, NJ: Prentice-Hall).

Feinberg, J. (1980) *Rights, Justice, and the Bounds of Liberty* (Princeton, NJ: Princeton University Press).

Feinberg, W (1998) *Common Schools/Uncommon Identities. National Unity and Cultural Difference* (New Haven and London: Yale University Press).

Ferrier, J.F. (1842) 'Berkeley and Idealism', in Ferrier *Philosophical Works*, Vol. III.

Ferrier, J.F. (1875) *Philosophical Works of James Frederick Ferrier*, ed. A. Grant and E.L. Lushington (Edinburgh: Blackwood); reprinted (2001) with an introduction by John Haldane (Bristol: Thoemmes).

Fish, S. (2002) 'Don't Blame Postmodernism', *The Responsive Community*, 12 (3).

Fleischacker, S. (2003) 'The Impact on America: Scottish Philosophy and the American Founding' in *The Cambridge Companion to the Scottish Enlightenment*, ed. A. Broadie (Cambridge: Cambridge University Press).

Fletcher, G.P. (1988) *A Crime of Self Defense: Bernhard Goetz and the Law on Trial* (Chicago: University of Chicago Press).

Fletcher, G.P. (2002) 'On Justice and War: Contradictions in the Proposed Military Tribunals', *Harvard Journal of Law and Public Policy*, Spring 2002.

Fowler, E. (1980) 'Some Interesting Connections Between the Common Sense Realists and the Pragmatists, Especially James' in *Two Centuries of Philosophy in America*, ed. P. Caws (Towata, NJ: Rowman & Littlefield).

Frader, J. (1993) 'Have We Lost Our Senses? Problems With Maintaining Brain-Dead Bodies Carrying Fetuses', *Journal of Clinical Ethics*.

Frank, J. (1930) *Law and the Modern Mind* (New York: Coward-McCann Inc.).

Frank, J. (1945) *Fate and Freedom* (New York: Simon and Schuster) .

Frank, J. (1949) *Courts on Trial* (Princeton, NJ: Princeton University Press).

Freeman, S. (1990/91) 'Constitutional Democracy and the Legitimacy of Judicial Review', *Law and Philosophy*, 9.

Freeman, S. (1992) 'Original Meaning, Democratic Interpretation, and the Constitution', *Philosophy and Public Affairs*, 21.

Freeman, S. (1994) 'Political Liberalism and the Possibility of a Just Democratic Constitution', *Chicago-Kent Law Review*, 69.

Fried, C. (1969) 'The Value of Life' *Harvard Law Review*, 82 (7).

Friedman, D. (1996) 'A World of Strong Privacy: Promises and Perils of Encryption' *Social Philosophy and Policy*, 13 (2).

Fukuyama, F. (1992) *The End of History and the Last Man* (London: Penguin).

Galbraith, J. K. (1984) *The Affluent Society* (Boston, MA: Houghton Mifflin).

Gardiner, M (1977) 'A New Kind of Cipher That Would Take Millions of Years to Break,' *Scientific American*, 237 (2).

Garrard, E. and McNaughton, D. (1998) 'Mapping Moral Motivation', *Ethical Theory and Moral Practice*, 1, pp. 45–59.

Garth, H. and Mills, C.W., ed. (1945) *Max Weber: Essays in Sociology* (Oxford: Oxford University Press).

Geras, N. (1998) *The Contract of Mutual Indifference* (London: Verso).

Gibson, W. (1986) *Neuromancer* (New York: Ace Books).

Goldstein, M. (1998) 'Surgical Management of Male Infertility and Other Scrotal Disorders', in *Campbell's Urology*, 7th edition, ed. P.C. Walsh, A.B. Retnik and E.D. Vaughan (Philadelphia, PA: W.B. Saunders).

Graham, G. (1999a) *Universities: The Recovery of an Idea* (Exeter: Imprint Academic).

Graham, G. (1999b) *The Internet: A Philosophical Inquiry* (London: Routledge).

Gramsci, A. (1978) 'The Intellectuals', in Gramsci, *Selections from Prison Notebooks*, ed. and trans. Quentin Hoare and Geoffrey Nowell Smith (London: Lawrence & Wishart), pp. 5–23.

Grubb, A. (1999) 'Posthumous Taking and Use of Sperm: A.B. v Attorney General of Victoria', *Medical Law Review*, 7 (1).

Gutmann, A. (1987) *Democratic Education* (Princeton, NJ: Princeton University Press).

Halstead, J.M. and McLaughlin, T.H. (2005) 'Are Faith Schools Divisive?' in *Faith Schools: Conflict or Consensus?*, ed. J. Cairns, R. Gardner and D. Lawton (London: RoutledgeFalmer)

Gutmann, A. and Thomson, D. (1996) *Democracy and Disagreement* (Cambridge MA: Harvard University Press).

Habermas, J. (1990) 'Discourse Ethics: Notes on a Program of Philosophical Justification,' in *Moral Consciousness and Communicative Action*, trans. Christian Lenhardt and Shierry Weber Nicholsen (Cambridge, MA: MIT Press).

Haldane, J. (2000) 'The State and Fate of Contemporary Philosophy of Mind', *American Philosophical Quarterly*, Vol. 37.

Haldane, J. (2001) 'Has Philosophy Made a Difference and Could it be Expected To?', in *Philosophy at the New Millennium*, ed. A. O'Hear (Cambridge: Cambridge University Press).

Hall, J and Ikenberry, G. (1989) *The State* (Minneapolis: University of Minnesota Press).

Hare, W (1993) *What Makes a Good Teacher? Reflections on Some Characteristics Central to the Educational Enterprise* (London Ontario: The Althouse Press)

Harris, J. (1998) 'Rights and Reproductive Choice', in *The Future of Human Reproduction*, ed. J. Harris and S. Holm (Oxford: Oxford University Press).

Harris, K. (1984) *Attlee* (London: Weidenfeld and Nicholson).

Hart, H.L.A. (1968) 'Prolegomenon to the Principles of Punishment,' and other essays in *Punishment and Responsibility: Essays in the Philosophy of Law* (Oxford: Oxford University Press).

Hart, H.L.A. (1999) *The Concept of Law* (Oxford: Clarendon Press).

Hegel, (1837/1988) 'The Geographical Basis of History' from *Lectures on the Philosophy of History* (c. 1820; published posthumously in 1837) excerpt in Rauch, L. trans. *Introduction to the Philosophy of History* (Indianapolis, IN: Hackett Publishing Company).

Hill, J. (2003) 'Dissecting Room: Conduct and Compassion: Posthumous Sperm Retrieval', *The Lancet*, 361.

Honoré, A. (1999) *Responsibility and Fault* (Oxford: Hart).

Hume, D. (1748, 1975) *An Enquiry Concerning Human Understanding*, ed. L. A. Selby-Bigge (Oxford: Clarendon Press).

Ignatieff, M. (1995a) 'Nationalism and the Narcissism of Minor Differences', *Queen's Quarterly*, 102 (1).

Ignatieff, M. (1995b) *Blood and Belonging: Journeys into the New Nationalism* (London: Viking).

Jackson J. and Doran, S. (1996) 'Evidence' in D. Patterson's *A Companion to Philosophy of Law and Legal Theory* (Oxford: Blackwell).

Jacobs, J. (2001) *Choosing Character: Responsibility for Virtue and Vice* (Ithaca, NY: Cornell University Press).

Jacobs, J. (2003) 'Some Tensions Between Autonomy and Self-Governance', *Social Philosophy and Policy*.

Jaeger, C. Renn, O, Rosa, E.A. and Webler T. (2001) *Risk, Uncertainty and Rational Action* (London: Earthscan Publications).

James, W. (1902) *The Varieties of Religious Experience* (London: Longmans Green & Co,).

James, W. (1902/1920) 'Letter to Schiller' 1902, in *Letters of William James* Vol. 1, ed. H. James, H. (1920).

James, W. (1909) *A Pluralistic Universe* (London: Longmans, Green and Co.).

James, W. (1911) *Some Problems of Philosophy* (London: Longman).

Johnson, S. (2001) *Emergence* (New York: Scribner).

Jones, M.W., ed. (1982) *The Value of Life and Safety* (New York: North Holland Pub. Co.).

Jones, P. (1985) 'William James' in *American Philosophy*, ed. Marcus G. Singer (Cambridge: Cambridge University Press).

Kagan, S. (1998) *Normative Ethics* (Boulder, CO: Westview).

Kant, I. (1785/1976) *Foundations of the Metaphysics of Morals*, trans. Lewis White Beck (Indianapolis, IN: Bobbs-Merrill Company, Inc).

Kant, I. (1793, 1960) *Religion Within the Limits of Reason Alone*, trans. Theodore M. Greene and Hoyt H. Hudson (New York: Harper & Row).

Kant, I. (1797/1996) *The Metaphysics of Morals*, ed. and trans. Mary Gregor (Cambridge: Cambridge University Press).

Keeney R. (1984). 'Ethics, Decision Analysis and Public Risk', *Risk Analysis*, 4 (2).

Keeney, R. (1986) 'The Analysis of Risks of Fatalities', in *Risk Evaluation and Management*, ed. V.T. Covello, J. Menkes and J. Mumpower (New York: Plenum Press).

Kelly, K. (1994) *Out of Control* (London: Addison–Wesley).

Koehane, R. and Nye, J. (1998) 'Power and Interdependence in an Information Age', *Foreign Affairs*, 77 (2).

Kohlberg, L. (1971) 'From Is to Ought: How to Commit the Naturalistic Fallacy and Get Away with it in the Study of Moral Development', in *Cognitive Development and Epistemology*, ed. T. Mischel (New York: Academic Press).

Korsgaard, C. (1997) 'The Normativity of Instrumental Reason', in *Ethics and Practical Reason*, ed. G. Cullitty and B. Gaut (Oxford: Clarendon Press), pp. 215–54.

Krasner, S. (2001) 'Sovereignty', *Foreign Policy*, 20.

Kusserow, R. (1996) 'The Government needs Computer Matching', in *Computers and Controversy*, ed. R. Kling (San Diego, CA: Academic Press).

Kymlicka, W. (1990) *Contemporary Political Philosophy* (Oxford: Clarendon Press).

Kymlicka, W. (1991) *Liberalism, Community and Culture* (Oxford: Clarendon Press).

Kymlicka, W. (1995a) *Multicultural Citizenship: A Liberal Theory of Minority Rights* (Oxford: Clarendon Press).

Kymlicka, W. (1995b) 'Misunderstanding Nationalism', *Dissent*, Winter.

Lane, H. (1954) *Talks to Parents and Teachers* (London: Allen and Unwin).

Lang, B. (1990) *Act and Idea in the Nazi Genocide* (Chicago: Chicago University Press).

Lawrence, D.H. (1973) *Lawrence on Education*, ed. J. and R. Williams (Harmondsworth: Penguin).

León-Portilla, M. (1963) *Aztec Thought and Culture: A Study of the Ancient Náhuatl Mind* (Norman, OK: University of Oklahoma Press).

León-Portilla, M. (1964) 'Philosophy in the Cultures of Ancient Mexico' in *Cross-Cultural Understanding: Epistemology in Anthropology*, ed. F.S.C. Northrop and Helen H. Livingston (New York: Harper and Row).

Levinson, M. (1999) *The Demands of Liberal Education* (Oxford: Oxford University Press).

Lichtenberg, J. (1998) 'Consuming Because Others Consume' in *Ethics of Consumption*, ed. D.A. Crocker and T. Linden (Oxford: Rowman and Littlefield Publishers).

Lubbers, R. (1997) 'The Dutch Way', *New Perspectives Quarterly*, Fall.

Lyotard, J. F. (1992) *The Postmodern Condition: A Report on Knowledge*, trans. G. Bennington and B. Masumi (Manchester: Manchester University Press).

McCarthy, T. (1994) 'Kantian Constructivism and Reconstructivism', *Ethics*, 105 (4), pp 44–63.

McCloskey, H.J. (1965) 'Rights', *Philosophical Quarterly*, 15.

McCloskey, H.J. (1976) 'Rights: Some Conceptual Issues', *Australasian Journal of Philosophy*, 54.

McDonough, K. and Feinberg, W., ed. (2003) *Citizenship and Education in Liberal-Democratic Societies. Teaching for Cosmopolitan Values and Collective Identities* (Oxford: Oxford University Press).

McKerlie, D. (1996) 'Equality', *Ethics*, 106.

McLaughlin, T.H. (1992) 'The Ethics of Separate Schools' in *Ethics, Ethnicity and Education*, ed. M. Leicester and M.J. Taylor (London: Kogan Page).

McLaughlin, T.H. (1999) 'Distinctiveness and the Catholic School: Balanced Judgement and the Temptations of Commonality' in *Catholic Education: Inside-Out/Outside-In*, ed. J. Conroy (Dublin: Veritas).

McLaughlin, T.H. (2003a) 'The Burdens and Dilemmas of Common Schooling', in *Citizenship and Education in Liberal-Democratic Societies. Teaching for Cosmopolitan Values and Collective Identities*, ed. K. McDonough and W. Feinberg (Oxford: Oxford University Press).

McLaughlin, T.H. (2003b) 'Teaching as a Practice and a Community of Practice: the Limits of Commonality and the Demands of Diversity', *Journal of Philosophy of Education*, 37 (2).

Mackie, J. L. (1973) *Truth, Probability, and Paradox* (Oxford, Clarendon Press).

MacLean, D. ed. (1986) *Values at Risk*, Maryland Studies in Public Philosophy (Totowa, NJ: Rowman & Allanheld).

McMahan, J. (1994) 'Self-Defense and the Problem of the Innocent Attacker', *Ethics*, 104.

Macedo, S. (2000) *Diversity and Distrust: Civic Education in a Multicultural Democracy* (Cambridge, MA and London: Harvard University Press).

Martin, C.B and Heil, J. (1999) 'The Ontological Turn', *Midwest Studies in Philosophy*, 23.

Martin, R. (1980) 'Human Rights and Civil Rights', *Philosophical Studies*, 37.

Martin, R. (1985) *Rawls and Rights* (Lawrence, KS: University Press of Kansas).

Martin, R. (1991) 'The Problem of Other Cultures and Other Periods in Action Explanations', *Philosophy of the Social Sciences*, 21.

Martin, R. (1993) *A System of Rights* (Oxford: Oxford University Press).

Martin, R. (1998) 'Rights', *Routledge Encyclopedia of Philosophy*, Vol. 8 (London: Routledge).

Martin, R. and Griffin, S. M. (1995) 'Constitutional Rights and Democracy in the USA: The Issue of Judicial Review', *Ratio Juris*, 8 (2).

Mayo, B. (1965) 'Human Rights', *Proceedings of the Aristotelian Society Supplementary Volume*, 39.

Marx, K. (1975) 'Theses on Feuerbach', in Marx and Engels, *On Religion* (Moscow: Progress Publishers), pp. 62–4.

Melden, A.I. (1988) *Rights in Moral Lives* (Berkeley, CA: University of California Press).

Mellor, D.H. (1971) *The Matter of Chance* (Cambridge: Cambridge University Press).

Miller, D. (1995) *On Nationality* (Oxford: Clarendon Press).

Mill, J.S. (1848/1965) *Principles of Political Economy* (London: Routledge & Kegan Paul).

Mill, J.S. (1859/1977) *On Liberty*, in *Collected Works of John Stuart Mill*, Vol. XVIII, ed. J.M. Robson (Toronto: University of Toronto Press).

Minow, M. 'Justice Engendered' in *Feminist Jurisprudence*, ed. Patricia Smith (Oxford: Oxford University Press).

Mishan E. J. (1971) 'Evaluation of Life and Limb: A Theoretical Approach' *Journal of Political Economy*, 79.

Monbiot, G. (2000) *Captive State: The Corporate Takeover of Britain* (Basingstoke: Macmillan).

Montague, P. (1983) 'Punishment and Societal Defense', *Criminal Justice Ethics*, 2.

Montague, P. (1995) *Punishment as Societal-Defense* (Rowman and Littlefield).

Moore, A. (2000) 'Posthumous Reproduction', *Otago Bioethics Report*, 9 (1).

Moore, M. (1995) 'The Moral Worth of Retribution,' in *Punishment and Rehabilitation*, 3rd edn, ed. J. G. Murphy (Belmont: Wadsworth Publishing Company).

Morris, C. (1998) *An Essay on the Modern State* (Cambridge: Cambridge University Press).

Morris, H. (1995) 'A Paternalistic Theory of Punishment', in *Punishment and Rehabilitation*, 3rd edn, ed. J. G. Murphy (Belmont: Wadsworth Publishing Company).

Mulgan, G. (1998) *Connexity* (Cambridge, MA: Harvard Business School).

Mumpower, J. (1986) 'An Analysis of the *de minimis* Strategy for Risk Management', *Risk Analysis*, 6 (4).

Murphy, J. G. 'Hatred: A Qualified Defense', in *Forgiveness and Mercy*, J.G. Murphy and J. Hampton (Cambridge: Cambridge University Press).

Nagel, E. (1939) 'Principles of the Theory of Probability', in *Foundations of the Unity of Science*, 1 (6) (Chicago: University of Chicago Press).

Nagel, T. (1986) *The View from Nowhere* (Oxford: Oxford University Press).

Nagel,, T. (1987) 'Moral Conflict and Political Legitimacy', *Philosophy and Public Affairs*, 16 (3) pp. 215–240.

Nagel, T. (1991) *Equality and Partiality* (New York: Oxford University Press).

Nieir, A. (2002) 'The Military Tribunals On Trial', *New York Review of Books*, February 14, pp. 11–15.

New Zealand Law Commission (2004) *New Issues in Legal Parenthood: A discussion paper* (Wellington, NZ).

Nizan, P. (1971) *The Watchdogs: Philosphers of the Established Order*, trans. Paul Fittinghoff (New York: Monthly Review Press).

Nordic Journal of Philosophical Logic (1998) Special issue on MacColl Vol. 3 (1).

Norman, R. (2001) 'Practical Reasons and the Redundancy of Motives', *Ethical Theory and Moral Practice*, 4.

Nussbaum, M. (1998) 'The Good as Discipline, the Good as Freedom,' in *Ethics of Consumption*, ed. D.A. Crocker and T. Linden (Oxford: Rowman and Littlefield Publishers).

Nussbaum, N. (2000) *Women and Human Development* (Cambridge: Cambridge University Press).

Nuttall, A.D. (1998) *The Alternative Trinity: Gnostic Heresy in Marlowe, Milton and Blake* (Oxford: Clarendon Press).

Oakeshott, M. (1989) 'Learning and Teaching' in *The Voice of Liberal Learning: Michael Oakeshott on Education*, ed. T. Fuller (New Haven and London: Yale University Press).

O'Neill, O. (2003) 'Some Limits of Informed Consent', *Journal of Medical Ethics*, 29.

Orr, R. and Siegler, M. (2002) 'Is Posthumous Semen Retrieval Ethically Permissible?', *Journal of Medical Ethics*, 28 (5).

Parfit, D. (1991) *Equality or Priority?*, The Lindley Lecture, University of Kansas (Department of Philosophy, Lawrence, Kansas).

Peirce, C.S. (1905) 'Issues of Pragmatism', *Monist*, 18.

Perkins, R. (1969) *Criminal Law*, 2nd ed. (New York: The Foundation Press).

Plato, *Gorgias*, trans. W.C. Helmbold (Indianapolis, IN: Bobbs-Merrill Company, Inc., 1952).

Plato, *Statesman*, trans. Christopher J. Rowe (Indianapolis, IN: Hackett Publishing Company, Inc.).

Putnam, H. (1999) *The Threefold Cord* (New York: Columbia University Press).

Putnam, H. (2002) 'Comment on John Haldane's paper "Realism with a Metaphysical Skull"', in *Putnam: Pragmatism and Realism*, ed. J. Conant and U. Zeglen (London: Routledge).

Quinn, W. (1985) 'The Right to Threaten and the Right to Punish', *Philosophy and Public Affairs*, 14.

Raine, K. (1970) *William Blake* (London: Thames and Hudson).

Ramsay, S., (2000) 'Parents Want Access to Dead Son's Frozen Sperm', *The Lancet*, 355, p. 50.

Rawls, J. (1955) 'Two Concepts of Rules', *The Philosophical Review*, 64.

Rawls, J. (1971/1972) *A Theory of Justice* (Cambridge, MA: Harvard University Press; 2nd edition 1999).

Rawls, J. (1993) *Political Liberalism* (New York: Columbia University Press; revised edition 1996).

Rawls, J. (1999) *The Law of Peoples* with 'The Idea of Public Reason Revisited' (Cambridge, MA: Harvard University Press).

Raz, J. (1984) 'Legal Rights', *Oxford Journal of Legal Studies*, 4.

Raz, J. (1986) *The Morality of Freedom* (Oxford: Oxford University Press).

Raz, J. (1990) 'Facing Diversity: The Case of Epistemic Abstinence', *Philosophy and Public Affairs*, 9 (1).

Reich, R (2002) *Bridging Liberalism and Multiculturalism in American Education* (Chicago and London: University of Chicago Press).

Robertson, J. (1998) 'Posthumous reproduction', in *Fertility and Reproductive Medicine*, ed. R.D. Kempers, J. Cohen and A.F. Haney (New York: Elsevier Science).

Rorty, R. (1990) 'Truth and Freedom: A reply to Thomas McCarthy', *Critical Inquiry*, 16, pp.636–9.

Rosecrance, R. (1999) *The Rise of the Virtual State* (New York: Basic Books).

Rousseau, J.J. (1762/1978) *The Social Contract*, trans M. Cranston (London: Penguin Books).

Rousselot, P. (1935) *The Intellectualism of St Thomas* (London: Sheed and Ward).

Royce, R. (1899) *The World and the Individual*, Vol. I (New York: Macmillan).

Russell, B. (1949) 'Philosophy and Politics' in *Authority and the Individual* (Boston, MA: Beacon Hill).

Russell, B. (1951) *The Autobiography of Bertrand Russell 1872-1914* (Boston, MA: Little Brown and Company).

Sacred Congregation for Catholic Education (1977) *The Catholic School* (London: Catholic Truth Society).

Sacred Congregation for Catholic Education (1982) *Lay Catholics in Schools: Witnesses to Faith* (London: Catholic Truth Society).

Salomone, R.C. (2000) *Visions of Schooling. Conscience, Community and Common Education* (New Haven and London: Yale University Press).

Scanlon, T. (1998) *What We Owe to Each Other* (Cambridge, MA: Harvard University Press).

Schelling, F.W.J. (1827/1996) *Samtliche Werke* (Cotta) Vol. 10.

Shrader-Frechette, K.S. (1991) *Risk and Rationality* (Berkeley, CA: University of California Press).

Seelye, K.Q. (2002) 'Pentagon Says Acquittals May Not Free Detainees', *The New York Times*, March 22, 2002, p. A13.

Segal, J. (1998) 'Living at a High Economic Standard: A Functionings Analysis,' in *Ethics of Consumption*, D.A. Crocker and T. Linden (Oxford: Rowman and Littlefield Publishers).

Sen, A. (1984) 'The Living Standard', *Oxford Economic Papers*, 36, Supplement.

Sen, A. (1987) *The Standard of Living* (Cambridge: Cambridge University Press).

Shattuk, J. (1996) 'Computer Matching is a Serious Threat to Individual Rights', in *Computers and Controversy*, ed. R. Kling (San Diego, CA: Academic Press).

Shirley, J. (2000) *Eclipse Corona* (Northridge, CA: Babbage Press).

Shue, H. (1996) *Basic Rights: Subsistence, Affluence, and US Foreign Policy,*2nd ed. (Princeton, NJ: Princeton University Press).

Shue, H. (1996) 'Solidarity Among Strangers and the Right to Food', in *World Hunger and Morality*, ed. W. Aiken and H. LaFollette,2nd ed. (Upper Saddle River, NJ: Prentice-Hall).

Smith, A. (1976) *The Wealth of Nations* (Chicago: University of Chicago Press).

Sockett, H (1993) *The Moral Basis for Teacher Professionalism* (New York and London: Teachers College Press).

Spryt, H. (1994) *The Sovereign State and Its Competitors* (Princeton, NJ: Princeton University Press).

Soules, M.R. (1999) 'Commentary: Posthumous harvesting or gametes: A physician's perspective', *Journal of Law, Medicine, & Ethics*, 27 (4).

Standage, T. (1998) *The Victorian Internet* (New York: Walker and Company).

Stephenson, N. (1992) *Snow Crash* (New York: Bantam Books).

Strange, S. (1996) *The Retreat of the State* (Cambridge: Cambridge University Press).

Strike, K.A. (1990) 'The Legal and Moral Responsibility of Teachers', in *The Moral Dimensions of Teaching*, ed. J.I. Goodlad, R. Sodor and K.A. Sirotnik (San Francisco and Oxford: Jossey bass Publishers).

Strong, C. (1999) 'Ethical and Legal Aspects of Sperm Retrieval After Death or Persistent Vegetative State', *Journal of Law, Medicine and Ethics*, 2 (4), pp. 347–8.

Strong, C., Gingrich, J. and Kutteh, W. (2000) 'Ethics of Postmortem Sperm Retrieval', *Human Reproduction*, 15 (4).

Sumner, L.W. (1987) *The Moral Foundation of Rights* (Oxford: Oxford University Press).

Taylor, C. (1989) *Sources of the Self* (Cambridge: Cambridge University Press).

Teichman, J. (1989) 'How to Define Terrorism', *Philosophy*, 64.

Temkin. L. (1993) *Inequality* (New York: Oxford University Press).

Thiessen, E.J. (2001) *In Defence of Religious Schools and Colleges* (Montreal: McGill-Queen's University Press).

Thorson, T.L. (1962) *The Logic of Democracy* (New York: Holt, Rinehart, and Winston).

Tillers, P. (1988) 'Mapping Inferential Domains' in *Probability and Inference in the Law of Evidence: The Uses and Limits of Bayesianism* (Dordrecht: Kluwer.

Tomasi, J. (1995) 'Kymlicka, Liberalism, and Respect for Cultural Minorities', *Ethics*, 105 (3), pp. 580–603.

Tornquist M. and Ehrenberg, L. (1984) *Environmental Health Perspectives*, 102, Supplement 4, October 1984.

Tropp, A (1957) *The School Teachers. The Growth of the Teaching Profession in England and Wales from 1800 to the Present Day* (London: Heinemann).

Truman, N.E. (1901) 'Pragmatism' *Philosophical Review*, Vol. 10.

Twining, W.L. (1990) *Rethinking Evidence: Exploratory Essays* (Oxford: Oxford University Press).

Updike, J. (1998) *Toward the End of Time* (New York: Random House).

Van Creveld, M. (1999) *The Rise and Decline of the State* (Cambridge: Cambridge University Press).

Vlastos, G. (1965) 'Degrees of Reality in Plato', in *New Essays on Plato and Aristotle*, ed. Renford Bambrough (London: Routledge & Kegan Paul), pp. 1–20.

Von Mises, R. (1957) *Probability, Statistics and Truth* 2nd ed. (New York, Unwin).

Waldron, J. (1990) 'Rights and Majorities: Rousseau Revisited', in *Majorities and Minorities*, *Nomos* 33, ed. J.W. Chapman and A. Wertheimer (New York: New York University Press).

Walzer, M. (1980) 'The Moral Standing of States: A Response to Four Critics', *Philosophy and Public Affairs*, 9.

Walzer, M. (2000) *Just and Unjust Wars: A Moral Argument with Historical Illustrations*, 3rd ed. (New York: Basic Books; 1st ed. 1977; 2nd ed. 1992).

Walzer, M. (2002) 'The Argument about Humanitarian Intervention', *Dissent*, (Winter).

Watson, G. (1996) 'Two Faces of Responsibility,' *Philosophical Topics*, 24, (2).

Weatherford R. (1982) *Philosophical Foundations of Probability Theory* (Routledge & Kegan Paul).

Williams, B. (1981) 'Practical Necessity', in *Moral Luck* (Cambridge: Cambridge University Press).

White, P. (1996) *Civic Virtues and Public Schooling. Educating Citizens for a Democratic Society* (New York and London: Teachers College Press).

Wiggins, D. (1991) 'Claims of Need', in Wiggins, *Needs, Values, Truth*, 2nd ed. (London: Blackwell).

Wilkinson, M. (2002) 'Last Rights: the Ethics of Research on the Dead', *Journal of Applied Philosophy*, 19 (1).

Wittgenstein, L. (1953) *Philosophical Investigations* (Oxford: Blackwell).

Yergin, D. and Stanislaw, J. (1998) *The Commanding Heights* (New York: Simon and Schuster).

Young, I.M. (1990a) *Justice and the Politics of Difference* (Princeton, NJ: Princeton University Press).

Young, I.M. (1990b) 'The Ideal of Community and the Politics of Difference', in *Feminism/Postmodernism*, ed. Linda J. Nicholson (New York: Routledge).

Zimring, F.E. and Hawkins, G. (1995) *Incapacitation* (Oxford: Oxford University Press).

Index